The Handbook of

Palmistry

Also by Ray Douglas:

Teach Yourself Palmistry
Dreams and the Inner Self
Decoding Your Dreams
Dream Analysis
Understanding Your Family's Dreams
Astrology and the Inner Self
The Essence of the Upanishads

Contents

1 **Influences:** The Nature of Palmistry   *p7*
2 **Thinking and Feeling:** The Major Lines   *p12*
3 **Permanent and Variable:** The Secondary Lines   *p16*
4 **Cheirotypes:** Distinctive Hand Categories   *p20*
5 **Thumbs and Fingers:** Character Clues   *p24*
6 **The Background of the Palm:** Ancient Gods, Soul, and the Mounts   *p37*
7 **The Pendulum of Karma:** Fate, Fortune, and the Rascette   *p44*
8 **Inherited Characteristics:** Left Hand, Right Hand   *p50*
9 **The Heart Line:** Directing the Emotions   *p56*
10 **The Rising of the Feelings:** Pride, Ambition and Greed   *p60*
11 **Inner Feelings:** The Girdles of Venus   *p67*
12 **Emotional Instability:** Chains, Islands and Breaks in the Heart Line   *p72*
13 **The Marriage Lines:** Affection and Child Lines   *p79*
14 **The Head Line:** Directing the Thoughts   *p84*
15 **The Sensitive Mind:** Business Brains, Dreamers and Social Skills   *p88*
16 **Attitudes and Obsessions:** Head and Heart Line Links   *p98*
17 **Common Sense and Uncommon Sense:** Branch Lines and the Supernal Zone   *p104*
18 **Mental Instability:** Islands, Chains and Breaks in the Head Line   *p110*
19 **The Life Line:** Energy, Time, Travel and Health   *p113*
20 **The Line of Fate:** Timescale of Fate   *p126*
21 **The Ups and Downs of Fate:** Dominance, Islands, Chains and Breaks   *p133*
22 **The Line of Fortune:** Timescale and the Seven-year Cycle   *p137*
23 **Characters and Predictions:** Simple and Complicated Patterns   *p144*
24 **Romance:** Stars of Venus and Lines of Influence   *p147*
25 **Jealousy:** Negative Relationships   *p154*

26 **Infidelity and Separation:** Elongated Islands
    and the Line of Dominance   *p157*
27 **Money:** The Gambler's Cross   *p161*
28 **Ambition:** Stars and the Strengthening
    of Passion   *p164*
29 **Success:** Eminence and Security   *p167*
30 **Vigour:** The Competitive Athlete   *p171*
31 **Stress:** Nervous Exhaustion and Guilty Secrets   *p173*
32 **Sociability:** Mixers, Loners, and Timidity   *p176*
33 **Assertiveness:** Domineering and Submissive
    Types   *p180*
34 **Physical Problems:** Hypochondria, Illness,
    Excess and Solomon's Seal   *p183*
35 **Creativity:** Sideways Thinking   *p192*
36 **Sensitivity:** Intuition, Concern, the Occult
    and the Spiritual   *p195*
37 **Compassion:** Caring, Sympathy and the
    Mark of Mercy   *p199*
38 **The Grand Cycle:** The Basis of Ancient
    Psychology   *p203*
39 **Giving a Reading:** Basic Principles; Permanent
    Impressions   *p216*
40 **Practical Analysis:** Outward and Inward Events   *p222*
41 **Quick Character Sketches:** Distinctive types   *p234*

Summary A: Signs on Mounts and Lines   *p246*

Summary B: Detailed Features   *p253*

Summary C: The Principle Lines   *p264*

Index: *p266*

1 Influences: The Nature of Palmistry

DOUBTERS will always doubt. Healthy scepticism is a useful asset, and it is only sensible to value personal experience above dogma and hearsay. It is best to keep an open mind until you are in possession of evidence. However, many people reject the whole notion of palmistry, even when offered firm evidence. Some of these are born disbelievers who accept nothing but concrete material facts. But not a few are religious people – religious both in the normally accepted sense of the word and in its more abstract sense, taken to include those who are 'spiritually orientated'.

It is not that such people see palmistry as sheer nonsense. On the contrary, they tend to take this negative attitude of rejection for two very specific reasons. First, a set of 'signs' to them implies that our fate is fixed and preordained, which thus seems to rule out the possibility of free choice – the choice to do right or wrong, the desire to improve, to do good, to atone. Second, they take exception to palmistry because it refers mainly to the base 'passions'. These coarse influences of life, these 'devices and desires', seem in devout eyes to overcloud the human soul and lessen or even preclude the possibility of spiritual expansion, of escape from everyday life.

In a way they are right. The passions certainly have this effect, so when they accuse palmistry (and, by implication, palmists too) of committing the offence of analysing such things, we have to agree with them. In its defence, though, I would point out that palmistry doesn't produce passions and desires or strengthen them, it merely *symbolizes* these things. Everybody is constantly surrounded by influences, whether good, neutral or evil, and plainly if they feel a certain influence to be bad, then for them at that moment it probably *is* bad. They may not realize it, but their attitude is the result of at least *two* influences: the 'bad' influence itself and the counter-influence that they are accepting. Certainly, it would be neither the right time nor the right place for them to take an intelligent interest – or even a healthily sceptical interest – in the art of reading the hand.

Ultimately, the nature of our lives surely depends on our personal needs and karmic contents. Life is, after all, a continuing cycle of events. As palmistry acknowledges, we are not spiritually devoid of contents, even at the moment of birth. Situations or characteristics are not really fixed, but they often seem that way because when people are static in themselves it looks as though nothing changes for them.

Static people will probably regard some object, some principle, in exactly the same light next year as they did last year – as they did twenty years ago. As far as they are concerned, if a thing is bad, then bad it is for all time. For them, if something makes its appearance on a certain level, then that is its level for evermore. Many, indeed, think this is a virtue. Politicians, for instance, are always asserting that their viewpoint is constant, even when they keep chopping and changing. They insist they 'have always said' such and such, as though to change your mind is a sign of weakness or inefficiency. Perhaps they don't like to admit that they are capable of being wrong.

It is no use arguing with a fixed point of view. But when people are developing, growing, learning, imbibing, expelling, they must inevitably go through a process of change, and their perceptions have constantly to be changing too. Of course, circumstances seem to change. As a wise man wrote in the Book of Ecclesiastes over 2,000 years ago:

For everything its season, and for every activity under heaven its time: a time to be born and a time to die; a time to plant and a time to uproot; a time to kill and a time to heal; a time to pull down and a time to build up; a time to weep and a time to laugh; a time for mourning and a time for dancing...

To change your perception does not necessarily mean that you were wrong before, or are wrong now. What seemed abhorrent a few years back may seem highly desirable today. Who knows, tomorrow it may seem abhorrent again. In short, it is not objects or principles that have innate levels so much as people who have levels of perception, of differing needs and differing understanding.

Hand readers too have their differing levels of understanding and perception, of course. I am not for one moment implying that all palmists should be taken seriously. The fact is, palmists and astrologers and fortune-tellers, like priests, doctors and psychologists, *can* have a powerful influence on people who consult them, and they should never forget the responsibility that this entails. People are vulnerable, people are suggestible – and 'people' means not just 'them' but you and me too.

A hand reader can interpret the signs in your hand only according to his or her own level of understanding. This is common sense, I suppose. But understanding runs very deep, and becoming proficient in this subject is not merely a case of learning a new set of signs and symbols. Ideally, all people should be known to one another, simply by becoming aware. It is my belief and, that all people are akin deep down ultimately, all things are known and knowable. The palm of the hand serves only as a token in a transaction.

Fashions change, and so do scientific perceptions. For instance, in my old pre-war set of encyclopaedias the subject of 'Palmistry' is given a very bad press – a dismissive paragraph describing it as the pursuit of simple minds, with no basis for rational discussion. But in the very same volume the entry on 'Phrenology', now an utterly discredited subject, runs to several thousand words, ending with an impressive bibliography.

Palmistry *has* had a hard time, ever since the Age of Reason dawned in the eighteenth century, when simple religious minds were persuaded to become simple atheistic minds instead. Unscrupulous fortune-tellers have not helped, of course. Palmistry should be a pleasure, not a pain.

Whether *your* mind is particularly simple or not, if 'fortune' means a lot to you, it is probably better to read your own hand if you can, rather than rely on someone else to do it. You might merely be curious to discover what is written there or you might be eager to explore your own possibilities, to further your urge to 'know thyself' (and this is the best possible motive for studying the subject); alternatively, you might actually want to don a headscarf and sit in a fortune-teller's booth for the sake of 'filthy lucre'. Either way, there can be no better time or place to learn this ancient art than here and now.

Actually, palmistry has never really been in the same boat as fortune-telling. Sensitive, psychic seers of the human soul *can* use the hand as a useful aid to their inspiration, but you certainly don't have to be a medium, or a gypsy, or a witch, or even a wizard, to read hands. The rules are fairly simple and easy to learn.

The hand by itself cannot reveal the future, any more than a computer can; but it can show you tendencies and probabilities. It can tell you about a person's character. Even without the extra dimension of psychic sensitivity, which many claim to have but few actually possess, people's hands can tell you fairly accurately how they habitually behave when everything is going right, and how they are liable to react when things start going wrong.

I believe you can be fairly certain about whether someone is likely to fly into a temper at the drop of a hat or remain calm under incredible stress, to step forwards boldly in an emergency or stay quietly in the background, hoping that the emergency will go away, and so on.

Further, you can tell if someone is a romantic dreamer or a more down-to-earth, scientific type, and you can get a pretty shrewd idea about whether they are clever or stupid, kind or cruel, healthy or sickly, lucky or unlucky ... Most people belong to neither one extreme nor the other; the majority fit in somewhere along a sliding scale.

I caution you not to *tell* anyone that they seem to you to be ill-favoured, unintelligent or unfeeling. Above all other considerations, palmists should be aware of the law of karma – the great and holy law which decrees that wrong you do to others will eventually be heaped on your own head: a fate to be avoided! If those 'others' are seeking to discover deep truths about themselves, and you claim to be able to reveal those truths, karma is waiting and listening, so:

DON'T tell anyone anything hurtful.

DON'T tell anyone they are going to suffer a disaster.

DON'T tell anyone when you think they are going to die.

The hand cannot be sure of anything like that. And even if it could, to break these rules is to put oneself automatically on the side of the evildoers, the spreaders of fear and despondency! It makes more sense to stay on the side of the good, and always be the bringer of good tidings. How much better we all feel when someone says something nice about us! It can be very upsetting when some idiot hurts our feelings, and it can be positively dangerous to cloud another's mind with worries and fears, whether we feel justified in so doing or not.

Those happy, healthy and wealthy people who are blessed with good fortune are usually ready to deny indignantly that there is any such thing as luck. 'What nonsense,' they say. 'I worked damned hard to get where I am today...' Of course they did! You can give it any name you like – 'talent', 'innate ability', 'sheer hard work' – but it all amounts to exactly the same thing. If these qualities belong to people's individual physical, mental and emotional make-up – their inheritance – the results of their ability to make the right efforts will show in their own history...in their own good fortune...in their own hand.

If you happen to be gifted with a particularly good brain, you cannot really, in all honesty, take personal credit for it. No more can you reasonably take credit for owning a magnificent body. You may work eight hours a day building it up, but why? Because it is in your character. Equally, you cannot be blamed for failing to make the grade. We are all children of fate, even those special people who really do seem to have a divine destiny.

All who study the law of karma come to the same conclusion, that sooner or later we all get exactly what we deserve, so it behoves us to do the best we can, while we can. If we expect to reap as we sow, we are doing ourselves a favour if we try to do right by others. Even from a selfish viewpoint, long-term, it is safer trying to improve another's lot, rather than trying to drag them down. Certainly, this is what palmists believe. Everything points in the same direction. At the very least, to 'do as you would be done by' is a sensible precaution to take, and it certainly makes the world a pleasanter place to live in.

2 Thinking and Feeling:
The Major Lines

BEFORE trying to read someone else's hand, it is necessary to appreciate the difference between *thoughts* and *feelings*. This difference is not always clear in practice, and our idiomatic way of speaking often obscures the issue still further. The managing director may say, 'I feel that our accountant's appraisal is correct...', when it would be more accurate to say. 'I think...' In other words, he *feels* that to say 'I feel...' lends weight or depth to the subject.

It is not something that normally we consider requires analysis. Yet certainly we can feel happy or sad, even when the brain sees no particular reason for it. We can put our mind to work on some problem, can stick grimly to the daily grind, even when our feelings would far rather be doing something else. We can entertain warm feelings for someone, even when common sense disapproves, and we can take a dislike to a person without any apparent logical explanation. Science-fiction writers like to visualize dangerous super-beings of the future who are all brains and no feelings. Animals have feelings, even if their brains are not very well developed. Their feelings tell them which of their pack members they like and which they hate the very sight of. Their brains simply tell them when to run, when to bite, when to stand up and when to lie down.

The head – the brain – is the abode of a person's thoughts: the cold seat of logic. The hot seat of a person's feelings or emotions is said to be the heart. There is no need to mistake the symbol for the reality. It doesn't really matter if doctors insist the heart is just a muscular blood-pump; it is a convenient and rather romantic way of describing feelings to say that they belong to the heart.

Almost all of us tend to use one function more than the other, to be either 'hot-headed' or cool and calculating. The ideal personality, I suppose, would possess an even balance between the two. In palmistry it is the Head Line that tells us something about the thought processes and the type of brain a person has. The Heart Line tells us something about the individual feelings.

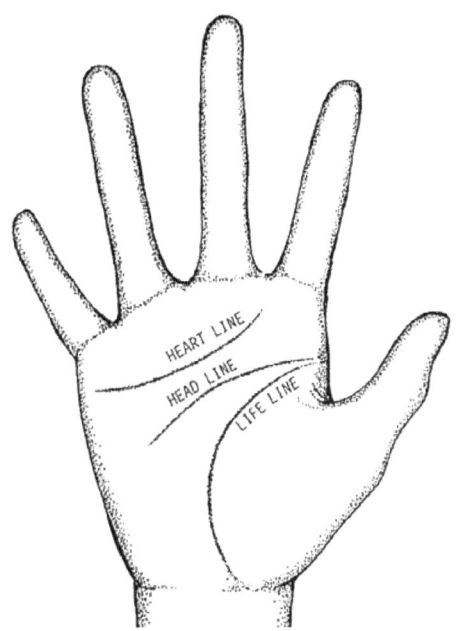

The three major lines

Of course, you can *feel* with the fingers, through the skin. But this kind of 'feeling' with the body has nothing to do with emotional feelings. Bodily feeling is better described as 'sensation', and in palmistry it is the Life Line that tells us something about a person's physical sensations, lifestyle, health, sense of security, and how he or she seems to fit in with the rest of the world.

Imagine as the norm a firm, symmetrical hand, with the three basic lines clearly marked. Your own hand, or the hand to be read, will probably be seen to vary from the norm in so many different ways, and these are the factors that, in their combinations, indicate individual idiosyncrasy.

If you can further imagine a normally staid and not particularly imaginative, averagely clever, and not unduly excitable, ordinarily amorous, reasonably self-possessed and completely unremarkable person, that person will probably possess the average hand. Everything that differs from the unremarkable bestows individuality and makes that person remarkable. These are the features that will stand out and need to be identified.

However, complete normality is itself rare enough to be quite remarkable. If there is nothing outstandingly good about someone, there will probably equally be nothing outstandingly bad. As any portrait painter will tell you, if you can find someone whose looks are completely average, you will have found not an 'ordinary' but an extraordinarily good-looking face. And by the same token, I believe that to possess 'average' characteristics is a blessing rather than a curse. At least it suggests that the owner of such a hand has a well-balanced personality.

There are many types of action. At the one extreme is the purely instinctive, animal reaction to circumstances that comes into play whether the emotions and the intelligence are well developed or not. At the other extreme there is the carefully considered judgement, exclusive to the human species. The intellect needs to be functioning correctly to make meaningful decisions. But the emotions – the feelings – are needed if we are to assess likes, dislikes and values of a more abstract nature: thoughts, if you like, without the solid base of materiality on which to rest.

Television has taught us all a lot about this. In televised confrontations or discussions, opponents can be seen to argue a case from their 'heart' or from their 'head'. Political disputes in particular tend to isolate the two functions and leave them clearly differentiated. Often we see the hotly emotional surge towards a goal that may seem so obviously desirable at the time but would not perhaps survive a more intellectual analysis. Then there is the cold, logical, unassailably correct view that may, in fact, prove completely unacceptable to any warm, caring person.

Where one set of perceptions is virtually missing, unpleasantness may ensue. In those rare cases where the two functions are indistinguishable – and in palmistry, when the two representative lines are combined so that there is no differentiation between the two – the circumstances are sure to portend for the individual concerned a problem that will probably need no comment.

So, with the Life Line tracking the progress of physical energy, of health and well-being, the three major lines of the hand refer to the individual quality of the three basic functions. They record the quality of human relationships, whether these are likely to be sympathetic, selfish, understanding or unconcerned. Whether the heart rules the head, or whether emotional feelings tend to be pushed into the background when decisions are to be made. Whether the body enjoys robust health, and whether the chances of a long and healthy life are good or poor. Whether the brain can concentrate keenly on the cut and thrust of life, or whether it habitually prefers to concern itself with abstract, intuitive, 'creative' values.

But neither cut and thrust nor creative talent can be put to use without a field of action, and the way in which these lines relate to their fleshy backgrounds expresses the continuous flow of perceptions on and in which the psyche operates. From the so-called mounts, each in itself representing a basic passion, we can understand the influence of ancient gods upon the human animal. We can assess to what extent the individual covets material wealth, whether financial resources are frittered away or painstakingly conserved, whether a living comes hard or easy. Whether conscience, integrity, culture, spirituality – all the finer principles of life – are all-important or well-nigh meaningless. These are the basics of palmistry.

3 Permanent and Variable:
The Secondary Lines

MANY PEOPLE who should know better, even some doctors and scientists, completely misunderstand the nature of the lines of the palm. They are not formed haphazardly in the womb by the fist-clenching of the foetus; they are arranged in a fairly consistent pattern common to the whole human race. In each individual, to a greater or lesser degree, they vary only enough to show individuality in a pattern already decided for us at our conception, by way of our parents' and our ancestors' genes.

This is especially true in the case of the three major lines which we have already considered. In anatomical terms, the outer skin or epidermis over most of our body tends to be fairly loosely arranged over the deeper layers of the cuticle or the 'true skin'. When you rub your body the skin tends to move about. But the chief function of the palm of the hand is to grasp, and if the skin on that part of the body were unstable, we would not be able to grip firmly and efficiently.

The skin of the palm also needs to bend very neatly and tightly along with the movements of grasping, as when we clench our fists. In order to fulfil these functions efficiently the flexion folds throughout their length are firmly tied by connecting fibres, or fibrillar tissue, to the deep layers of the dermis, and to the sheaths of the flexor tendons. These folding lines, or *sulci*, form the distinctive and clearly marked lines with which we are familiar. They are further emphasised by subcutaneous layers of fat arranged between them, which serve to pad the skin so as both to strengthen the grip and at the same time to protect the underlying tendons from damage. These raised areas are known anatomically as the *monticuli*, in palmistry as the mounts.

If you study your own hands you may notice that, whilst the three main firmly tied-down lines are clearly recognizable, there is another type of line that may or may not be present in the individual palm. This second category consists of lines that are *not* tied to the deep layers, or tied only very lightly, so that unlike the three fixed lines could be said to be to some extent haphazardly disposed, though they too will be found to follow a fairly precise pattern. They form a sort of lateral or transverse counter-movement to the

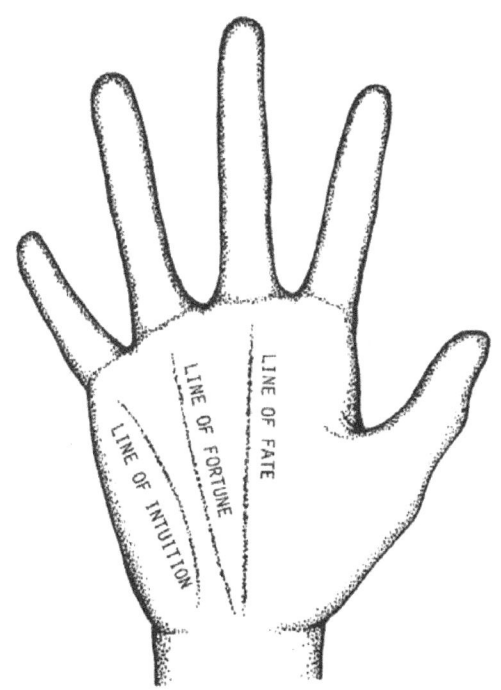

The three secondary lines

straightforward gripping function catered for by the three main, permanent lines.

The most distinct and deeply anchored lines, then, are the personal lines fixed and decided for you by your genes. As permanent and unique symbols of your personal inheritance, from the viewpoint of palmistry they can be seen as tracks along which your strength of will and actions, the quality of your thoughts and emotions, your physical vigour and habitual lifestyle, may be said to flow. The unfixed or only lightly fixed secondary lines, which tend to run up the length of the palm from the wrist towards the base of the fingers, have a different connotation. Being to a large extent acquired not through the genes but apparently by chance, brought about by transient or at least less permanent factors, these secondary lines form apposite symbols of the non-inherited, impersonal influences that sometimes arise quite unexpectedly to affect our lives.

To the extent that some of these transverse or ascending lines are, however, fixed and permanent, the implication is that in the individual case, and during the individual lifetime, fate itself is fixed and permanent. The difference between the two sorts of lines represents the difference between what is inborn in the individual and what is not. In broader terms it can be said that the function, influence or impulse symbolized by a fixed line is fixed and permanent during the life of its owner. The lines that are not permanently fixed represent those factors that time and cir-cumstances may change. Together, they give us an idea of the day-to-day fate to be encountered during our lifetime, and our probable reactions to all these factors.

Genetic abnormalities which may affect the personality often have physical signs which a doctor will recognize. But the normal range of personalities and the happenings of fate, though obvious enough during our life, have an abstract nature. They cannot be plotted physically; they cannot be dissected or discovered during a *post mortem* examination. Their only real proof is their experience. You are unlikely to succeed in proving the validity of palmistry through a process of logic, any more than that of religious faith. A sceptic might demand to know, for example, what and where precisely is this connection between the Head Line and the mental processes? Or where is the neurological link between the emotional centre of the brain and the Heart Line? And, of course, this sceptical type of question will get no sensible answer.

But if you study your own hand in the light of your own knowledge of yourself, and the hands of your family and friends in the light of your knowledge of them, you will very soon say: 'It really does work!' It all boils down to the distinction between art and science: art, like personality, has an abstract base; science, like the physical body, has a material one. The art of reading the hand works chiefly by way of symbolism and synchronicity. As a uniquely personal map carried by each individual, a pattern which corresponds with a person's past and present life, the hand can equally well provide a forecast of routes to be taken, or probabilities for the future.

It used to be thought that personality was largely decided by a person's upbringing, but this turns out not to be true. Personality is decided almost entirely, not by our environment, but by our genes. Academic studies on identical twins who have been separated since birth have demonstrated this fact quite conclusively. Their hand patterns, we can assume, will be very similar, and when these twins have finally been brought together in middle age, the researchers have discovered that their lifestyles, health, mannerisms, and their patterns of speech, habits of thinking and feeling, are all virtually identical too. Even the things that have happened to them during their years apart, good fortune and misfortune alike, have also corresponded to an uncanny degree. When twins grow up together, of course, they often strive to be different, and usually succeed. An examination of their fingerprints may point to these minor variations, because these are said to be truly unique. But the nature of these minor differences of direction are liable to be such that they will not show up during a study of their palms.

    To summarize the difference between the permanent and the variable, it should be remembered that the hand shows two directions or tides of movement in individual human affairs. The three major lines, running down or across the palm of the hand from near the base of the fingers, arise from personal impulse, from the will, from the brain, from the physical motivation, from conscious, deliberate actions. The three secondary lines, running from near the wrist upwards towards the base of the fingers, can be said to arise not from conscious actions, but without the power of will, from unconscious happenings and influences. All in all, the two directions mark the difference between what is inborn and personal, and what is imposed and impersonal.

4 Cheirotypes: Distinctive Hand Categories

THE SIZE, proportions and general appearance of the hand can tell an observant palmist a great deal about its owner. Comparatively large hands tend to belong to calm, phlegmatic people: ponderers, deep thinkers and slow speakers − people who usually shun the limelight and seem to prefer a back seat. Comparatively small hands usually belong to the more 'pushy' types: quick thinkers and ready speakers, masters of instant appraisal and appropriate response.

Similar definitions apply when referring to the smoothness or knottiness of the finger joints. Smooth-fingered people are the quick-reactive and impulsive ones. Gnarled-finger types tend to be more stolid and seemingly content. Typically, knotted fingers belong to the introvert, smooth ones to the extrovert. People with short fingers are usually more practical than reflective; those with long fingers are inclined to be more thoughtful and sensitive.

But it is best to avoid carrying this observation to any false conclusions. Some apparently practical people are nevertheless hopelessly inefficient (like the sitcom DIY enthusiast whose shelves keep falling down), while some predominantly sensitive, artistic people can be very efficient indeed. A more accurate picture of a person's capabilities may be obtained by assessing the general proportions of their hand − their cheirotype − coupled with the shape of their fingertips.

A cheirotype sums up the comparative length and width of the palm and the length of the fingers, expressing these as percentages. Two related factors are involved: P, the percentage by which the palm is narrower or broader than its length; and F, the percentage by which the fingers are longer or shorter than the width of the palm. The diagram shows the necessary measurements as X, Y and Z. The factors may be calculated using the following simple equations:

$$P = \frac{X}{X+Y} \times 100 \qquad F = \frac{Z}{Z+X} \times 100$$

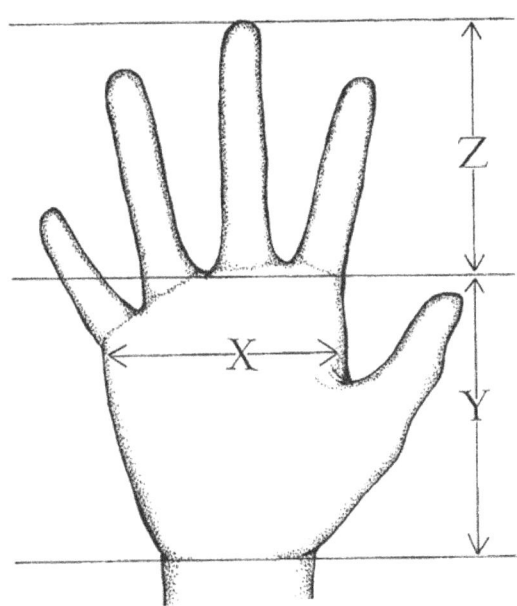

Cheirotypes: basic measurements

Basically there are five cheirotypes, which include two common variations and two less common extremes on either side of the average. At one extreme, the 'rugged' types of hand (AA) are short and thick, with stubby fingers and a palm more or less as broad as it is long. Typically, the fingertips are square and solidly thick. At the other extreme, the 'sensitive' types of hand (BB) are just the opposite: long and slender with delicate fingers with, usually, finely shaped and quite sharply conical fingertips. The 'normal' hands (O) are average, with fingers about equal in length to the width of the palm, and usually with firmly rounded fingertips.

Cheirotype	P factor	F factor	Compatible fingertips
Rugged AA	48 plus	below 45	Square
Practical A	48–46	45–48	Blunt or Spatulate
Normal O	46–45	49–50	Rounded or Spatulate
Artistic B	45–44	51–52	Conical or Spatulate
Sensitive BB	43 or less	53 or more	Pointed

AA   A   O   S   B   BB

Pointed Fingertips: AA *Square;* A *Blunt;* O *Rounded;*
S Spatulate; B *Conical;* BB *Pointed*

Measurements need to be fairly precise to give reliable results, but with a little practice individual cheirotypes will be evident on sight, without the need for measurements. The majority of hands slot somewhere into the A-O-B range, and their cheirotypal names reflect the basic characteristics of their owners. Possessors of an average hand can confidently be expected to prove down-to-earth all-rounders, reasonably practical, reasonably artistic, reasonably hard-working.

The 'practical' types (A) take the 'square' characteristics a stage further. Their fingertips too are usually square and firm. Good providers, they work hard in a sensible way and value material security, are usually conventional in their attitude towards society and accept the morals of the day.

Owners of the 'artistic' type of hand (B) tend towards the opposite set of characteristics: they will be individualists, often valuing freedom of personal choice above security and conventional morality. Such people like to 'do their own thing' in the fields of artistic creation, entertainment and romance. Their fingertips are usually conical – that is, ovoid rather than smoothly rounded.

AA and BB are, of course, extreme versions of the A and B types, and their distinctive characteristics are also exaggerated, perhaps to a fault. At the one extreme, in AA, finer emotional feelings may seem to be lacking or even absent altogether. At the other extreme, in BB, individual feelings are so intensely developed and all-devouring that practical considerations may tend to be overlooked.

But don't be dogmatic about your assessment. Having established the apparent cheirotype, check it by turning the hands over and studying the knuckle side. It sometimes happens that, when seen palm-uppermost, the proportions of the hand indicate a strongly practical type, while when seen from the rear, the fingers appear long and delicate. It is as though an artistic or sensitive type of person has had the palms of his or her hands modified by heavy work – and indeed quite frequently this is exactly what happens. Many people may find themselves stuck for life in heavy labouring work when they would far rather be inventing or painting, writing poetry or composing music. There may have been dramatic circumstances that forced an unsuitable lifestyle on an artistic subject, like an intellectual dissident being sent to work in some inhuman labour camp. But, if not a simple matter of opportunity and cultural expectations, it is far more likely to illustrate some kind of voluntary psychological escape. An attempt, it may be, to modify an adolescent character trait seen at the time to be undesirable – a young man, perhaps, who feared to be labelled weak or effeminate, suppressing his artistic instincts in what he saw as an aggressively macho world. All this will influence your character reading and you must modify it accordingly.

People who display characteristics of more than one cheirotype in their hands may be expected to show commensurate variability in their personality and basic outlook. Thus an A-type hand which also has conical fingertips may well belong to a practical worker with an unusually delicate touch, a producer, perhaps, of exquisite artefacts. Conversely, the owner of a B-type hand, yet with squarish fingertips, may well put his or her artistic feelings and creative talents to work in practical ways – in sculpture perhaps, publishing, or fashion design.

There is another fairly common fingertip shape that does not belong to any one cheirotype – the spatulate or bulbous type, in which the soft underside of the top phalange, when viewed from the front or rear, has a distinctively swelling outline. This characteristic also indicates practical creativity and is often to be found in the hands of craftspeople and musicians. The feature is usually to be seen within the central range A–O–B and seems to add a whimsical, vaguely eccentric and often obsessive flavour to any of the cheirotypes.

5 Thumbs and Fingers:
Character Clues

THE 'OPPOSING THUMB' able to be used both for gripping and for more delicate handling is a physical characteristic that sets human primates apart from the simian apes, and it serves as a primitive symbol of tenacity and the ability to manipulate material objects. In fact, thumbs vary individually to a surprising degree, and can tell us quite a lot about their owners' character.

Length of thumb has significance in the spheres of will-power and logic. The longer the thumb, by and large, the more forthright the character, the more strong-willed and, unfortunately perhaps, the more domineering and closed to reasonable objection he or she will seem to be. Oliver Cromwell was said to have had a thumb 'of great length', and I dare say so did many of the tyrants of history.

An unusually short thumb, as we might expect, portrays the opposite set of characteristics, suggesting a mind that, far from being dominant in company, is submissive to the point of suppression. If the long-thumbed person is a bully, the short-thumbed individual is a natural victim – a frequently over-emotional person who is easily swayed, and even more readily led. The ideal, as usual, lies somewhere between the two extremes. It must be said, however, that an element of 'longness' is a favourable indication of the type of determination that marks the quality of fair leadership, without any unpleasant implications.

In a closed hand, the difference may not be readily apparent, but length of thumb is not to be confused with its 'set' – depending upon whether it springs from low down on the hand towards the wrist, or higher up towards the index finger. A high-set thumb again recalls the origins of this useful natural tool as a sensitive grasping instrument opposing the fingers, for its grasping nature may be interpreted in metaphorical terms: the owners will most likely seem lacking in the 'milk of human kindness', and will want to keep all their acquisitions – including emotional feelings and social talents – to themselves. Conversely, the low-set thumb suggests generosity and a readiness to offer sympathy to others when needed. A natural carer (or a respected welfare worker) will almost inevitably own a low-set thumb, and so will any who work or simply long for freedom from want and oppression for the world's underprivileged people.

A stiff, straight thumb is a sure sign of obstinacy coupled with excessive caution. The owner of a thumb like this will feel emotions, but as a rule these feelings will be held severely in check. For this reason, people with stiff thumbs will seem to live their lives on an even keel. Notably self-controlled, they are usually reliable but, not being very adaptable, tend to be somewhat intolerant of the shortcomings of others.

A supple thumb, particularly one which bends itself slightly backwards when relaxed, is the badge of an adaptable person. Such people dislike rules and regulations, and have few unbendable views of their own. Because they tend to take things as they come, they are likely to be reasonably tolerant of faults and failures, both in themselves and in others.

A distinctive hourglass waist to the thumb implies a mind which is sharp but tends to lack the power of logic. Its owners will be private people who think a great deal though they may be reluctant to speak their thoughts. When they do give an opinion, it is likely to be a 'red herring', for they seldom say exactly what they mean. The full-waisted thumb suggests just the opposite: its possessors will speak their mind readily and therefore, though they may be faultlessly logical in both premise and conclusion, they tend to lack the virtue of tact.

A full, straight thumb which, when viewed in profile, appears shaped like a club, the top phalange bulbous on the fleshy underside, betrays a tendency towards violence, and a quick temper - a case of obstinacy and tactlessness both carried to extremes and likely to be put into physical practice. It has been called 'the pugilist's thumb', and with good reason.

Fingerprints (including thumbprints) are said to be unique, not only to each individual but also to each individual finger, and they certainly add individuality to the general attributes of a person's hand. But despite all the millions of combinations that must exist, they can be classified into just a few distinctive types. These basic patterns can tell the palmist, if not the detective, something about their owner's character. The five categories recognized by palmists are set out overleaf.

THE WHORL

Said to be the sign of independent, self-contained, somewhat dogmatic characters. High powered business people are likely to have this type of print, and it is seldom to befound on the fingers of yes-men and underlings.

THE LOOP

This pattern is said to be a sign of versatility, identifying the mercurial type, a darting mind and lightning quick emotional responses. It is possessed by wide-ranging jacks of all trades rather than single-track specialists.

THE HIGH ARCH

This type of print, like the loop, indicates quick and responsive minds. These characters are usually impulsive and very sensitive, possibly highly strung. It is often to be found on the fingers of outstandingly artistic or musical people.

THE LOW ARCH

Somewhat the opposite of the high-arch finger-printer, these types will always keep their emotions in check. They find it difficult to accept anything on its face value, and they always play things down. Sometimes guarded to the point of surliness, though they may in fact be affectionate and caring.

THE COMPOSITE

This type of print seems to be composed of opposing swirls or loops, and is said to indicate a 'dual personality', apt to change his or her mind frequently. Circumstances for such a person always overrule principles. They may not intend to be untruthful, but they are apt to say one thing and do another.

As far as the detective searching for clues to a crime is concerned, any one of these patterns could belong to a criminal, as it well may. But the very general character sketches that they offer can point to the *type* of criminal involved.

The whorled pattern may at first seem to suggest that 'Mr Big', the master criminal, has been involved – but this would probably be a false conclusion. A whorled finger-printer, if of criminal bent, would certainly focus all his skill and resources on the successful commitment of his crime. He would, in short, act in a professional manner and would therefore be highly unlikely to leave his own prints behind as damning evidence. In such a case, I would surmise that someone has been acting out of character – a high-flyer, perhaps, who has got himself into financial difficulties and is taking desperate measures.

The loop finger-printer, as a criminal, suggests the lightning-quick in-and-out raider. He may specialize in theft from cars, or car theft itself; he may well be a 'drummer' who can clear your house of valuables in two minutes flat. He is unlikely to operate on his own doorstep, but spreads his talents far and wide, and for this reason will be a slippery fish to catch. Individually, his crimes will not be carefully planned, but they will be carried out with great precision.

The high arch pattern suggests the sort of villain who makes an art form out of his crimes. Not for him the lightning raid. He will take his time and enjoy every moment of it. If cars are his target, his main interest will be the driving of them rather than their material value – a born joyrider. When property is involved, if it is not the greatest bank robbery of all time, he is likely to leave his mark behind in the form of graffiti and purposeful vandalism.

The low arch print, on a criminal, indicates a person who is probably addicted to petty theft. This fingerprint type is no more likely to turn to crime than any other, but when he does fall into temptation the low-archer will show little respect for other people's feelings or sentimental values. His attitude will be: 'if they leave their things lying around, they can expect to get them nicked – it's their own fault!' If he has a conscience, it will apply mainly to his own closest relationships – and this is where one can find a chink in his emotional armour.

Finally, the composite finger-printer, when he turns to crime, will be the least predictable of crooks. Opportunism is the key, and spur of the moment impulse is the trigger. He is not likely to carry out his crimes very efficiently and will probably make mistakes – such as leaving behind his finger-prints – that will lead to his being caught. He is liable to make hoax calls and is the sort of person to start a fire just to watch the brigade arrive. Once his crime has been committed, he will probably not be far away.

Individuals may possess more than one type of print on different fingers. This mixing of prints reflects their mixed character: they are likely to possess a complex personality. Palmists may glean some clue as to the particular areas of action in which differing characteristics apply by noting which finger bears which prints, and relating them to their appropriate mounts (see the next chapter). Many people quite unconsciously display one distinct attitude where material possessions are concerned and quite another when it comes for instance to religious belief, sensuality, person-to-person confrontation or communication. What to the onlooker may seem sheer hypocrisy often has an inbuilt explanation, and such a case may well be found symbolized in the fingertips.

More easily observable is the length of a person's fingers, and this factor is highly significant too, apart from the general tendency for the AA type of hand to have short fingers, and the BB type to have comparatively long ones. Take the first or index finger and compare its length with the third or ring finger. When these two fingers are more or less the same length, we can assume that the subject is a well-balanced person who gets on reasonably well with others. The longer the index finger seems in relation to the third finger, the more domineering and ambitious the person is likely to be. Pride and an unspoken sense of superiority will be inbuilt. In a woman, too, a long index finger indicates a high level of oestrogen in the body. The shorter the index finger when compared with the third finger, the more will the opposite apply. The possessor of a very short index finger is likely to be particularly cautious and may well suffer from feelings of inferiority. These are the two extremes, and the hand will usually reveal a tendency one way or the other.

A study of the next chapter will show that the index finger is 'ruled' by Jupiter and related to ambition and assertiveness. The second finger is 'ruled' by Saturn, relating to the Saturnian type of personality and the habitual ways in which we cope with the limitations of material resources, and our place within the environment. When this second finger is particularly long and seemingly well developed, it suggests a person well able to cope with a modicum of hardship and, indeed, one to whom a certain amount of hardship is sure to come. Such people have great self-discipline, and are quite likely to be found living under difficult conditions. These are usually serious, philosophical people, quite unlike one in whose hand the second finger is scarcely longer than its neighbouring fingers. Such a person will have very little patience with suffering. He or she will naturally gravitate to wherever life seems to promise the fewest problems.

The third or ring finger is 'ruled' by the Sun. We have already noted that when this finger and the index finger are of equal length, the owner's character will be equally evenly balanced and self-confident. When the first and second fingers are in proportion, but the third finger is particularly long, all the ambition indicated by the index finger will be directed along the path of abstract rather than material good fortune – towards the attainment of prestige and good publicity, particularly when the lowest phalange of this finger is noticeably longer than the two phalanges above it. In men, too, a long third finger suggests a high level of testosterone.

Finally the little finger may be considered: it should reach more or less to the upper joint, or the base of the top phalange of the adjacent third finger, to be considered of average length. The little finger is 'ruled' by Mercury, and its characteristics are traditionally related to the principle of communication. An unusually long little finger implies that its owner may seem unable to stop talking for very long. Good actors and impressionists are likely to display this feature, and it can be a great asset when a person's calling in life demands the gift of loquacity – but something of a trial to everyone around when it does not. This is the finger most closely connected with business skills, too, and a lack of business ability is suggested when the little finger seems to be unusually short.

Comparative length of the phalanges is ascribed significance too. The topmost phalange in each case relates to the intellectual or rational application of the quality represented by that particular finger. The middle phalange reflects the emotional application, or value-judgement of that quality. The lower phalange relates to the practical, physical application of that quality. A long phalange expresses comparative exaggeration of a characteristic; a short phalange expresses a shortcoming within this facet of the personality.

SUMMARY: *When phalanges are unusually long*

Index finger

TOP: *Ambition pursued for intellectual satisfaction.*
MIDDLE: *Ambition pursued for emotional satisfaction.*
LOWER: *Ambition pursued for physical satisfaction.*

Second finger

TOP: *Given to factual analysis.*
MIDDLE: *Fondness for the natural world.*
LOWER: *Acquisitive nature.*

Third finger

TOP: *Broad cultural interests.*
MIDDLE: *Love of art and music.*
LOWER: *Practical expertise in art or music.*

Little finger

TOP: *Inventive in communication.*
MIDDLE: *Guarded in communication.*
LOWER: *Brashness of display.*

SIGNIFICANCE OF OVERALL FINGER LENGTH:

Index finger

Long: *Ambitious. For a woman, a high level of fertility.*
Short: *Cautious.*

Second finger

Long: *Self-disciplined.*
Short: *Self-indulgent.*

Third finger

Long: *Publicity-seeking. For a man, a high level of fertility.*
Short: *Retiring.*

Little finger

Long: *Talkative.*
Short: *Reserved.*

   A finger which shows a natural curve can tell you something about its owner. Flexibility, and the lack of it, can both give the fingers the appearance of a curve: bent slightly forwards towards the palm when stiff and inflexible, backwards when flexible. A forwards curve is said to imply a somewhat grasping nature, and it certainly demonstrates a certain inflexibility of character. It typifies the stickler for rules and regulations, with a prudent and strictly practical nature. A backwards curve shows flexibility of character, with little regard for rules or conventions. Backwards-curving fingers often belong to born entertainers who frequently seem to have a poor sense of business and financial management.
   Perhaps of more significance for the palmist's first impression of the general shape of the hand is the sideways type of finger curve. Any of the fingers may curve either way, and the index finger quite often shows a distinct curve towards its neighbouring fingers. This indicates great determination and will-power with a stubborn streak, the sign of an achiever. The implication is that the Jupiterian or Jovian impulse, everyone's basic driving force, is being strengthened by the Saturnian force of materiality: ambitions being brought to reality.

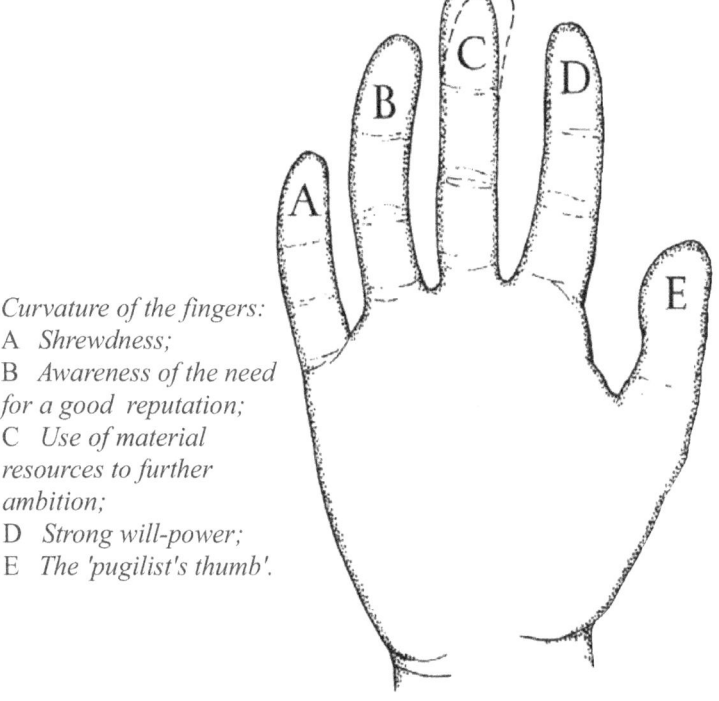

Curvature of the fingers:
A Shrewdness;
B Awareness of the need for a good reputation;
C Use of material resources to further ambition;
D Strong will-power;
E The 'pugilist's thumb'.

   The third or Sun finger often shows a bias towards the middle or Saturnian finger, implying a tendency towards the best use of material resources with regard to the principle of wholeness: that is, time and money will be spent on the aims of personal fulfilment and prestige, the feel-good factor rather than mere acquisition. For the possessor of an inwards-curving Sun finger, it is as though an unspoken question accompanies many day-to-day decisions regarding what is to be done for the best. When pronounced, the trait can indicate a touch of neurotic anxiety or a defensive attitude connected with the idea of self-worth. Such a person will be very concerned about what others may think of them.
   Finally, there may be a bias of the little finger, the Mercurial symbol of communication, towards the cultural sphere of the Sun and the material, resourceful and ambitious fields of the other two

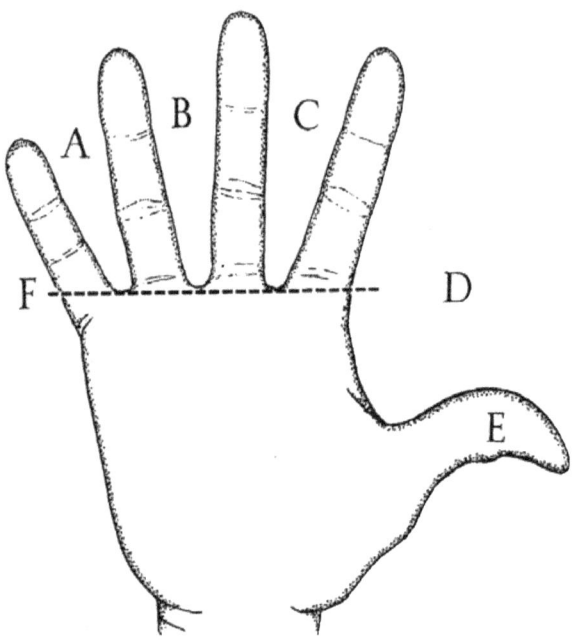

*Finger span and alignment:
a comparatively wide spread shows:*

A *Dislike of convention;*
B *An easy-going, relaxed personality;*
C *Self-confidence and determination;*
D *Generosity and sympathy;*
E *Flexible thumb indicates a flexible nature;*
F *Even alignment at the base of the fingers
indicates a high achiever.*

fingers. The possessor of an inwards-curving little finger is likely to demonstrate a good head for business, and a shrewd capacity for devising money-making schemes. He or she will also be tactful and diplomatic, an expert mediator when disagreements are in the air.

There is another curve associated with the fingers – the curve of the set or alignment. In the great majority of hands the Saturnian finger is set higher or further forward than the others, so that the four fingers are aligned on a curve. In cases where this normal characteristic is exaggerated and the curve is more pronounced than usual, the implication is that life is fated more than usually to prove a struggle for the person concerned. A markedly low-set Jupiter finger will imply a lack of confidence and self-assertion. A low-set little finger will imply a shortage of the Mercurial qualities of communication, social and business skills. The opposite applies when the base of the fingers shows a more or less even set, as near as possible to a straight line. The fingers then will appear more equal in length than average. A straight set of fingers and worldly success usually seem to go hand in hand, though a perfectly straight alignment is rarely to be seen. Top politicians and people in high public office, however, almost invariably possess a straighter than average set of fingers.

When someone lays their hand flat on a table top in a way that is relaxed and unselfconscious, you may notice that their method of doing so differs from person to person. Some individuals spread their fingers wide, others hold them tightly together. In many cases there will be a pronounced gap between two fingers in particular – let us say the little finger and the Sun finger – whilst the others are held fairly close to each other. We can read significance into this.

Fingers that are all spread fairly widely when relaxed in this fashion tend to belong to frank and open people, those who probably feel they have nothing to hide, and who can face the future without apprehension. When the opposite is the case, and the fingers are held stiffly together, we can be sure that their owner is excessively cautious, not very sociable, and probably given to worrying constantly about what the future may bring.

When a pronounced gap is left between the little finger and its neighbouring Sun finger, the person concerned will prove to be an independent type who dislikes rigid rules and conventions. He or she is likely to be full of original ideas, and will probably feel the need to communicate them in a friendly manner. A wide gap between the second and third, the Saturn and the Sun fingers, implies that the principle of limitation and discipline as typified by Saturn is not allowed to infringe upon the Sun principle of cultural expectations and social status. This person will be easy-going, if not devil-may-care, and will seem to care nothing at all about saving for a rainy day.

When the most pronounced gap appears between the first, the index or Jupiter finger, and the second or Saturn finger, the subject is likely to keep these two principles apart in real life. The driving power of Jupiter – personal ambition, the fulfilment of that individual's sense of morality and worth – is not allowed to be thwarted by outside considerations. The principle tends to be more important even than practical considerations. This is the sign of a person who is not really interested in what others may think or feel.

Finally, the relaxed hand may show a particularly wide gap between the thumb and the first finger. This is really a sign of the best and most civilized, the most 'human' of qualities. Such a person is likely to be generous and out-going, always sympathetic and ready to lend a hand or do a favour. This interpretation is the same as that given when the thumb is low-set, that is, when it springs from the hand comparatively low down near the wrist. A low-set thumb indicates a character we can all admire: humane, courageous, generous and thoroughly urbane. A high-set thumb, by contrast, is said to indicate a somewhat tight-fisted attitude, both to money and to information or conversation.

All these characteristics need to be assessed in the light of all the other information available. Never be too dogmatic when reading a hand. Always remember that you are assembling a mind-picture of the whole person, and people amount to far more than the mere sum of their various parts. You may be assessing the fingerprints, the general cheirotype or the individual lines and signs, but none of these can be taken as cut-and-dried indications of a person's character. All these things go towards building up a portrait of the whole person, and will be modified as the portrait begins to take shape.

6 The Background of the Palm:
Ancient Gods, Soul, and the Mounts

TRADITIONAL palmistry involves the study of often minute details to reveal subtle aspects of the personality. The basic features are simple enough: the Head Line, reflecting intellectual qualities; the Heart Line, indicating emotional qualities; and the Life Line, recording the qualities of health and vitality. But we all know, or at least suspect, that there is far more to life than these obvious things.

The fleshy background to the basic lines, the slightly raised areas known as mounts, are still referred to by names which identify them with the influence of ancient gods. Many centuries ago, when these mounts were named, only the innermost planets were known, and the gods of old shared their names with these planets. Perhaps nowadays we would have named the mounts differently. We may have invoked the names of Uranus, Neptune and Pluto. The principles traditionally connected with these three names are not really concerned with the personality, as such. They relate to a far more mysterious region of the psyche: the collective unconscious. We can now say that these three principles are symbolized by the three wrist 'bracelets' known to palmists as the 'Rascette', which is described more fully in the next chapter. Names are a mere convenience, and there is no need to take them or 'planetary influence' too seriously. A study of the diagrams in this chapter will show that these names are used to identify the mounts and describe their respective natures, the functions and qualities that palmists traditionally ascribe to them.

What are these qualities, you may wonder, but the base passions mentioned in the opening chapter? Fundamentally, that is indeed all they are – the background of personality. Traditional palmistry describes the interplay of fate with these individual passions, the occurrences they have apparently wrought and the effects they are likely to have in the future. But as usual there is more to it than 'just that'. The list that follows suggests that the symbolism both of the mounts and of the lines fits into the pattern of human life on a far grander scale.

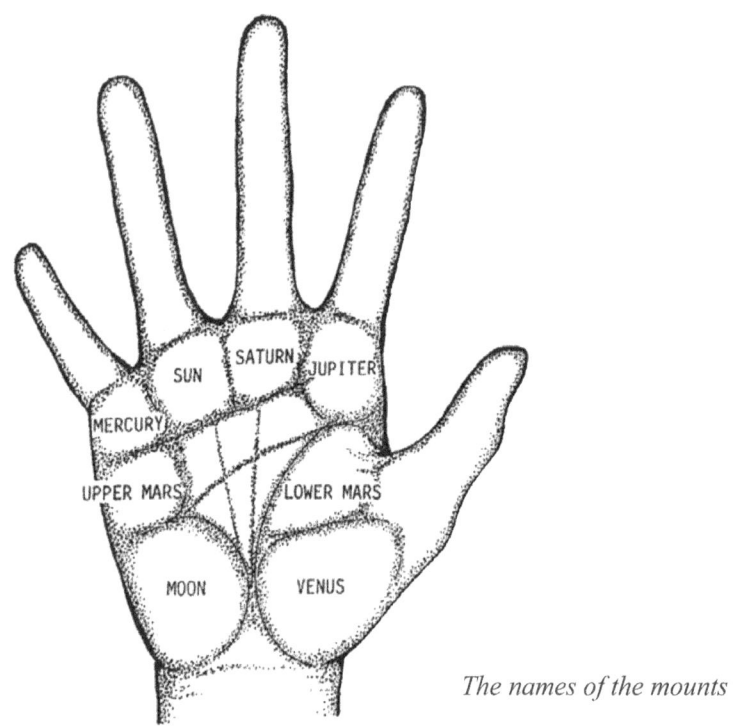

The names of the mounts

The 'invisible planets'

PLUTO	Collective unconscious:
NEPTUNE	energy visualized as
URANUS	flowing from the Rascette

The 'visible planets'

SATURN	Boundary of time and death
JUPITER	Seat of the 'lower soul'
MARS	Seat of the passions
EARTH	Seat of the physical body
MOON	Instinctive responses
VENUS	Emotional responses
MERCURY	Mental responses
SUN	Principle of life

This listing makes it clear that not only the body and its passions but the soul itself – what is known as the 'lower soul' to distinguish it from the immortal spirit – is surrounded by the orbit of Saturn, by Old Father Time, by the boundary of death. Finding a way for the soul to exceed this boundary and thus attain immortal spirit is, or should be, the concern of palmistry and palmists, for it is certainly the point and the aim of all religions and the beginning of true spirituality.

Perhaps in the past palmistry has concentrated too much on surface values. There has seldom been any real hint of hoped-for spiritual attainment, or even an awareness of the collective unconscious mind. The old-fashioned superstitious aspects have not entirely gone away: the fortune-telling imagery of imminent fate; the myth of the tall dark stranger. But now, more than ever before, we all need an additional pointer or guide.

Personality is no less real because of spiritual needs. Many people would say that the brain is the seat of the individual psyche, the governing principle. Others would claim that the emotional centre, the 'heart', is the seat of wisdom. A few might regard the governing principle as synonymous with the physical body, the instinctive 'I am', centred, perhaps, in the region of the solar plexus.

Each may be correct in his or her own individual case. Intellectuals can truly say that their highest principle, their own guiding light, resides in the brain. Devout people, or perhaps ardent lovers, might equally well claim the heart as the centre of action. Fakirs, or anyone who holds their own body in particularly high, or particularly low esteem, might claim that the material body rules, or must needs be conquered as a dangerous obstacle.

All these claims, however – particularly perhaps if in the individual case they are true – indicate, I think, a falling short of the ideal. The human soul should be the central guiding force of the individual, from whatever higher power the soul may or may not derive its energy. The soul *should* be higher than the brain, or the heart, or the body. But it would be a mistake to think of 'soul' as something quite distinct from everyday life, of concern only to particularly pious or religious people, or sincere 'seekers after the truth'. Soul is indeed the earthly seat of spirituality, but it is also the seat of everyday experience. All influences have first to enter soul before they can reach our worldly functions and come to our worldly attention. In the case of most individuals, soul never comes to awareness and would seem quite irrelevant to daily affairs. In a few cases, soul is so active, so aware, that it possesses and projects of its own volition the full range of conscious functions. It can see, hear, speak, understand and impart information quite independently of the ordinary brain or emotional feelings, or the eyes and ears and mouth.

Intellect tends not to be friendly towards soul. Intellect likes and, indeed, needs to take credit for all kinds of psychic activity, conscious and unconscious. The function of intellect is to analyse, and analysis – by definition the rendering of wholes into identifiable parts – destroys wholeness. But wholeness is the concern, the very purpose, of the soul.

As for the heart, it feels very insecure whenever it senses soul, for it sees soul as a threat to its own sense of importance and as a harbinger of death. Both intellectual and emotional people, therefore, may claim that 'soul' is no more than a label, a convenient term to describe cultural background, religious feeling, emotionally-held opinions and so forth. But the soul is not meant to be understood. Soul is intangible but it is no mere theory. It is the only gateway we have to true spirituality and thence to immortality.

The *physical* residence of the soul, the personal powerhouse governing heart, mind and body, is symbolized in the palm of the hand by the Mount of Jupiter, the fleshy area beneath the base of the forefinger. Connected with this mount is a channel that can symbolically be focused through the index finger. When you point, you are said to direct your life powers towards the person or thing pointed at. In many cultures it is 'rude' to point. In some shamanistic or animistic societies where demons are very real, it can be positively fearful!

The line which culminates in the index finger, running from the Rascette at the wrist across the slanting palm to the fingertip, represents the line of force serving your own soul – your own inner feelings, the driving force, the primary aim – and the underflowing current of life, running through the sea of the collective unconscious. Your own karma is being focused and hurled against the object of your pointing. On the map of the hand, only the barrier of the Head Line – the logical workings of your own brain – prevents this process from coming to awareness.

On a materialistic scale of reckoning, the Mount of Jupiter is considered to be the seat of ambition. And what, indeed, is ambition but a basic driving force? From this point of the palm, the main features of the hand derive and radiate.

From this symbolic point, the soul can rule the heart, the

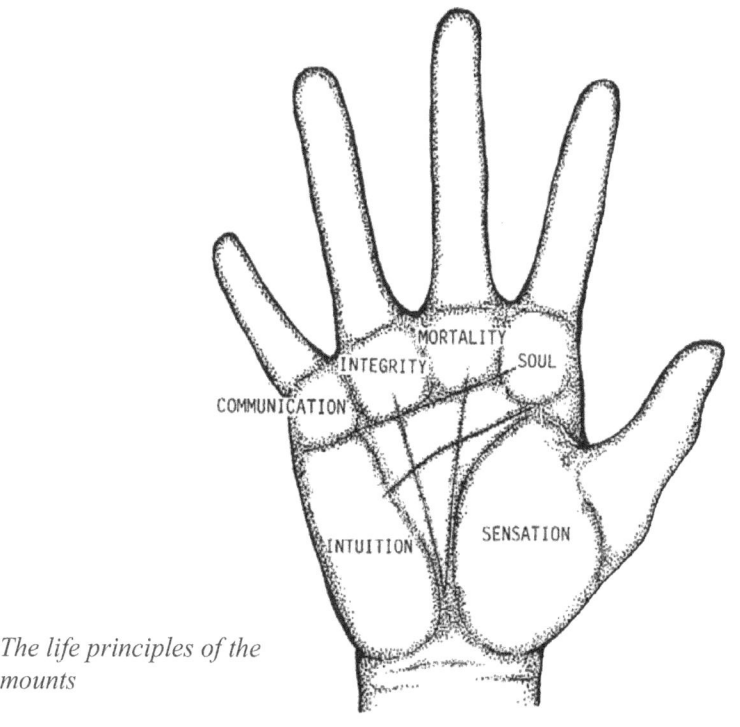

The life principles of the mounts

head, the body and individual life itself. Directly below, bound by the Life Line, the Mounts of Mars and Venus represent the physical body, its desires, passions and needs.

As the feelings derive from the soul, via the heart, so from the Mount of Jupiter, as a rule, runs the Heart Line. But its starting point may be said to be shared equally with the Mount of Saturn, beneath the second finger, as both are frequent tributaries. In traditional palmistry, this Mount of Saturn is known as the area relating to resources, to materiality, and is often connected with melancholia or depression. The reason for this connection could hardly be plainer: Saturn, of course, is another name for Chronos, the Grim Reaper, Old Father Time – the limiting principle of human life. This in real life is so often where deep depression starts: at those times when the progress of the feelings, traced by the Heart Line, has been denied the fullness of Jupiter, the unlimited contents of the soul; in those cases where life's ruling principles have become bound by the conventions, laws, rituals and material possessions under Saturn's

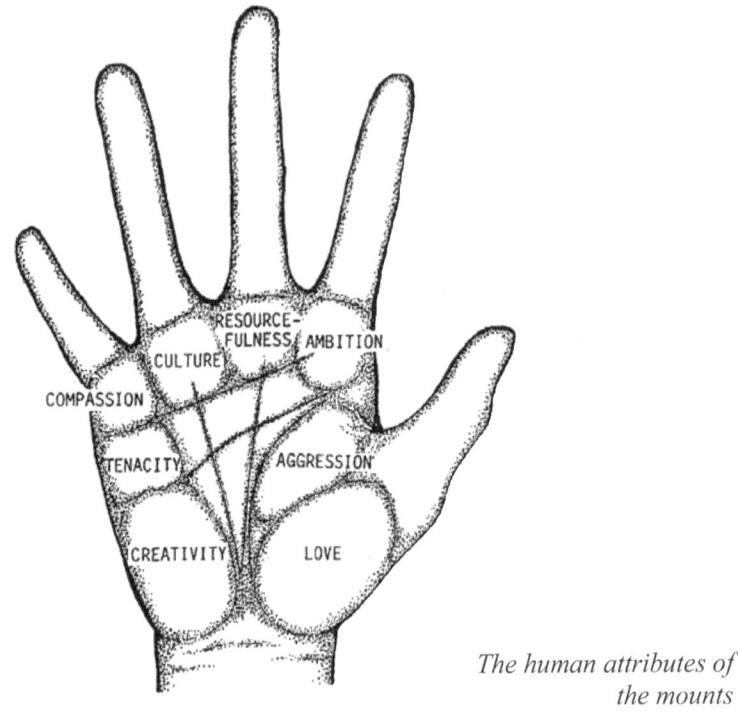

The human attributes of the mounts

sway. It is a real, practical situation that happens all too often. Your soul tells you in which direction your life should run but, for whatever reason, you *dare not* respond.

You can look at it as 'soul' or 'ambition', but in either case Jupiter is the primary source of our three main streams of consciousness, the mental, the emotional and the physical, modified in terms of practical considerations by the power of Saturn. The indication is that 'soul comes first', whether acknowledged as a fact or not. The way in which these three principles of heart, mind and body respond to the influences of fate may be charted as they trace their course among and towards the principles that attract them. Your life is recorded symbolically as these three main lines, washed by the stream of karma, approach and respond to the Mounts of the Sun, Mercury, Mars, Venus and the Moon.

The traditional significance of the mounts, the life principles and human values ascribed to them, and the innate nature of these principles and values, may be summarized by the table opposite.

Mount	Principle	Value	Nature
Jupiter	Soul	Ambition	Impetus
Saturn Sun Mercury	Morality Integrity Communication	Resourcefulness Culture Compassion	Intention
Lower Mars Venus	Sensation	Aggression Love	Action
Upper Mars Moon	Intuition	Tenacity Creativity	Reaction

7 The Pendulum of Karma:
Fate, Fortune and the Rascette

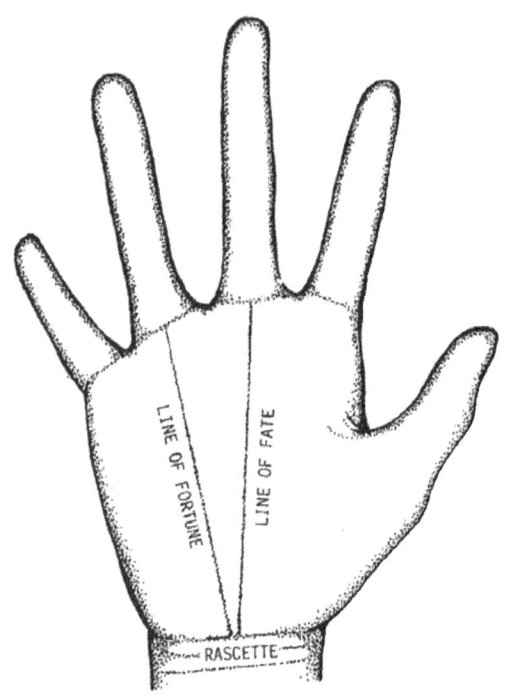

The Lines of Fate and Fortune

THE GRIM REAPER is not to be denied. Neither birth nor death can take place without the permission of Saturn, without the involvement of the Saturnian principle of time and materiality. So it is with this significance in mind that we note an additional line known as the Line of Fate, which may or may not be present on any individual palm. When present, the Line of Fate runs to the Mount of Saturn from the three wrist bracelets known as the Rascette, which itself signifies the basic quality, the unconscious motivation, the current of life that flows beneath our conscious awareness.

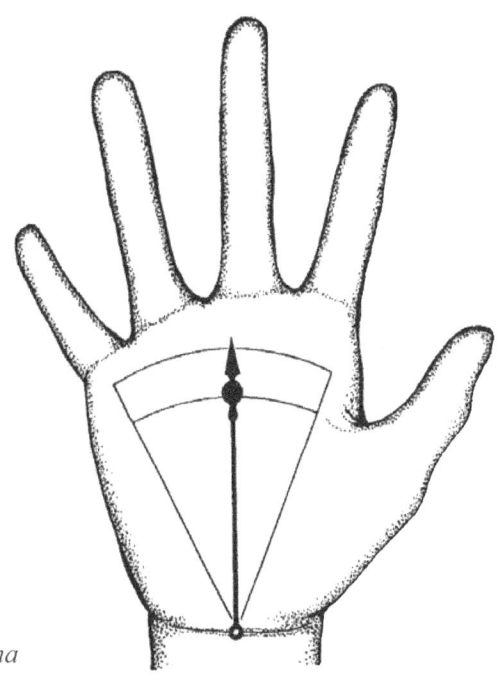

The Pendulum of Karma

    The three rings of the Rascette, you will remember, serve to represent the three 'invisible' planets symbolizing the collective unconscious – Uranus, Neptune and Pluto. Their symbolic role in this is not concerned with personality or personal content so much as the higher, or deeper, aspect of humanity: the condition perhaps wherein all people are as one – a condition which does not as a rule come to our awareness. It is outside the province of the thoughts, the feelings and the sensations of our ordinary lives. This is the region from which the Line of Fate is drawn. It is not, as I say, present on every hand, When it does appear, it is said by palmists to represent those factors in our lives which seem to be preordained and beyond our capacity to foresee. It does not imply that these unconscious factors are able to bring the mind to awareness, but rather the opposite.

    As the Heart Line draws level with the third finger, it skirts the base of the Mount of the Sun, known traditionally as the seat of culture. In deeper terms, whereas Jupiter represents the soul and Saturn the principle of time and mortality, the Sun represents the

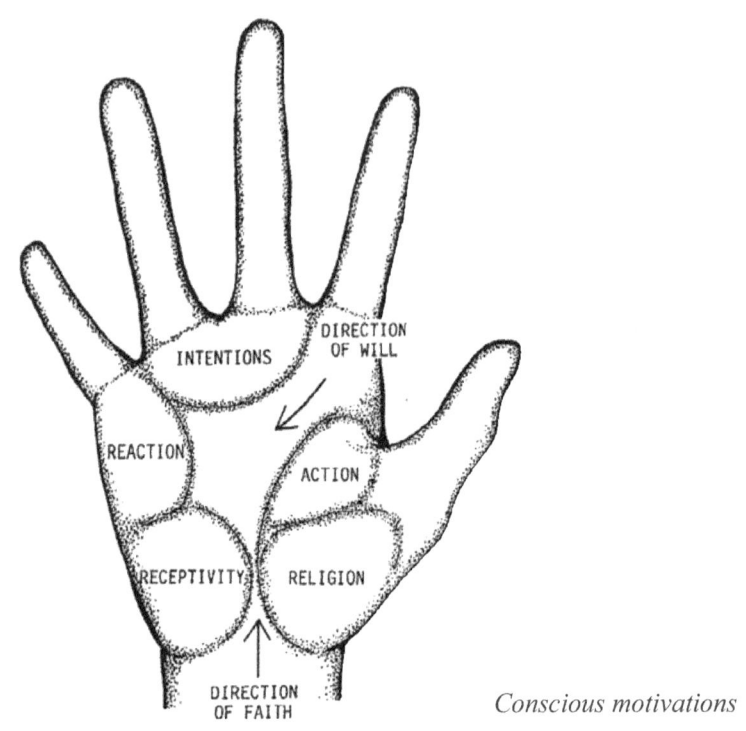

Conscious motivations

integrating principle in humanity, the urge towards wholeness that draws the feelings confidently through the bounds of mortality. On a more prosaic level, it records whether material resources are being used for the good.

There is another subsidiary line that, when present, runs to the Mount of the Sun from the Rascette, and this is the Line of Fortune, sometimes known as the Sun Line. Because inner culture of the type represented by this line takes on the appearance of outer good fortune, the Line of Fortune when it appears represents that brand of good luck which seems to come effortlessly to some fortunate people – to those perhaps, in tune with their own integrating principle.

Some of the popular notions associated with marriage – a man finding his 'better half', human integrity, psychic completion – may explain why the third finger, rising from the Mount of the Sun, is the traditional finger on which to wear a wedding ring. At the very

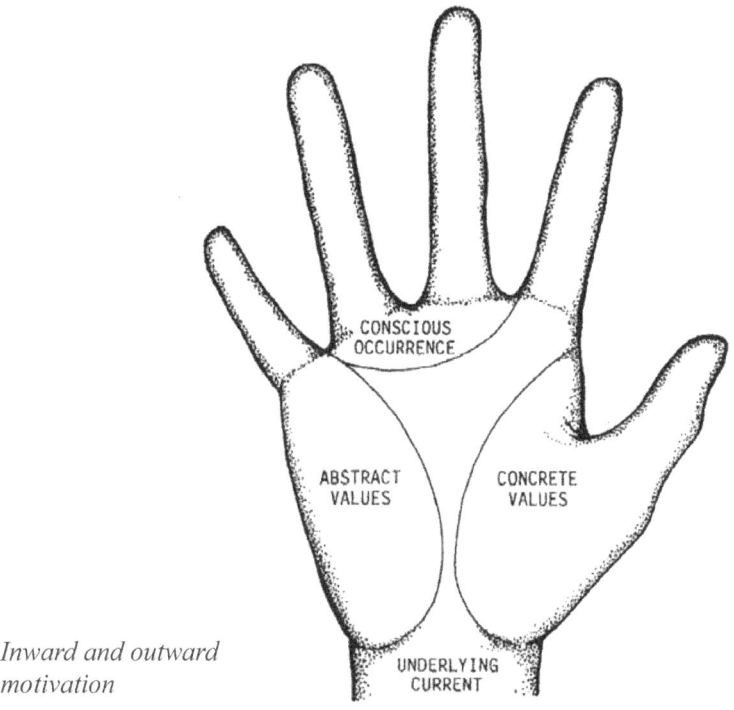

Inward and outward motivation

least, marriage represents integration and the potential to become complete on a physical scale.

Finally, the Heart Line, on most hands, passes beneath the little finger, often curving around the Mount of Mercury. Mercury, of course, is said to be the messenger of the gods, representative of darting thoughts, and this area is traditionally regarded as the seat of communication. It is at the end of the Heart Line that the lines of Marriage appear – and what more appropriate place could there be for the consummation of that special form of communication which, ideally, takes place at the culmination of the feelings?

If you look at the general plan of the hand, you will see that the zone connecting the unconscious current of life at the Rascette with the consciously active zone of the mounts is roughly triangular. This could be visualized as forming part of the pathway of the soul – a channel of influence flowing from and to the index finger. Inevitably it is the route, too, of karma.

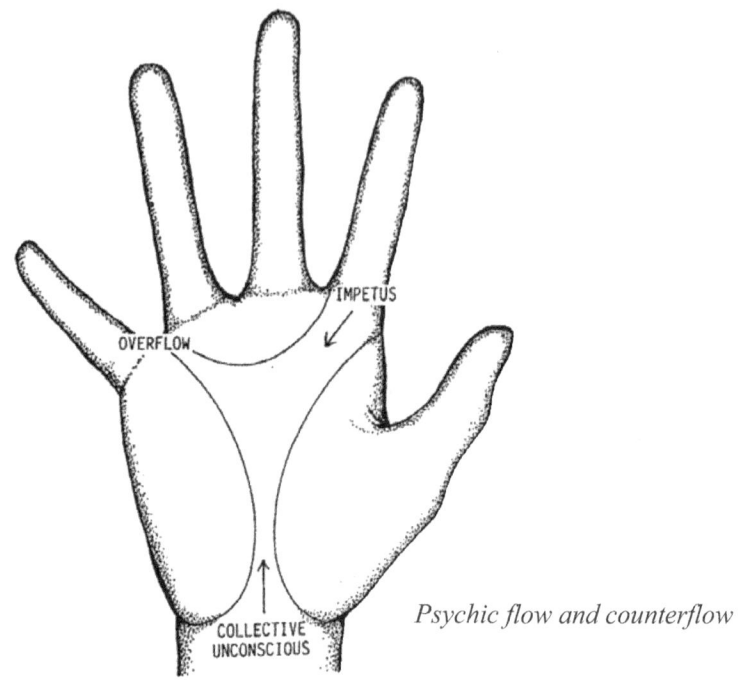

Psychic flow and counterflow

      With a little more imagination, this triangular zone could be visualized as being covered by a pendulum hinged on the Rascette, constantly swinging along the Head Line and the Heart Line, between Jupiter and Mercury, between soul and mind. As the tip of this pendulum sways through the cultural and material zones of consciousness, between the inward motivation of the soul on the one side and the outward thoughts and attitudes of the mind on the other, its motion touches and stirs in turn the concrete, physical zone based on the Mount of Venus and the abstract, intuitive zone based on the Mount of the Moon.

      Thoughts, in this scale, can be seen to be abstract. Along with tenacity, as represented by the Upper Mount of Mars, thoughts express the abstract side of action and intention. The idea of flow and counterflow through this channel expresses the interplay of *will* acting against *faith*. The former, flowing from the soul along the Heart Line, Head Line and Life Line, meets the latter, flowing between the opposing banks of religion on the side of concrete values and

48

receptivity on the side of abstract values. Both currents meet in the Supernal Zone, to which I shall return later.

In some people, it seems as if a proportion of this 'soul-stuff' leaks out, as it were, between the little finger of Mercury and the third finger of the Sun. When this happens, the individual concerned will feel an urge to communicate these deep, innately cultural values, emanating from the soul and the collective pool of the unconscious, to the world in general. Such people, it is said, 'wear their soul on their sleeve'. As a sign of this peculiarity, it will be noticed that their little finger spreads itself considerably wider than the other fingers. We have already seen that this characteristic also implies a communicative character who is not hidebound by rules and conventions – and I suppose this amounts to much the same thing.

Seen in the light of all this, neither the Line of Fate nor the Line of Fortune, when strongly marked, is a particularly welcome sign to possess. They suggest a karma that is in some way 'fixed' during the present lifetime on earth – a fate that may be happy, but one that cannot be altered until death. A successful lifestyle, perhaps, but one that will remain unmodified by conscience, or doubt, or recrimination, until Saturn finally has his way, and the lines are erased in death's decay.

It is a strange fact that the Rascette on the right wrist (see the following chapter for the difference between right and left hands) often becomes progressively less distinct when an individual's karmic load begins to be shed. No sooner is a soul 'opened' to release such unwanted contents, perhaps through contact with other 'opened' souls, than the clear three-ringed bracelet formation begins to break down, until sometimes, perhaps after many years, it has even disappeared altogether into a blur of fine lines. The Lines of Fate and Fortune, too, can appear unexpectedly, or just as mysteriously disappear. Palmistry can be seen to work!

8 Inherited Characteristics:
Left Hand, Right Hand

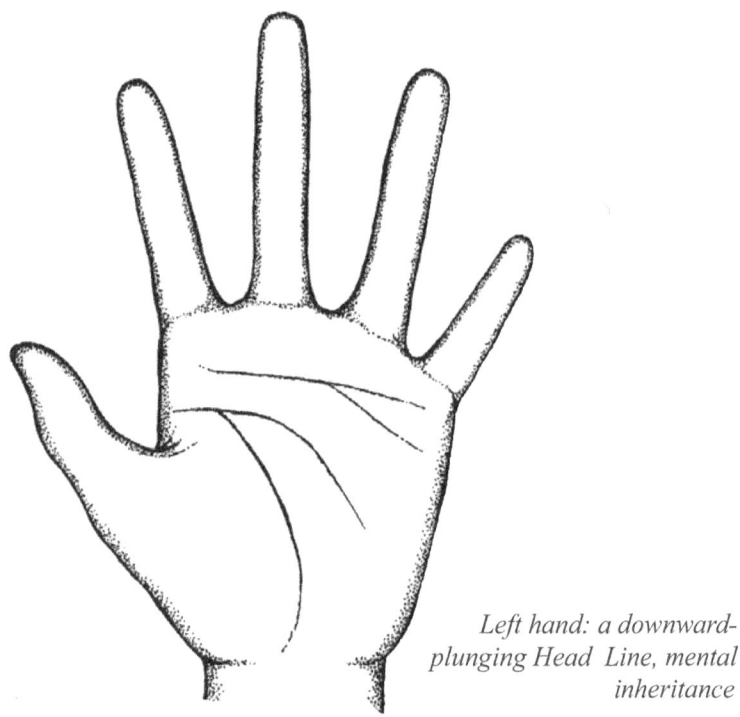

Left hand: a downward-plunging Head Line, mental inheritance

THE TWO HANDS placed side by side will often show very similar features, the one a mirror-image of the other. Usually, however, there are differences between the two sets of characteristics, and sometimes they are very different indeed. Either hand will offer a sketch of the personality, each with a slightly differing slant. Both hands placed together will show a sequence of events – a potted personal history. Reading from left to right, they tell the ongoing story of the individual life. They present a picture of the development of personality, and the way in which it reacts with the underlying power of soul.

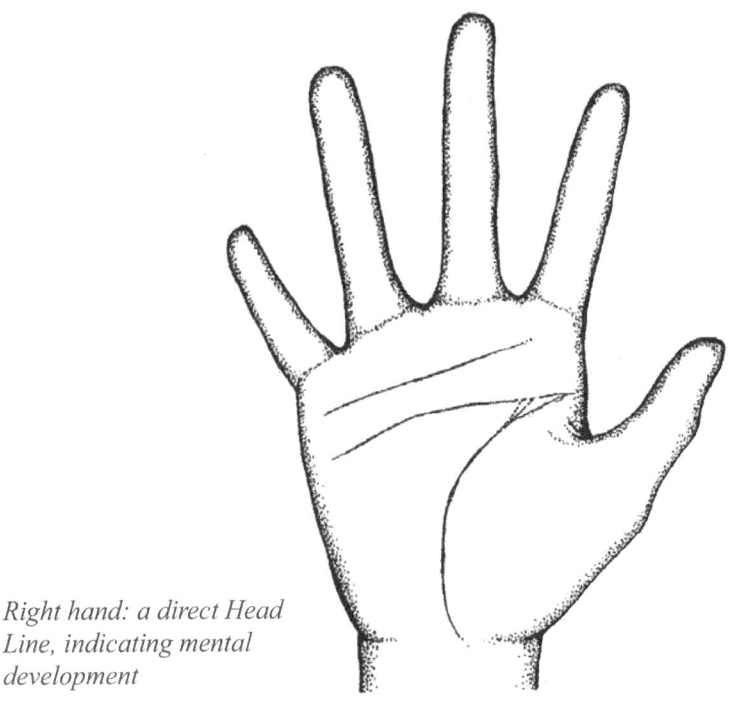

Right hand: a direct Head Line, indicating mental development

It is rare to get the chance to compare the hands of parents and their children. There is usually a very definite link between them and, if the opportunity presents itself, there is much room for interesting research in this field. Basically, the left hand represents our inheritance: everything that is fixed and unalterable; the material side of nature. Often (and certainly this is so in my own case) it happens that distinctive signs in the right hand of the parent reappear in reverse on their child's left hand. When this happens, it suggests that a certain set of characteristics has been passed on, and hints very strongly at their nature. When the left-hand pattern of the parent is repeated in the child's left hand, the root of that particular inheritance goes very deeply and will prove persistent during adult life. Particularly inflexible characters will probably have a very similar pattern on both hands, and their parents will probably exhibit precisely the same features in both their hands too.

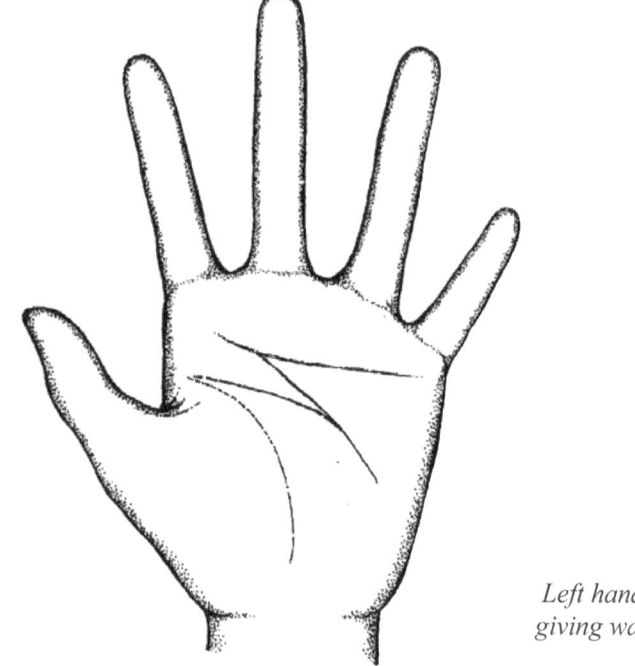

Left hand: feelings giving way to ideas

Armed with this knowledge, it is possible to tell by comparison between the hands which features seem to have developed as a direct consequence of inheritance and which (having no counterpart in the parents' hands) may seem to indicate characteristics that seem to be the exclusive, personal property of the child. Some characteristics may be inherited from the father, some from the mother. Unless there is evidence to the contrary and without sight of the parents' hands, it is probably best to assume that this line of inheritance operates through the father.

A downward-plunging Head Line on the right hand, contrasting with a straight inherited version on the left hand, for instance, will seem to indicate that a no-nonsense, intellectually orientated father has sired a head-in-the-clouds dreamer! But the reverse may equally well be the case. The right-handed characteristic in this respect may well be more 'favourable' than the left, depending of course on the cultural expectations of the subject. A child may have

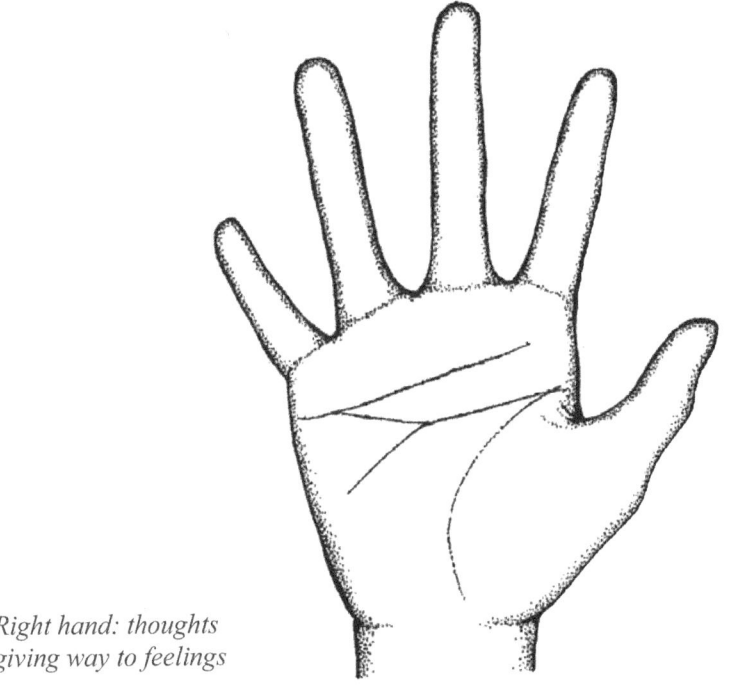

Right hand: thoughts giving way to feelings

inherited a mediocre mental capacity but, through hard work and tenacity, good fortune, good teaching, good advice and application, proved able to make the best of an unpromising start in life. A ne'er-do-well father *may* produce outstanding progeny. Inheritance is not always direct, and genius after all has to originate at some point in time and space.

    The more complicated the pattern of lines, the more complicated will be your conclusions, but all the more interesting for that. On the parent's right hand, for instance, the Head Line and the Heart Line may be joined by a strong branch-line, suggesting that the emotions and thoughts are powerfully linked, or that one function tends to overrule the other. Children inheriting this state of affairs will probably find the distinctive sign in their left hand but, through the modification of their personal karma, their right hand may be quite different. There may be a connecting line; or the branch-line may start, running upwards from the Head Line, but fail to make contact with the Heart Line, forming instead a major fork of its own.

This will indicate that the twin functions of thinking and feeling are more clearly differentiated in the child than in the parent. It may be that the fork has developed out of proportion, the upper prong leaving a moderately 'weak' Head Line behind, overtaking it and running straight and true across the palm. When such a fork is very pronounced and barely joined to the Head Line itself, it may be considered as an important line in its own right, the Supernal Line, and this may perhaps indicate the best possible use of this particular inheritance. In effect, the mind and heart of this person will have been joined by a third function, possibly more powerful and certainly more mysterious than either. In such a case the child (though the capacity will not become apparent until adulthood) may develop a detached kind of subtle reasoning that can understand and feel superior to thoughts and feelings, rising above both logic and sentiment. Owners of this sign will rarely be able to get the better of someone in an argument, however. They can always see the opposing view-point, and sympathize with it!

There will probably be a definite, recognizable time in the individual's life when the right hand takes over, as it were, from the left. It is in fact the onset of responsible adulthood. This can often be seen most clearly when the Line of Fate crosses or rises on the Life Line. When this happens, the system of measuring time on these lines, discussed later in the book, may be applied, and the age of the subject or the year when this transfer takes place can be accurately fixed.

Opposites or strong differences between right and left hands should always be noted, as they are highly significant. If a left hand branch-line switches direction in the right hand, as though carrying the flow of inherited influence back from one major function to another, a certain degree of psychological confusion may be suspected. The same sort of characteristic may be hinted at in the handwriting that veers erratically from forwards- to backwards-leaning styles. Such individuals are liable to vacillate between opposing poles, seeming so hopelessly split between conflicting ideas that they can barely achieve anything worthwhile. With a positive and a negative always working simultaneously, they tend to be the sort of people who worry endlessly over which course of action to take and end up doing nothing. But this is tension at its worst. Tension at its best is a source of energy, and this interplay, this tension between left and right, whether or not it takes a positive direction, can be a powerful indicator of soul.

The left hand, then, can be said to reflect the physical inheritance, while the right hand records the psychic response to that inheritance. Both hands must be considered together if you are to gain an inkling of soul by way of palmistry, because soul encompasses both the material and the spiritual, the give and the take, the positive and the negative. This is why our hands are instinctively placed together in prayer, as an indication of 'wholeness'. Such things are made clearer by having two hands to ponder. But when one seeks a material explanation alone, one searches for it in the left hand. A spiritual or more abstract explanation is to be found in the right hand. Thus signs denoting purely material events – journeys, inheritances, physical accidents, disabilities and illnesses – will tend to appear in the left hand. Signs denoting intellectual, emotional, religious and spiritual developments will appear in the right. The most significant events – the truly holistic phenomena – are recorded in both hands. Always examine both hands, as both sides of an argument, and 'read them like a book'.

9 The Heart Line: Directing the Emotions

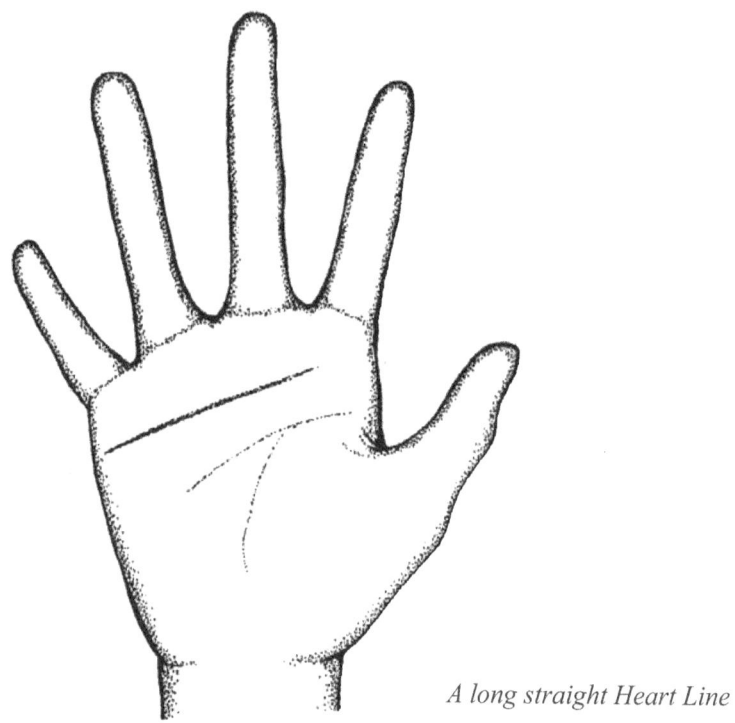

A long straight Heart Line

IT IS THE HEART LINE that plots the intensity and direction of our emotional feelings. In hands where this line is long and strong, there is every reason to suppose that their owner's emotions will be equally forthright. Where the Heart Line is short and faint, whether the subject be of a reasonable or unreasonable nature overall, you may be sure that he or she will not be an emotionally orientated person, but instead may seem to be rather markedly lacking in warmth and affection.

The tenderest affection habitually expressed – this is the happy side of a personal nature reflected in a long, clear Heart Line extending to the edge of the palm. A line that is deeply marked

Short, deeply marked Heart Line

but fairly short, however, especially if it commences late and does not extend beyond the Mount of the Sun, means that the subject will certainly be an emotional person and, indeed, a fiercely passionate one; but it is likely to be the brand of up-and-down passion in which, to an outsider at least, tenderness may seem to be absent. Such a one will be prone to violent all-consuming love affairs, involving love-hate relationships that lead inevitably to fights or shouting matches – punctuated, of course, with spells of passionate love-making. This, I think, will be the love of the scarlet lily rather than the white rose.

A markedly straight Heart Line implies a markedly straight, coolly staid emotional life. The owner of a line like this will be unlikely to do anything that would outrage the neighbours, and to such a one a marriage quarrel would be more likely to involve a quiet exchange of barbed sarcasm than a claws-bared screaming match.

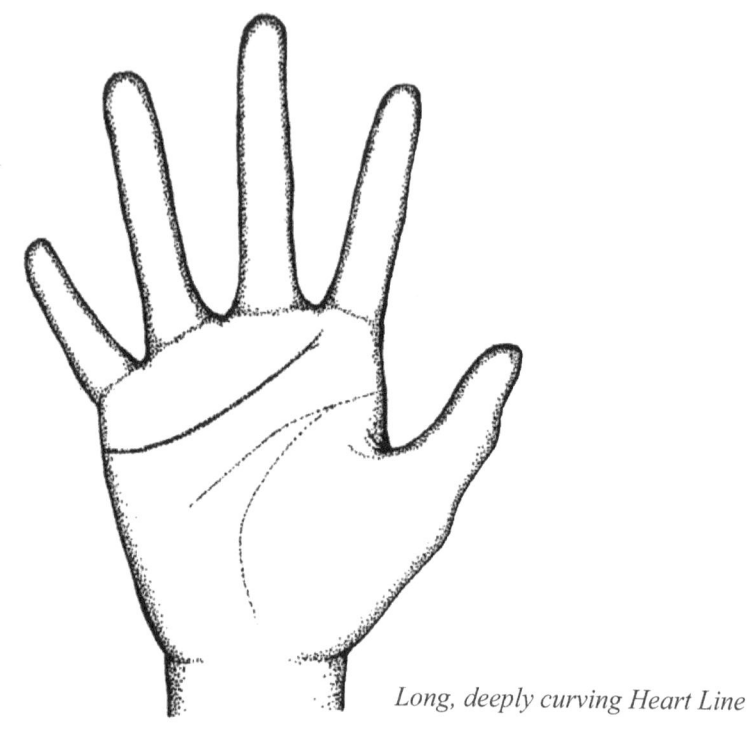

Long, deeply curving Heart Line

The long and deeply curving Heart Line is the sign of a deeply affectionate but often temperamental character. When such a person loves, their emotions run at a very deep level, gathering strength in the psyche. The owner of a firmly marked, deeply plunging Heart Line that carries on round the edge of the palm will not *necessarily* be a particularly out-going or extrovert person, but when his or her heart becomes attached to another person, the emotions involved will be quite extraordinarily outgoing. In cases where a person with a straight Heart Line would be discreet about an affair, the wearer of this deeply curving version will want the world to know about it. In this way its presence on the palm could be said to portend indiscretion. There will certainly be nothing secret about its owner's *affaires de cœur*.

In cases where the affections are orientated in a non-sexual direction, the deeply curving Heart Line tells of com-passionate devotion, but this wonderfully human characteristic may well become lost or swamped in an emotional tide of irrational feelings that can be a source of psychological trouble. Such a person will not necessarily be happy; the emotions are simply too powerful to be trained and steered along the rails of a smooth and peaceful lifestyle. Temperamentally, the deeply curving Heart Liner can be equally loving and savage, serenely happy when things are going well and utterly devastated when they go wrong.

The palmist often has to consider questions of compatibility. Talk of marriage quarrels may suggest that two different Heart Liners are bound to fall out. Perhaps they will, from time to time, but this need not be a disaster. Like attracts like in the short term, but in the long term there is also the more enduring attraction of opposites. Evenly balanced disagreements can cement a relationship, and both conflicting poles can complement the other. Each will act as a modifying influence on the excesses of the other partner. With a grain of luck and a pinch of intelligence on both sides (and all this is recorded in the palm), an emotionally 'odd' couple may well make a happy match. Once we realize our own uniqueness, or once this brand of uniqueness has been pointed out to us, we can begin to compromise where compromise is needed (and it always is, sooner or later) and bypass the more dangerous areas of dissent.

10 The Rising of the Feelings:
Pride, Ambition and Greed

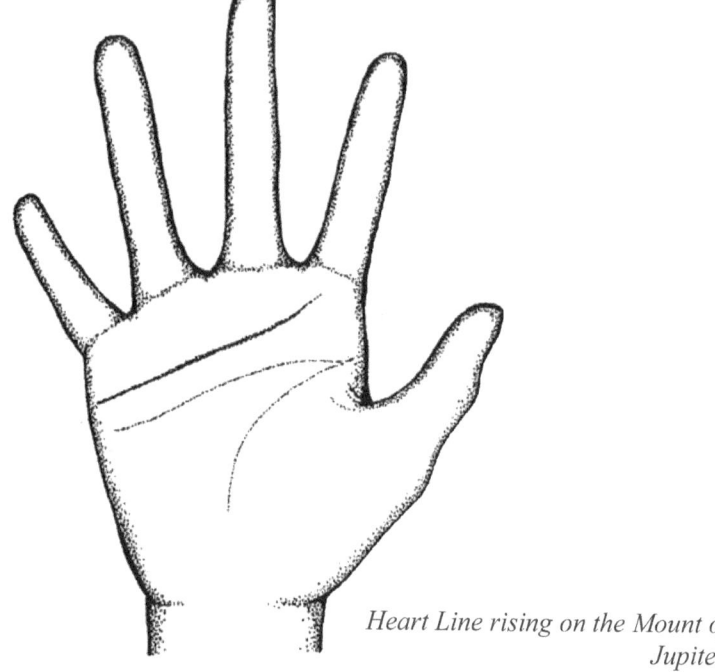

Heart Line rising on the Mount of Jupiter

LIKE THE TWO other main lines slightly lower down on the palm, the Heart Line rises in the general region of the Mount of Jupiter, and from this we can deduce that all three lines can symbolize a flow of messages from the human soul. But the precise starting point carries special significance. When the Heart Line rises clearly on the Mount of Jupiter itself, the features attributed to this mount will be transmitted, as it were, via the emotional life of the subject. They will flavour the flow of feelings.

When the Heart Line has different sources of origin on the left and right hands, this can be read in two ways. First, in the context of inheritance and the modification of personal karma. And second, in the context of feelings about material things on the left hand and feelings about abstract things on the right. But unless the two

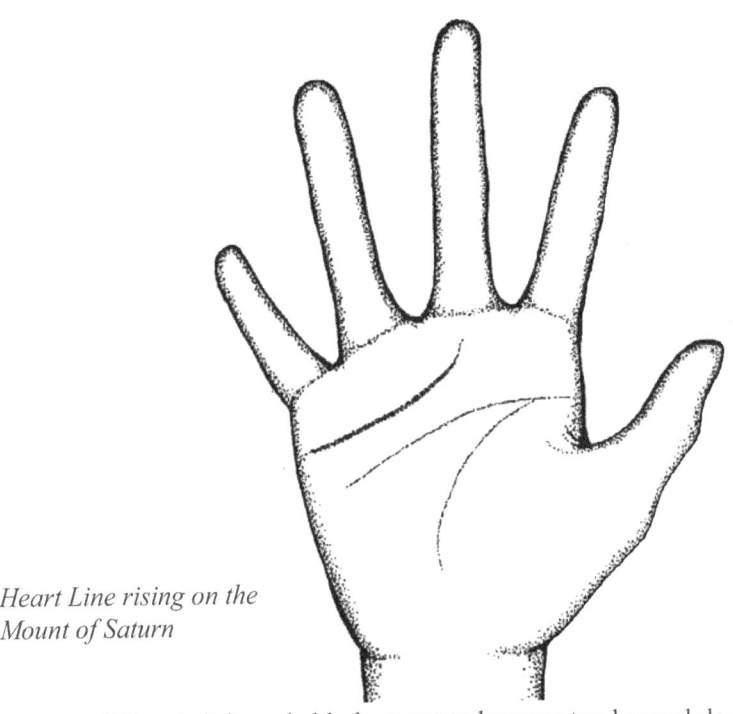

Heart Line rising on the Mount of Saturn

are very different, it is probably best not to become too bogged down with this distinction.

On the most basic level, people whose Heart Line rises directly on the Mount of Jupiter will have ambition in their heart! Compared with the bulk of humanity, their emotional driving force will seem exaggerated. Pride will never be too far away, never too deeply beneath the surface. Pride and ambition will play key roles in all their relationships, not least their marriage. Their sense of ambition will have ensured the best match possible, and pride will probably not allow them to stray too far from the formally approved path of faithfulness and morality. It would seem humiliating to an individual showing this characteristic on his or her palm, to be thought less than upright and honourable in this respect.

On a more rarefied level (and particularly in the right hand Heart Line), the emotional life of Jupiter-heart people will seem to be inspired directly from the soul – not, that is, from anything 'holy', but from the ordinary, unrefined, unpurified 'lower' soul. As the human soul is recipient of all influences, both high and low, such a person

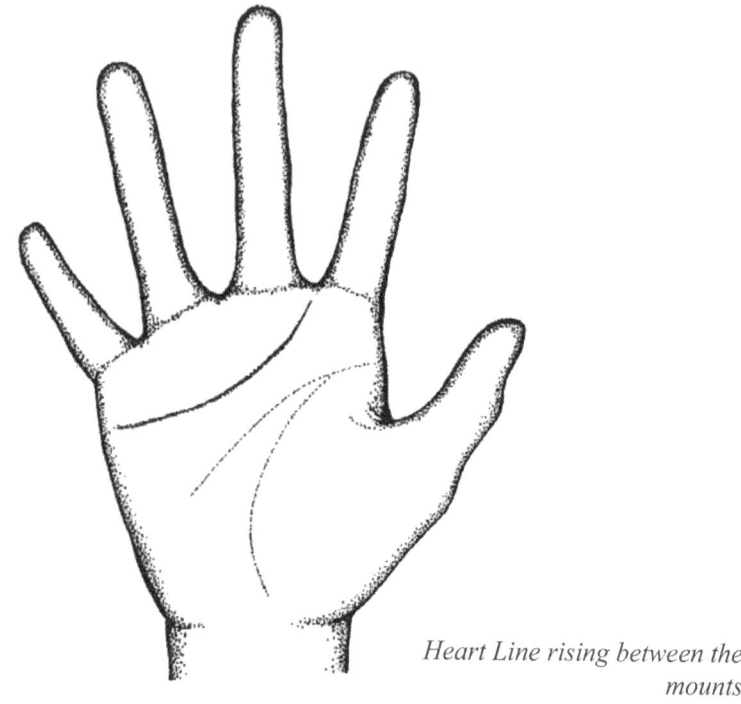

Heart Line rising between the mounts

will not necessarily act from the highest or the purist of motives. The heart may seem to act quite independently of, or even sometimes in spite of, the modifying influence of calm reason. Its stubborn course will be set and there will be no deviation, no sudden changes of mind.

To have a 'Jupiter-heart' is not at all the same as being spiritually inclined. But such people will be likely to follow the teachings of their religion, or inherited set of moral rules, with firmly imposed self-discipline. They will rarely question or deviate from this path. In religious terms, it will perhaps be difficult at times for them to differentiate between their faith and their own pride. Such people may act in extreme ways to guard their faith or traditions – in their own eyes – while to others they will seem simply to be satisfying their own sense of pride. Jupiter-hearts may perform some acts of supreme sacrifice, but they can be dangerous! They can become fanatical in their beliefs and actions.

The Heart Line that commences clearly on the Mount of Saturn denotes a very different character. Saturn-heart people's

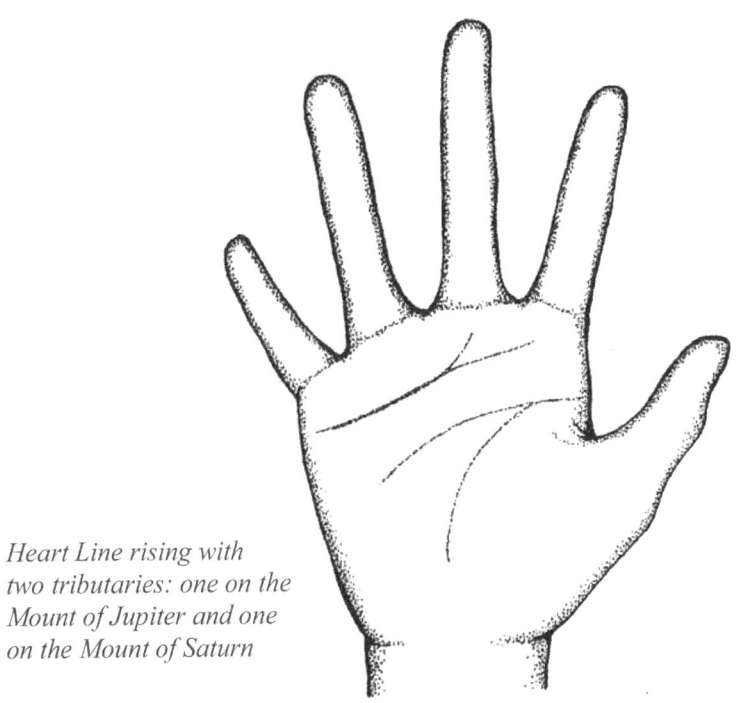

Heart Line rising with two tributaries: one on the Mount of Jupiter and one on the Mount of Saturn

emotional world will be attuned to the interests of materiality; the wealth of the world will be dear to their heart. They may not be misers – indeed, they may well be big spenders; they will seldom be short of the means to spend lavishly on luxuries. But they will be quite unperturbed by the finer feelings or even the suffering of others. Their emotional driving force will be 'gain', and they will act primarily not out of consideration for ethical principles, but for possession, for ownership. Charity for them truly 'begins at home'.

This is not the same as selfishness, and Saturn Heart Liners will look after anyone for whom they feel responsible. If you are indebted to someone, you 'owe' them, and in a subtle way you belong to them. Dependent people are in a sense possessions, and to Saturn-heart people the well-being of their dependants will be a matter of pride. In the case of a man with this feature, if his Heart Line is also clear and straight, he will certainly be highly sensual, but he may lack tenderness. Sensuality too is a possession, a taking in, and he will have satisfaction at whatever cost. Tenderness for him would be an unnecessary expense.

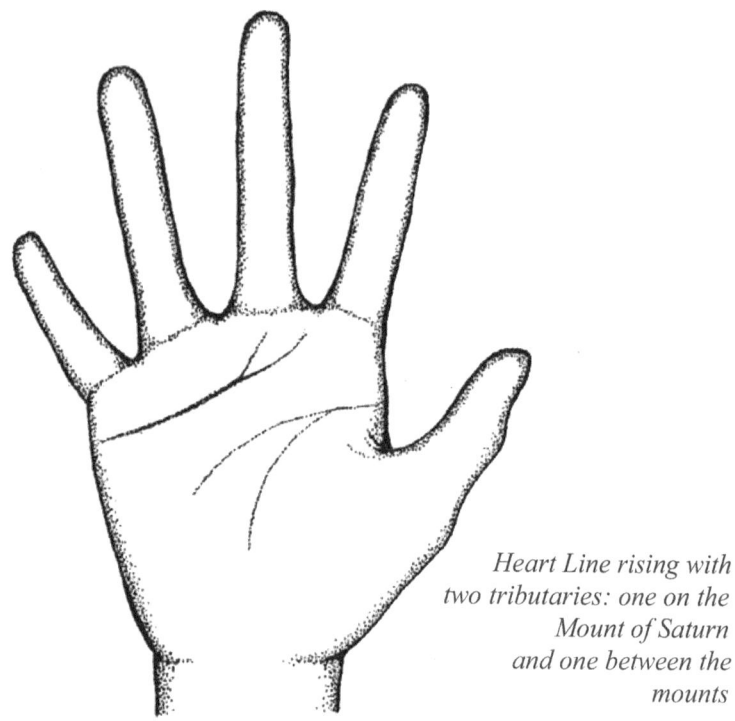

Heart Line rising with two tributaries: one on the Mount of Saturn and one between the mounts

These are the two polarities of emotional direction, but such extreme examples are rare and the great majority of people fall somewhere between the two. The Heart Line frequently commences with a fork, like the tributaries of a river, and the rising point of these tributaries is significant. The personality of a Heart Liner such as this will be that much more complicated, and that much more interesting – more 'human'.

When the Heart Line rises from a single point, as we have just seen, and continues unequivocally straight and clear, this is how his or her emotional path through life is sure to seem to its owner. To such a person, there will seem to be only one possible solution to any particular problem, and individual choice or outside influence will scarcely enter into consideration. But tributaries divide this blinkered view and give the subject a broader choice of action. Instead of having one fixed viewpoint, the subject can now 'feel' the other's point of view, can realize that there is more than one way of acting and reacting.

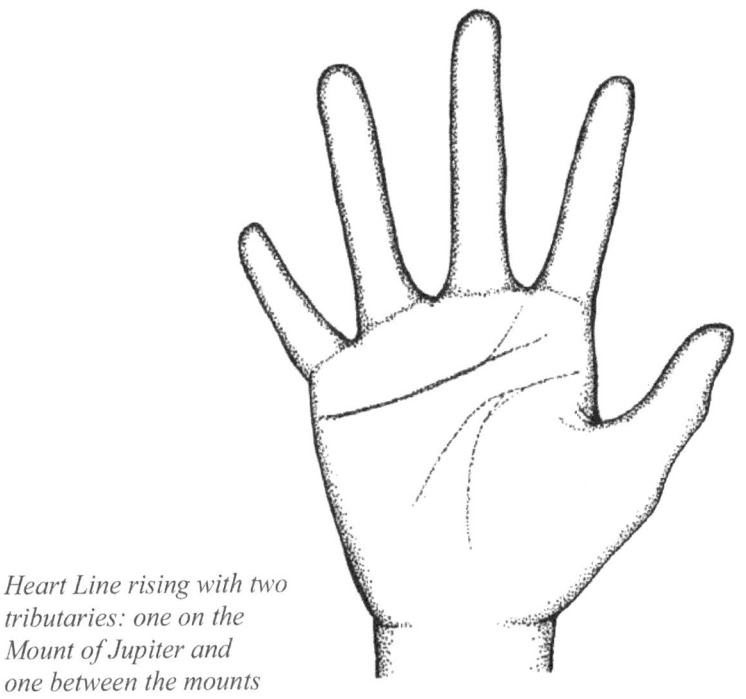

Heart Line rising with two tributaries: one on the Mount of Jupiter and one between the mounts

As tributaries denote duality or multiplicity, a division of responsibilities and priorities, and the mounts involved imply viewpoints that are fixed, so the areas between the mounts denote impartiality, a falling between two extremes. The middle ground between the Mount of Jupiter and the Mount of Saturn is neither all soul – that is, all ambition and abstract principle – nor all sensuality or the physical and material consolidation of possessions. Sometimes there is a threefold tributary, and the complication, or the dilution of purpose, will be increased according to the respective points of origin. In palmistry this principle holds firm; the qualities symbolized by the mounts express the driving force of the emotions, and the significance of every possible starting point of the Heart Line does not really need to be learnt as a matter of rote. It will be largely a matter of personal interpretation depending on whose hand is being read.

Basically, though, a subject with an equal tributary to their Heart Line, with one arm at Jupiter and the other at Saturn, will be an evenly though not necessarily 'well' balanced personality. The middle ground is not involved here; such people will tend to fluctuate between the two extremes. Their moods will vary accordingly, between the light-heartedness of Jupiter and the dourness of Saturn. In extreme cases the psychological fluctuation known as bipolar disorder, or the 'manic-depressive' syndrome, may be indicated by this feature.

A Heart Line that rises with one tributary on the Mount of Saturn and the other between this and the Mount of Jupiter betokens people who care deeply about material wealth and physical comforts, but their outlook will always be modified by the middle ground so that it is never too extreme. When they also possess a businesslike Head Line, they will be born fund-raisers. These are the characters who will found the metaphorical goldmine, part of the proceeds of which (once their own needs are taken care of) are to be dedicated to spiritual, charitable or cultural aims.

Perhaps the 'best' rising of the Heart Line involves one tributary arm between the Mounts of Jupiter and Saturn, and another on the Mount of Jupiter itself. This will imply *just enough* of the Saturnian concern with material benefits and sensations. It means in effect that its wearers can understand and sympathize with both Jupiter-heart and Saturn-heart types, and thus will tolerate two opposing views without necessarily agreeing with either. They should be able to keep their feet planted firmly on the ground, while appreciating all the abstract benefits available to them from higher realms. They will be unlikely to develop the unswerving attitudes and fanatical devotion that characterize the fixed Heart Liner.

In the Buddhist ideology, this is the type of character known as a 'faith-greed' person. Faith will be uppermost, but greed, as the corresponding opposite side of the coin, will always be present. Such people tend to take matters on trust and feel affection readily. They do not need sound intellectual reasons in order to believe something. And if they happen to like any particular person, thing, practice or quality, they will be unwilling to let that person, thing or custom go. A little of everything they have contact with tends to stick to these types of people, and they will therefore tend to have more 'contents', more virtues, and more faults, than any other Heart Line type – and infinitely more than people whose Head Line seems to rule the hand, whose brain overrules the heart. All these characteristics need to be read and interpreted in the light of all the other features on the subject's hand.

11 The Inner Feelings: The Upper and Lower Girdles of Venus

FAINTER than the Heart Line itself, an Inner Heart Line, also known as the Upper Girdle of Venus because of its association with the sex impulse, is an occasional feature of the palm near the mounts. This line is associated with the hidden, inner life rather than the superficial feelings of everyday expression. You will see from the diagrams that this Girdle outlines the area of 'conscious occurrence' and constitutes a sort of reception zone for karmic influences.

It is the working of this stream of unconscious impulses reacting on the soul that gives rise to the deeper, inner feelings – feelings which normally remain unexpressed; the heart functioning alone may be said to be the source of the coarse, outer feelings. Both these functions, however, are closely connected and interwoven; the difference between them is a subtle one. Inner feelings are the product of the whole human being and, though of an individual nature, are constantly being modified through the undercurrent of collective life – a real and truly spiritual force which, in the symbolism of palmistry, is visualized as flowing through the palm from the wrist. It is the Girdle of Venus that is said to catch and sift this modified flow, and these subtle inner feelings are displayed and pictured, if only sketchily, in this Inner Heart Line, as a faint scratchy soundtrack of the ancient voice of purification.

Inwardly, the inner feelings tend to congregate around certain human qualities or values, throwing an inhibitive emotional barrier around them. As an outward sign of this, the Girdle of Venus surrounds certain of the mounts, including, as a rule, the Mounts of Saturn and the Sun. It may or may not include the Mount of Mercury in its embrace, and when this is indeed the case, it seems in some way to inhibit this abstract, compassionate, communicative area of the psyche – the sign, perhaps, of an introvert.

Invariably it denotes great sensitivity, but it often seems to preclude others from partaking in what should be rightly the shared fruits of these deep areas of the human psyche. Its wearer can seldom be induced to talk freely about his or her deepest feelings, or their philosophy of life. It is really a case of 'still waters run deep'. This Upper Girdle of Venus has often been interpreted as a bar to marriage, or a sign of homosexuality, and with this implication in mind we

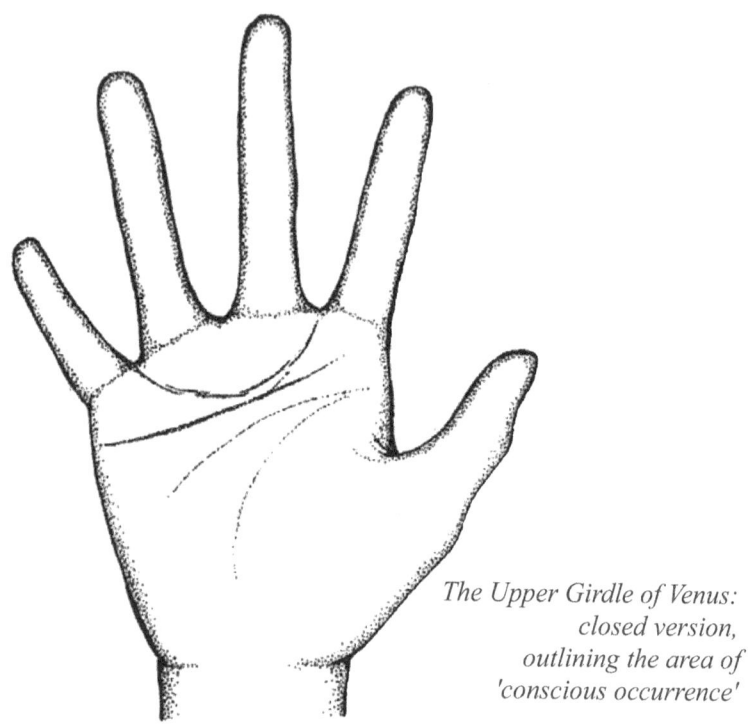

The Upper Girdle of Venus: closed version, outlining the area of 'conscious occurrence'

should note that it sometimes appears on the left hand of inheritance, to be either confirmed and strengthened or overruled and dispersed on the right. But to interpret this sign exclusively in terms of sex is to overlook the more subtle and wide-reaching aspects of the inner feelings.

There can also be an opposing girdle at the 'transmitting end' of this karmic flow above the wrist, as though to block off the underlying current – a dam to the inner feelings. When the Rascette appears to be enclosed or ringed, close to the Mount of Venus and the Mount of the Moon, and particularly when this ring is formed by the uppermost bracelet itself, looping unbrokenly upwards into the palm, there will seem to be a corresponding reluctance to let go of inner contents, even a denial that they exist. An unconscious fight will be taking place, as though to keep these karmic contents – this continuing subtle flow of universal life forces – from intruding on the awareness.

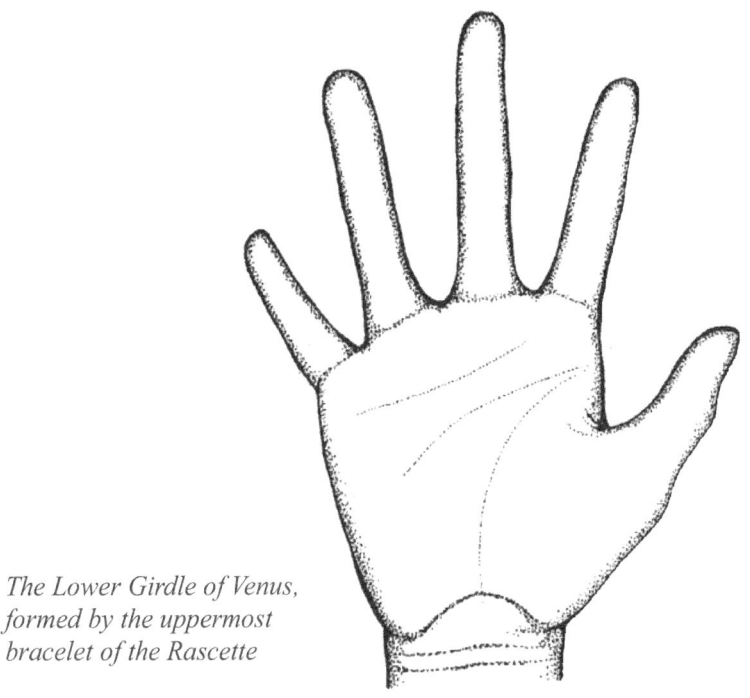

The Lower Girdle of Venus, formed by the uppermost bracelet of the Rascette

In this, there may be a bias towards one side of the palm or the other, towards abstract or concrete values. If the former, with the loop intruding on the Mount of the Moon, the wearer is liable to deny the validity of any influences apart from reason and logic. This is the man or woman who will proudly proclaim 'I did it my way!' If the latter is the case, however, when the looped bracelet, this Lower Girdle of Venus, impinges upon the Mount of Venus itself, traditional palmists have often noted, when the wearer is a woman, that she is likely to suffer difficulties associated with childbirth. The cyclic process of birth seems reluctant in such a case to proceed on a concrete level. Something within the karmic flow seems determined to obstruct the continuing cycle of human life, as far as that individual is concerned.

One less dramatic feature associated with a Rascette loop is the development of an unusually powerful external ego. The most frequently used word in its wearer's vocabulary will probably be 'I'.

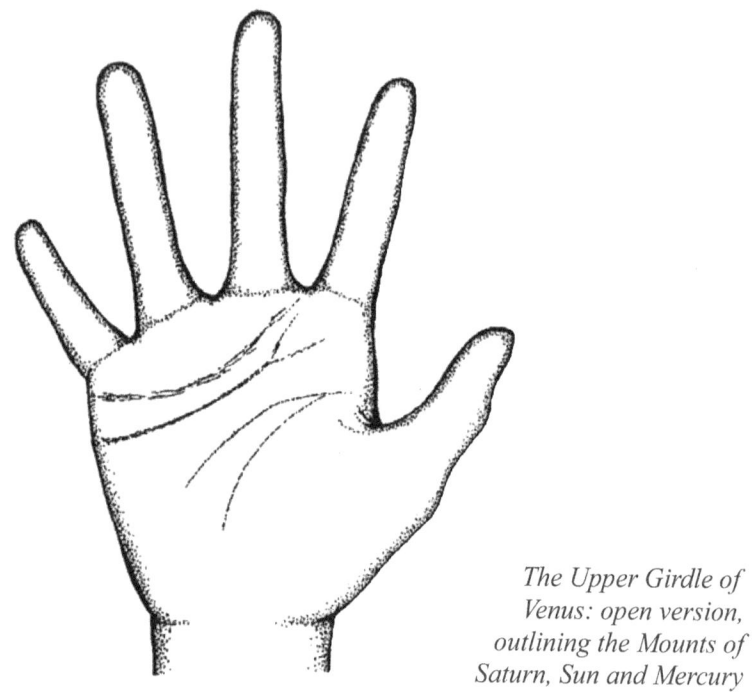

The Upper Girdle of Venus: open version, outlining the Mounts of Saturn, Sun and Mercury

This is rather the opposite of what happens to the wearer of an Inner Heart Line, when the zone of conscious occurrence – the Mounts of Saturn, the Sun, and possibly Mercury too – are ringed by the Upper Girdle of Venus. In such case, the inner contents will continue to flow freely and often come to awareness because these are sensitive, deeply thoughtful people; but they will experience difficulty in consolidating their worldly fortunes or in building a satisfactory external ego. Instead, it is the inner self that becomes strengthened at the expense of personality, setting abstract, thoughtful, spiritual values above those of a practical, material nature.

Wearers of this Inner Heart Line, the Upper Girdle of Venus, inevitably suffer a certain conflict of identity. Qualities that remain unconscious and hidden to most people are liable to come flooding to the surface. They may possess strange wisdom, but an obvious lack of balance in their personality, an over-sensitive vulnerability in their everyday social life, makes them very much the odd one out.

Such people often go to unusual lengths to achieve whatever they may have set out to achieve, defying criticism and opposition, as though their life depends on its completion. But suddenly and without warning, the flow of their life-current may change. Instead of following the voice of reason, they will veer and change course unpredictably. They may long for true spiritual contact (although they are unlikely to want to discuss it), but when they are fortunate enough to find it, as they often are, the course of their soul's purification, and their sex life with it, is often chaotic.

In sheerly practical terms, they may be seen to be erratic types, characterized by sudden enthusiasms and just as sudden loss of interest, and this characteristic will be reflected in their romantic associations too. They are liable to fall passionately in love with complete sincerity (often with a completely unsuitable partner) and feel violently let down when eventually their passion turns out to be unreciprocated. Their friends will say that they are 'temperamental'; but this up and down quality, this 'blowing hot or cold', is explained by the unpredictable changes of direction triggered at a level deeper than most people experience.

Occasionally this Inner Heart Line takes over the emotional function completely, replacing the normal course of the Heart Line itself. When this is seen in the hand, you can be sure that the compulsive drive of the inner feelings has come fully to awareness and taken over the subject's life. This is especially true when the left hand of inheritance shows faint traces of the Upper Girdle of Venus, while the right hand shows that the Heart Line itself has adopted this higher course, running deep and true. There is an example of this in the sample analysis in Chapter 40.

12 Emotional Instability:
Chains, Islands and Breaks in the Heart Line

AS WE HAVE SEEN, a strong, clear Heart Line implies, if not necessarily a loving one, at least a clear-cut emotional attitude to life and to people – a sign, in other words, of emotional stability; everyone concerned knows where they stand. Correspondingly, a strong Heart Line marked by a series of tiny islands, giving the appearance of a chain rather than a clear line, implies a degree of emotional instability. It could truly be said of subjects with this chain formation on their upper palms that they are 'all heart': they may seem to live on their emotions; their lives may seem to be regulated by emotional relationships, by their feelings for others, but these feelings will be wildly erratic.

Chained Heart Liners will prove quite unpredictable in any kind of partnership arrangement which depends on an emotional understanding. Family and friends have to learn to tread on tiptoe through a temperamental minefield. Such a person may gush enthusiastically one minute and shut up like a clam the next, so that nobody knows if they have run out of steam or taken offence at some imagined slight. In romantic affairs such people are liable to be fickle in the extreme. They are expert at setting up an instant and impenetrable emotional barrier when it is least expected. In purely platonic friendships and business relationships, they may prove either unexpectedly understanding and generous, or incomprehensively unreasonable. They are predictable only in their unpredictability. It is not that they want to be awkward, or do not care to be reliable, or wish anyone ill, or want to hurt people's feelings; not at all. It is they who are the victims of their own feelings. Like their Heart Line itself, their emotions are constantly turning and twisting and backtracking in close circles, swerving this way and that, instead of pursuing the steady course that makes for steady relationships.

If a Heart Line is only partly chained, take special note of the mount beneath which the chains occur. This will indicate the compartment of life in which emotional instability will be most apparent. The heart, or the emotional function, is where values are decided, and if these Heart Line chains are to be seen beneath the

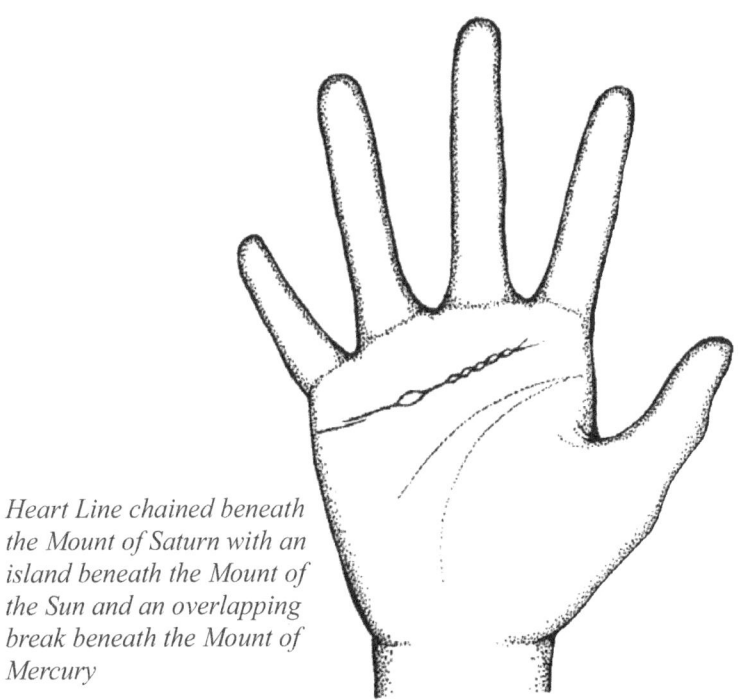

Heart Line chained beneath the Mount of Saturn with an island beneath the Mount of the Sun and an overlapping break beneath the Mount of Mercury

Mount of Saturn, the Saturnian compartment of material possessions, the subject's sense of values may prove topsy-turvy. Seemingly inconsequential items may be guarded fiercely, or other possessions valuable or valueless alike may be distributed where they are not really wanted.

If Heart Line chains appear beneath the Mount of the Sun, the solar zone of culture, art and enterprise, these cultural, civilized aspects may take unpredictable twists and turns in the subject's life. There may be emphasis on ideas which, to other people, will seem weird, or there may be fiercely guarded 'secrets', perhaps of an occult nature.

If these chained formations occur beneath the Mount of Mercury, the Mercurial zone of communication, this will be the area of imbalance and unpredictability. An innocent question may meet with an unexpectedly snappish reply, or the subject may seem to be unable to stop talking, gushing on and on however much the audience fidgets and giggles. This little-finger Mount of Mercury is the most 'abstract' of the mounts, and emotional instability in this zone could perhaps be synonymous with the 'confusedly discursive' personality in the ancient Buddhist classification of human types. In effect, the subject's feelings will have become unstable in the area not only of communication but also of tenacity, so that the compartment of life that should properly be filled with intuitive understanding, compassionate reaction and emotional support where it is needed has become bloated with an un-predictable excess of speech, unmodified by reason.

Every feature in the palm must be seen and interpreted in the light of all the other features of the hand. But where an emotional outpouring has an aggressive nature the effect of this will vary greatly according to the subject's cheirotype. When Mercurial chains are to be seen in an AA palm, the palmist should tread and speak warily, for excesses such as this can be positively dangerous.

The feature known as an 'island' is larger, more isolated and more distinct than a chain link. When considerably larger than an individual link in a chain formation, a solitary circular or oval island occurring along the Heart Line can point to an isolated (though it may well be protracted) and probably unhappy event fated to take place during the subject's life. Again, its nature may be guessed at according to its position in relation to the mounts.

A real island is surrounded by water, and thus to a certain extent isolated; an island on the Heart Line implies a state of emotional isolation. Herbalists of old held to the 'doctrine of signatures', reasoning that if part of a plant resembled a human organ such as the heart, it should have a medicinal effect on that organ in fact. In a sense, our study of signs or 'signatures' on the Heart Line recalls this ancient doctrine, for it too is a system of symbolism.

Traditionally, an island on the Heart Line is said to represent a romance that has caused or is fated to cause heartache or feelings of guilt, particularly when it occurs beneath the wedding-ring finger and the Mount of the Sun, the zone of culture and integrity. The emotional disturbance here will be deeply felt within the conscience; at the very least, it will mean a case of badly hurt feelings.

When an island occurs beneath the Mount of Saturn, relating to resources, the corresponding emotional hurt will involve material possessions. It could predict the sort of failed love affair that hurts the pocket more than the conscience – say maintenance paid only grudgingly – particularly when this feature is associated with a branch leading to the Head Line.

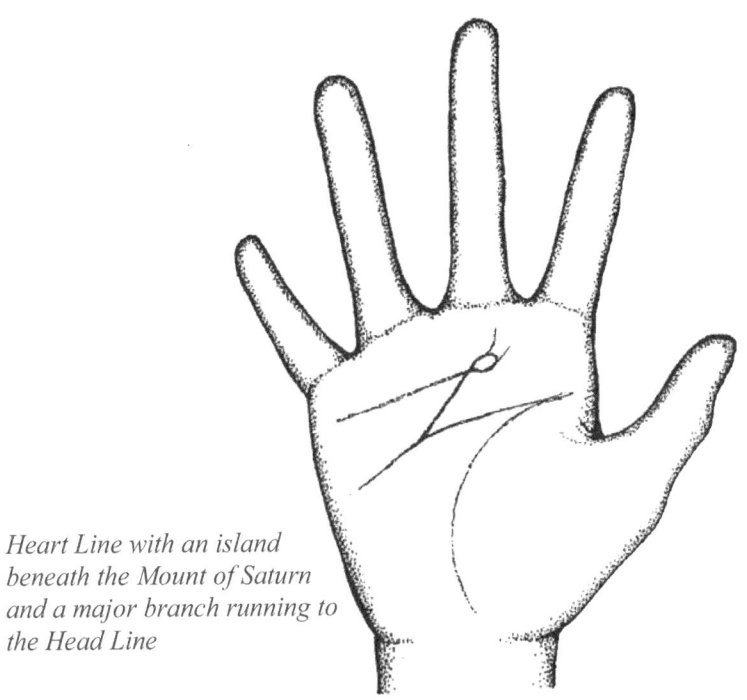

Heart Line with an island beneath the Mount of Saturn and a major branch running to the Head Line

Looked at from a broader, general angle, an island in the Heart Line is likely to represent a time in one's life when normal affairs become disrupted, with emotionally painful results. It does not always refer to an 'emotional attachment' in the generally accepted sense. In general terms, it simply indicates an injury received in the field of emotional combat – a disappointment so severe that it may change the course of your life. Instead of following a smooth course, the flow of feelings has met some hindrance, some boulder in the brook that causes them to eddy and swirl in wide circles before resuming their original course.

A break or series of breaks in the Heart Line may be interpreted similarly. Each break implies a corresponding hiatus in emotional attachments; not an impediment exactly, rather a check, followed by a change in the direction of feeling. A series of breaks will often be found in the hand of a temperamental romantic, someone who will readily form passionate attachments which, to the people concerned and to onlookers, will seem to mean a great deal at the time. Then suddenly there comes disappointment, an unkind word

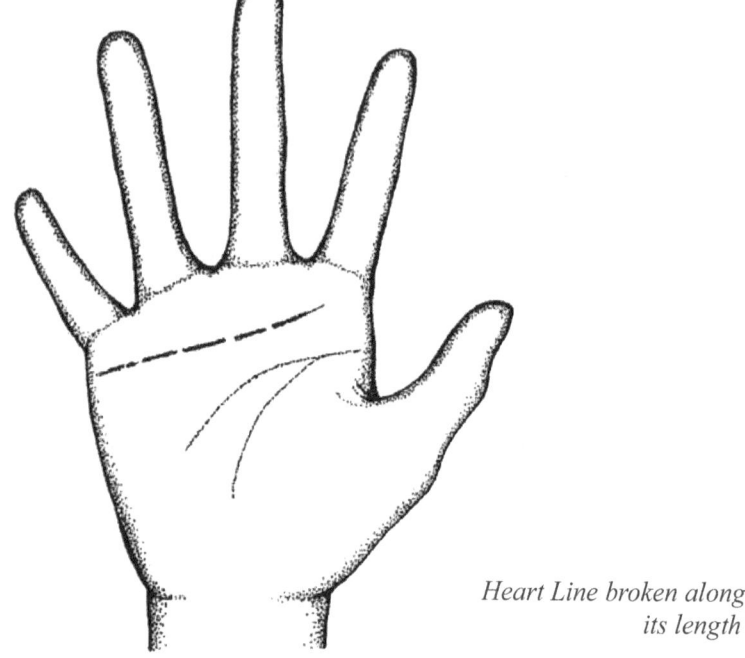

Heart Line broken along its length

perhaps, and the feelings are simply suspended. The emotions are withdrawn from their object and redirected elsewhere. There is no confusion involved, as there is in the case of islands or chained formations. There is no deep brooding or agonizing over a broken heart, though any of these things may well be experienced by the other party in the affair. There is simply a sudden and apparently wilful withdrawal of interest. A case of, 'Right, that's it! Sorry, but I've changed my mind!'

Breaks which overlap indicate an emotional break which is far less *final* than clean-gapped ones. They imply a patching over or a healing of the breach. Occasionally, overlapping breaks are extensive, stretching perhaps the whole length of the Mount of the Sun. These imply a certain duality of loyalties. When pronounced they may even indicate schizophrenic tendencies, with the contradiction of opposing principles, each held in place by powerful but conflicting emotional attachments.

One can often find an overlapping break in the Heart Line to

Heart Line with an extensive overlapping break

be associated with some kind of emotional disturbance – a neurosis perhaps which has seemed to take on menacing proportions. The contents of the soul itself can seem to stand in plain conflict with family interests, with the norms of society. Some deeply seated, perhaps inherited fault, frequently but not always connected with sex, seems to clamour for attention. When there is a neurotic struggle of this kind, a certain duality in the attachment of feelings is inevitable, and this duality may be mirrored in the overlapping break of the Heart Line. It is the sign of 'inner turmoil' and should be interpreted, tactfully, as such.

Conventional moralists and religious people in particular seldom realize, I believe, that 'immoral traits', either inherited, inbuilt at an early age or acquired later in life, lodge themselves uninvited in the human soul, whether their presence is consciously acceptable to the feelings or not. It is no use ignoring them; they will still be there and they cannot be dealt with by suppression. They *can* be 'concreted over' so that no-one knows they are there; but if they are to be shed, they have to be acknowledged and projected outwards. This is where tact by the palmist is specially called for.

Where unwanted emotional traits have been inherited, either from the parents or, more mysteriously, through karmic content, the overlapping break in the Heart Line is likely to occur in the left hand. But in individual cases where refinement of such features is destined to take place, perhaps through the catalysis of spiritual contact, the right hand will show a pronounced difference. The break will, symbolically, have been repaired and the smooth course of the Heart Line will continue, unmarked, across the right-hand palm.

One can see how it sometimes comes about that emotional traits which are 'on the way in' (the late arrivals) will make their appearance in the right hand; those features that are 'on the way out' however (the early arrivals), limit their appearance to the left hand. They are destined to be 'overcome' during the subject's lifetime. Without this variance, this field of conflict within the human soul, palmistry would be as meaningless as any random collection of lines, bumps and creases, and inherited characteristics of the human body.

13 The Marriage Lines:
Affection and Child Lines

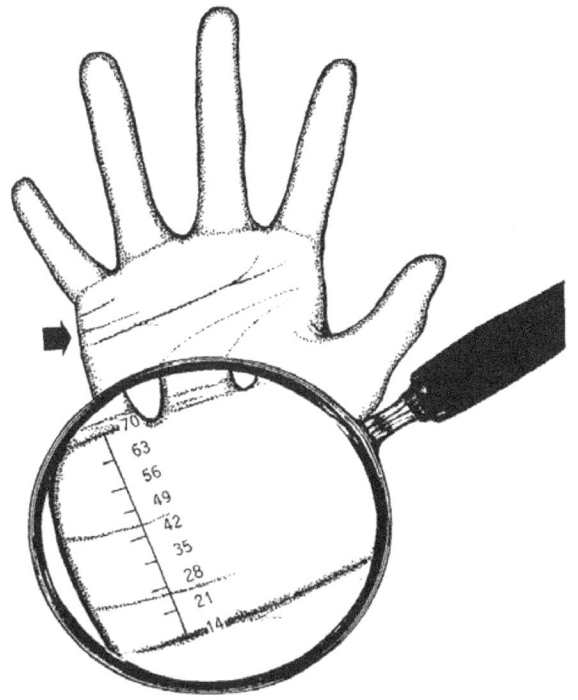

Timescale on the Marriage Lines: the diagram shows two separate periods of attachment, the first at around the age of twenty-six, the second at around the age of forty-five

THE SO-CALLED Marriage Lines are to be found on the Mount of Mercury, right on the edge of the palm. They may be absent altogether; there may be one, or several, each indicating a close tie of affection – a period during the subject's life when his or her 'heart goes out' to another. They are not the most reliable of guides on the hand and, needless to say, they know nothing of legality or 'churching'; but they do have some correspondence with the flow of love and affection. The more clearly marked the line, the more deeply involved and long lasting the attachment.

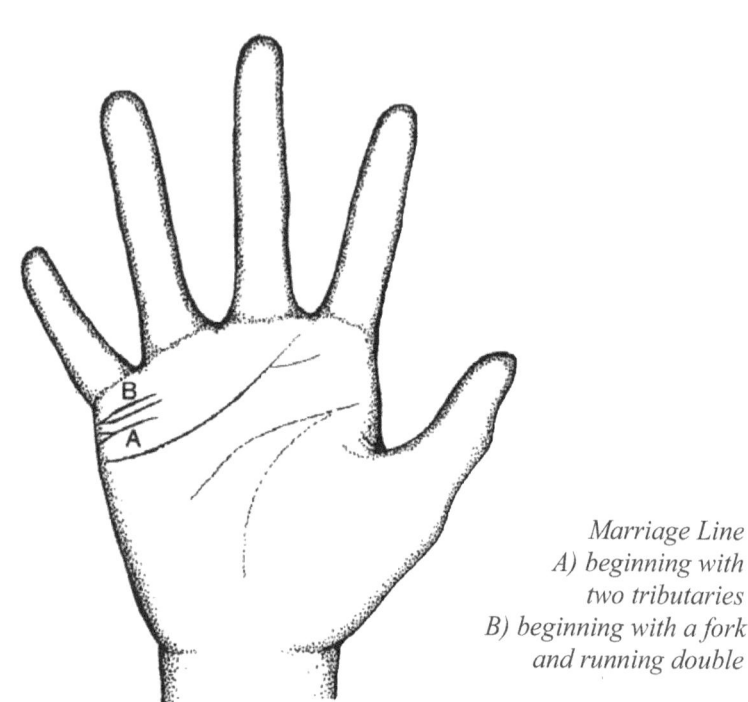

Marriage Line
A) beginning with
two tributaries
B) beginning with a fork
and running double

They rise on the edge of the palm and travel 'inland' from there. Where they are distinctly marked, with a good space between the boundaries of the Heart Line below and the baseline of the little finger above, it is possible to apply a timescale indicating the approximate age of the wearer at the onset of the involvement. This scale begins on the Heart Line at fourteen – the traditional age of puberty – and ends at the base of the little finger at the age of seventy. But because the area is not as a rule the most distinct and clearly marked part of the palm, it is no use measuring precisely, and you can scarcely hope to arrive at more than a very approximate conclusion.

A clear, straight and fairly short line is the most 'propitious'. In cases where a dominant Marriage Line rises (on the edge of the palm) with two tributaries, one can predict that there will probably be two 'loves' in the subject's life, even though he or she may be quite happily married. The marriage at least has two sources of dynamic energy. A Marriage Line which terminates in a fork, however, symbolizes a division of the ways, but as they are still linked, there will often be a tacit understanding whereby both partners are free

Overlong Marriage Line reaching to the Mount of Venus

to 'do their own thing' while remaining together in companionship.

A strong fork at the very beginning of a double line implies that there are two distinct lines of romantic interest, rather than two partners, and it hints at bisexuality. Where there is more than one line very close together, and not joined by a fork, there may well be a doubling up of affection – not exactly a guilty secret, but a case, perhaps, of continuing to love a 'ghost', an unobtainable ideal of a partner, while making the best of what one has.

A very long Marriage Line is not necessarily a propitious sign. Such a line can hint at an over-emotional relationship, and the wearer is unlikely to play the role of breadwinner, or caring mate and parent, with very much conviction. A line that curves downwards suggests a dull and not very happy marriage, particularly if it is long enough to cross the hand and actually reach the Life Line. If a Marriage Line crosses the Life Line and reaches the Mount of Venus itself – the seat, that is, of parental and family background – it portends dreadful family rows and recurrent in-law problems. The wearer should be tactfully informed of this danger, and remind both

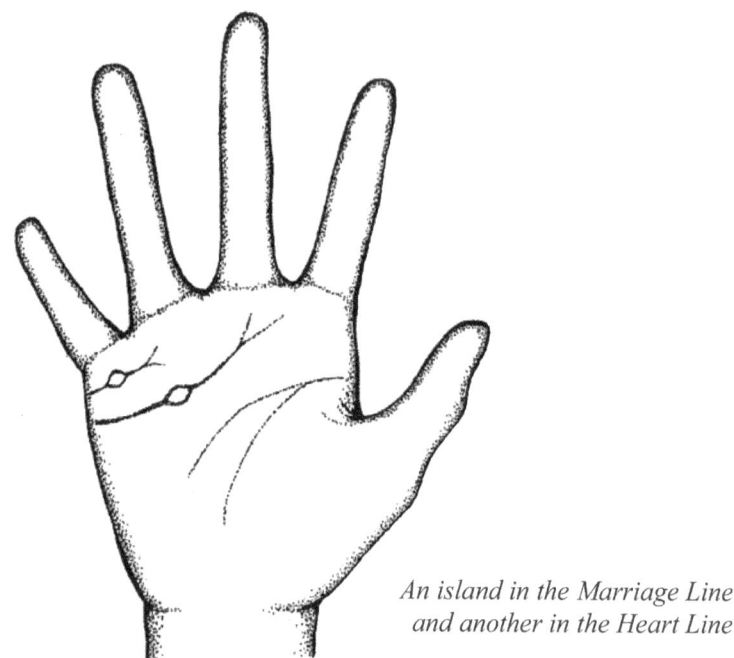

An island in the Marriage Line and another in the Heart Line

that the marriage vows include the words 'forsaking all others' and that there is a knot to be untied on entering a close relationship, as well as one to be tied. The present and future should have precedence over the past.

An island or islands along the Marriage Line hint at a disastrous extramarital affair. Breaks along the line indicate a withdrawal of affection by one partner or the other, but if these breaks overlap, the breach will probably be repaired and the couple reunited.

Child Lines are closely related to the so-called Marks of Concern, which also appear on the Mount of Mercury and often reach to the Marriage Line. The lines denoting a boy are thicker and often longer than those for a girl. You can differentiate these from the Marks of Concern chiefly by the type of person whose hand you are reading. Where the subject plainly *wants* to know about the possibility of having children, then that is the significance to be applied. When the subject is interested, not in romance or parenthood, but in 'personal development', or working for the good of the world – for the whole human family rather than any personal one – then you should

Child Lines on the Marriage Line: successively, a boy, a girl, and another boy

consider them in terms of general concern; they will represent metaphorical children. Child Lines may be found in the hands of childless people too, they will also be on the hands of those who would dearly love to have children but have been denied this type of fulfilment by fate. Their Child Lines will not necessarily indicate 'dream children', however. They may well indicate the children of relatives and friends who can, in some measure, take the place of the longed-for children in the subject's affections.

14 The Head Line: Directing the Thoughts

THE HEAD LINE traces the course of the mind, represented by the brain, as a lineal sketch of the mental processes. In the most general of terms, by its length this line suggests the standard of intelligence; by its depth or clarity it suggests the degree of dedication or ability to concentrate; by its direction it suggests the type of intelligence involved.

But this, of course, is an over-simplification. Classifying someone's brain is not quite so straightforward a matter. There are so many different *sorts* of intelligence. The concept of intelligence is itself a somewhat contradictory one, and its manifestations can be misleading. For instance, there are so many clever people about who seem to have no idea how *others* think. An academic may seem to be lacking in common sense. And we probably all know someone with a brilliant mind who behaves in what strikes us as a stupid manner, or who makes the most ill-considered or inappropriate comments. At times, such a person may seem as thick as those two proverbial short planks. Then again, we may know an obviously dull-witted fellow who, when the circumstances arise, proves himself a brilliant strategist.

The point is that cleverness does not necessarily go hand in hand with common sense, with clear-mindedness. Natural-born philosophers always suppose that others are less intelligent than themselves, and simplify their pronouncements accordingly. But in their attempts to accommodate others, they succeed only in lowering these same others' opinion of their own wit. Again, some may be too shy or otherwise inhibited from speaking out at the appropriate moment, so that they appear dull-witted in company, allowing their less-gifted associates to shine by comparison. All this amounts to a fragmented picture, like a jigsaw puzzle to be reassembled in the palm of the hand.

To a palmist, temperament is perhaps more important than intelligence, and the direction of the Head Line will certainly give some idea of this factor. The Head Line that travels straight across the palm towards the Upper Mount of Mars – the seat of tenacity – indicates a keenly calculating brain. Such people are the logicians of the world, those who at least think of themselves as the intelligentsia.

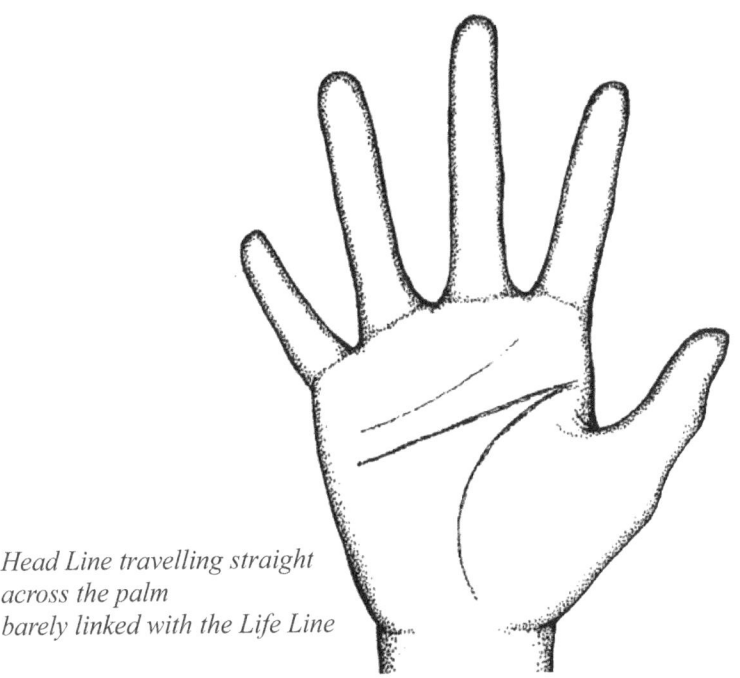

Head Line travelling straight across the palm barely linked with the Life Line

intelligentsia. They are nothing if not realistic. They tend to call spades spades, unless a scientific description is required, and have their roots firmly set in practical ground.

Straight Head Liners tend to fit into the ancient Buddhist system of human classification as examples of the 'intelligence-hate' type, for 'hate' is the flip side of the coin of intelligence. You cannot always be positive in your outlook. If your life is based on intelligence to the exclusion of feelings, of emotions, then when you are being negative you tend to hate everything that does not conform to the intelligent ideal. Tolerance is not the strongpoint of wearers of this straight, fearless Head Line.

The feelings are even further divorced from everyday life when the Head Line commences high, below the Mount of Jupiter, but at a point some little way above the commencement of the Life Line. The subject may seem quite normally affectionate and, indeed, in many respects easy-going. But when Head Line and Life Line are comparatively widely separated – perhaps by as much as 1cm (½ inch) – and there is also a straight alignment of the Head Line,

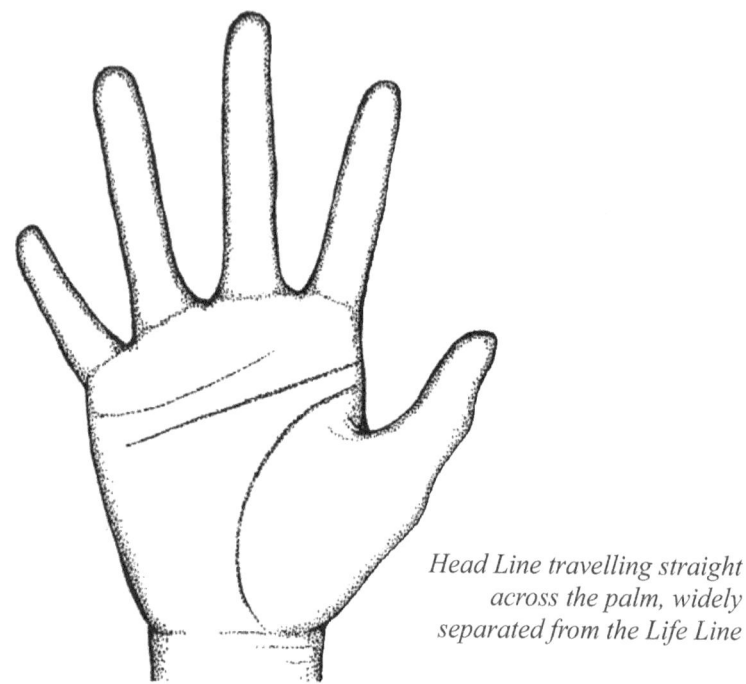

Head Line travelling straight across the palm, widely separated from the Life Line

such affectionate relationships will be planned and purposeful. There is no real feeling for others in people such as this. They may be the most pleasant people to know, but somehow you can always sense their inbuilt air of coldness, of detachment.

They may seem oddly out of touch with the way most people feel, as though unable to divine another's feelings. Sentiment is a quality quite unknown to them; everything must be judged by its logically perceived value, and because of this emotional lack, their judgement may sometimes prove faulty. Despite their obvious intelligence, their life may seem to lack a secure foundation, and business success will elude them. The feelings really are necessary when a balanced judgement has to be made. A straight Head Line, clearly separated from the Life Line in this way, may well be the sign of one who 'knows everything and achieves nothing'.

But there are compensatory advantages. The fact that the Head Line starts quite separately from the Life Line means that subjects will be fortunate in never suffering from shyness. They will always feel able to speak their mind – though others within range

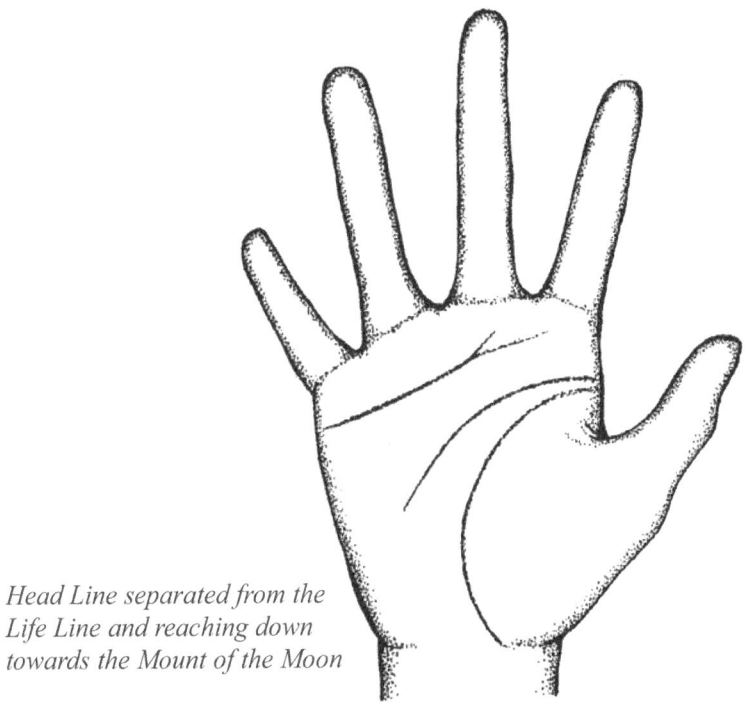

Head Line separated from the Life Line and reaching down towards the Mount of the Moon

may deplore the fact! This very lack of inhibition spells danger, however, for their physical life is barely under the guidance of their keen brain. It is as though the brain is functioning clearly but in isolation, leaving both the heart and the body to look after themselves.

Such people will often fail to see danger. If their mind tells them that they are needed (and they can indeed prove a blessed ally and a staunch friend), they will leap into the breach, oblivious to risk. They may thus display outstanding heroism, and many a successful soldier bears a Head Line widely spaced from the Life Line at its commencement. Usually, however, the soldier's Head Line, having started in isolation, in mental heroism, will proceed to curve gently down the palm towards more intuitive realms, leaving it to the Heart Line, to the emotional feelings, to surge determinedly into the Upper Mount of Mars. A soldier's courage may derive ultimately from his mental attitude, but his drive towards the courageous situation, his extreme dedication to the cause, his principles and patriotism will all be matters for his heart.

15 The Sensitive Mind:
Business Brains, Dreamers, and Social Skills

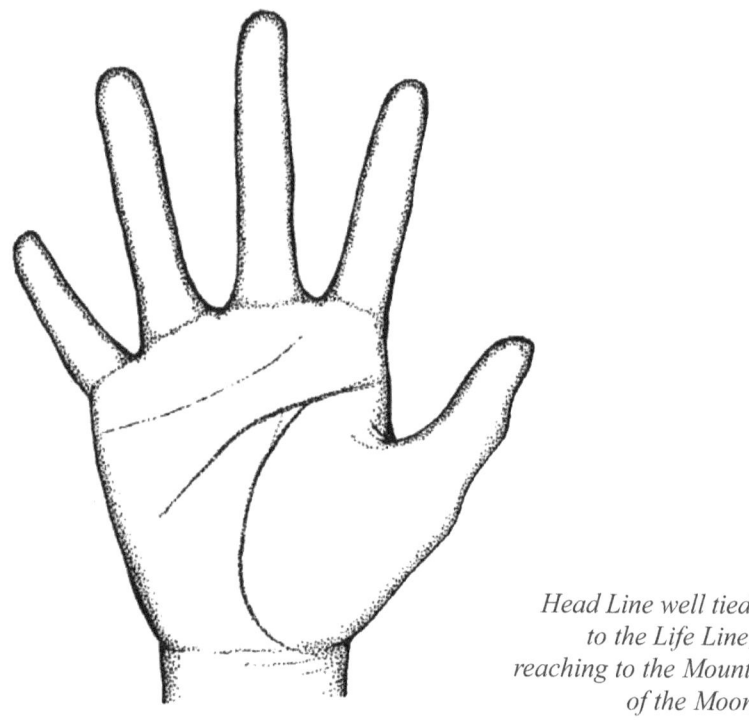

Head Line well tied to the Life Line, reaching to the Mount of the Moon

WE HAVE already seen that the perfectly straight Head Line denotes a perfectly straight, incisive, no-nonsense brain. The average Head Line starts out as though aiming for the opposite edge of the palm, but halfway along its course curves slightly downwards. However, the Head Line that dips down decidedly towards the Mount of the Moon portrays an aptitude to think in intuitive, creative, 'soft' terms. Sensitive, artistic people are sure to have a Head Line of this nature.

If a well-balanced fork is in evidence near the end of the Head Line, dividing two modes of thought, as though disposing both influences evenly, it may well symbolize the best of both worlds. This is probably the ideal: a firm, straight Head Line reaching to

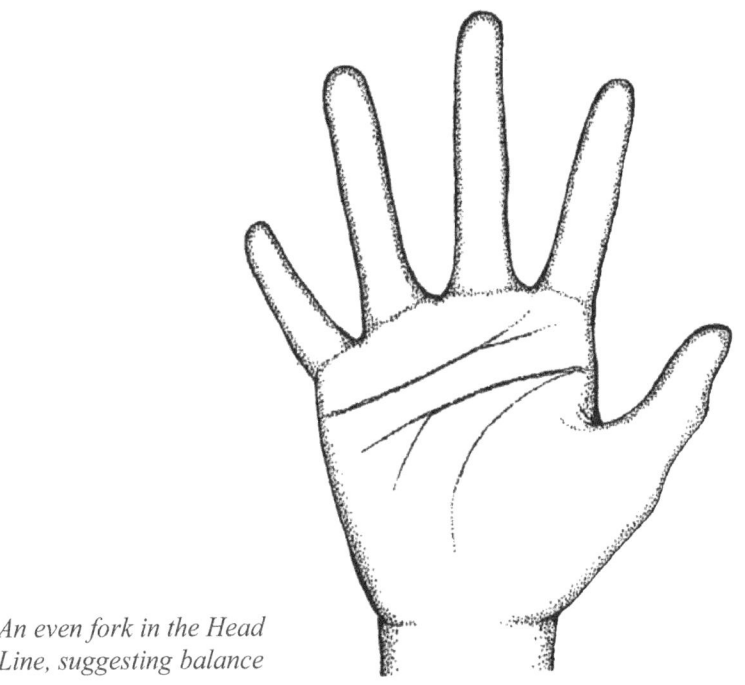

An even fork in the Head Line, suggesting balance

the tenacious, no-nonsense Upper Mount of Mars, but which forks cleanly beneath the Mount of the Sun and also runs an equal distance down the palm, into the more abstract area of creativity.

It is, though, all a matter of degree. When a fork occurs, but seems to be overlarge, or unevenly balanced, a palmist may assume the wearer's thought processes to be correspondingly exaggerated or unbalanced. An over-developed fork may imply that the individual seems always to be up against impossible decisions, as though forever torn between two conflicting possibilities, two possible courses of action, with the power of logic opposing the imagination, original creativity fighting unadventurous conformity. The unfortunate result will be that nothing of real value is ever achieved.

An unforked Head Line that slopes gently to touch the upper part of the Mount of the Moon indicates a realistic, well-balanced approach, not only to money and business matters but also to the less-materialistic values of life. It suggests an innate willingness to

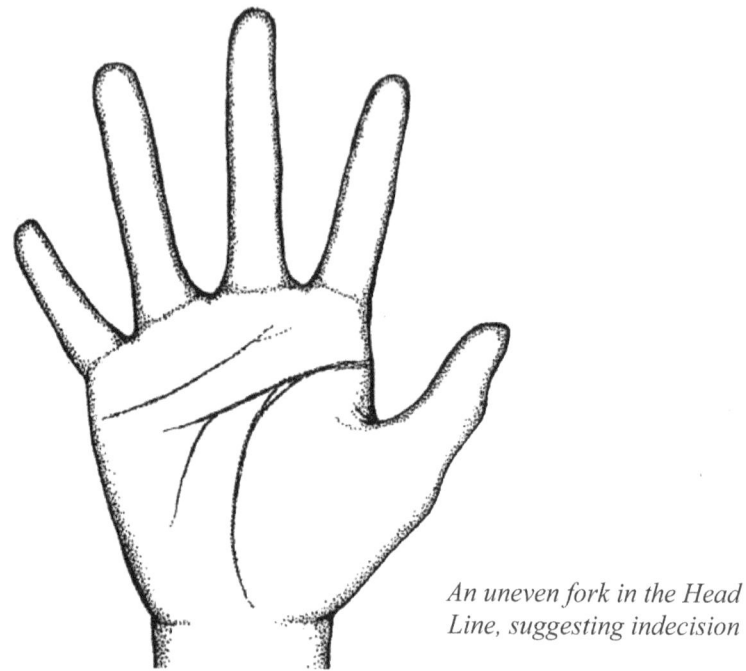

An uneven fork in the Head Line, suggesting indecision

accept the imaginative alternative to an over-logical approach. But a Head Line that plunges deeply into this abstract, intuitive area of thought, symbolized in the palm by the Mount of the Moon, suggests that the subject's head is liable to remain in the clouds, even when a realistic, material approach is called for.

The plunging Head Liner will be a mystic dreamer who does not readily fit into the world. He or she will be the daydreamer who, as though addicted to dreams, becomes upset when the dream bubble bursts: the exaggeratedly introverted thinker who always turns to ideas at the expense of hard facts. These factors will seem to be even stronger when the Head Line is tied to the Life Line for some distance, as though holding on to dependence – an unwillingness to be born into the real, uncomfortable world. A wide separation between the two lines speaks of a rather hazardous type of independence that indicates the opposite extreme and seems to see no connection between physical and mental welfare: a person who never successfully links the physical vehicle with the action to be taken – a strangely impulsive, illogical character.

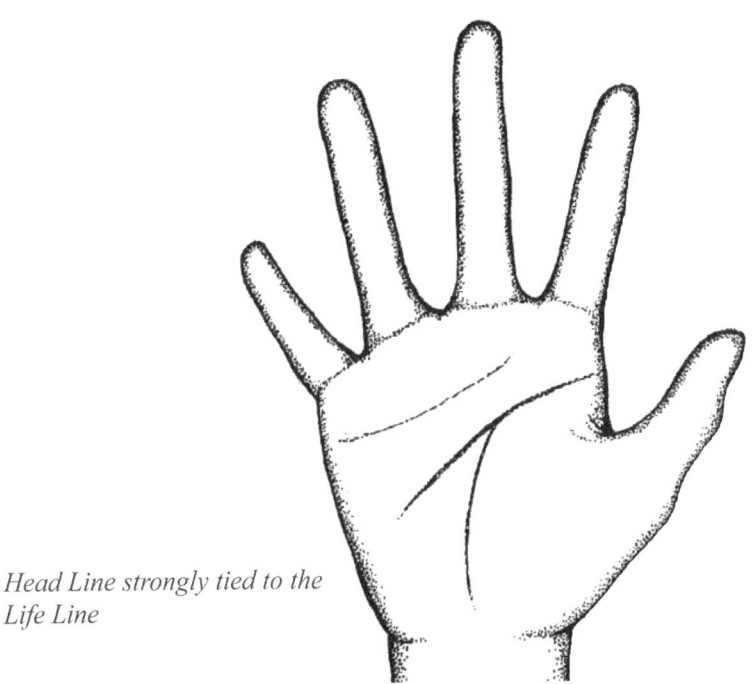

Head Line strongly tied to the Life Line

The Head Line that starts at the same point as the Life Line and shares its course for 2 cm (1 inch) or more across the palm means that the wearer's psyche cannot really feel free from physical restraint. Inevitably, shyness stems from the invisible psychological knots that this union symbolizes. Instead of venturing forth when boldness is called for, bearers of this overlong union between Head Line and Life Line – between the two functions of thinking and sensing – will tend to cling to the security of their own body, their own home base, their own lifestyle, and retreat into a shell.

Inhibition is the keyword. The tied start to the Head Line does not necessarily mean that the subject will be shy in the usually accepted sense. It certainly betokens a built-in caution, which will often show itself in a reluctance to make decisions and a wariness of social occasions. But there are always other psychological factors to be taken into consideration, and as far as cheirognomy is concerned, the shape and proportions of the hands themselves will have significance here.

As far as psychological freedom is concerned, perhaps the ideal rising point for the Head Line is just a little way above the Life

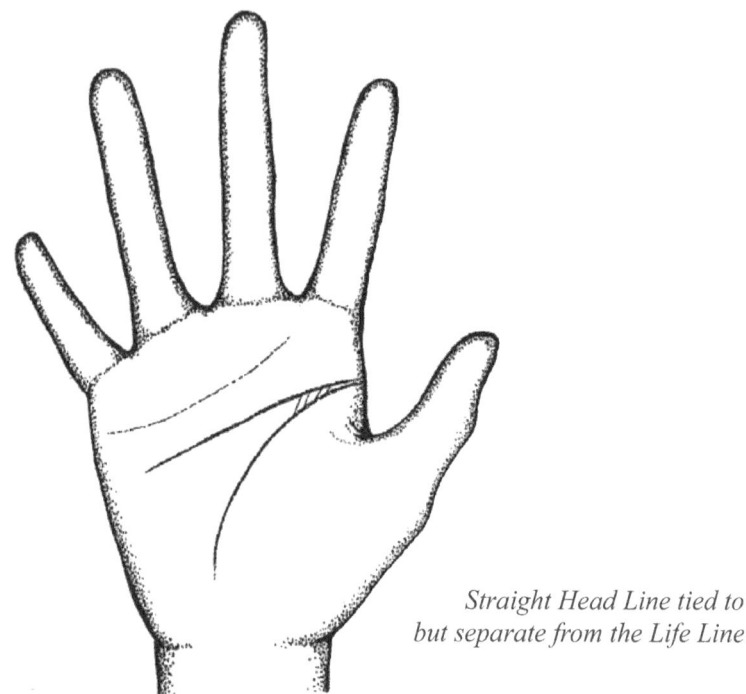

Straight Head Line tied to but separate from the Life Line

Line, for this balance denotes the best of both worlds. Such people will possess a confident, independent nature strong enough for them to feel free from the influence of other's opinions. Not only will they seem to care not a bit what the neighbours may say or think, but they also display the artless ability to talk to those neighbours persuasively enough to turn them to their own point of view. When outside viewpoints are not involved, they will still remain close enough and faithful enough to the generally recognized principles of social conformity to ensure that all their decisions, instinctively arrived at, are well balanced and basically sound.

It is always the case that our social skills and basic attitudes towards society are modified by the *direction* of our interests, and this point is well illustrated by the Head Line as it tracks across the palm. Assuming a reasonable length of line, implying that subjects are well endowed with basic intelligence, a Head Line tied to but narrowly separated from the Life Line at its commencement, and following a straight course throughout its length, suggests people who will be happiest when there are others round about to whom they can

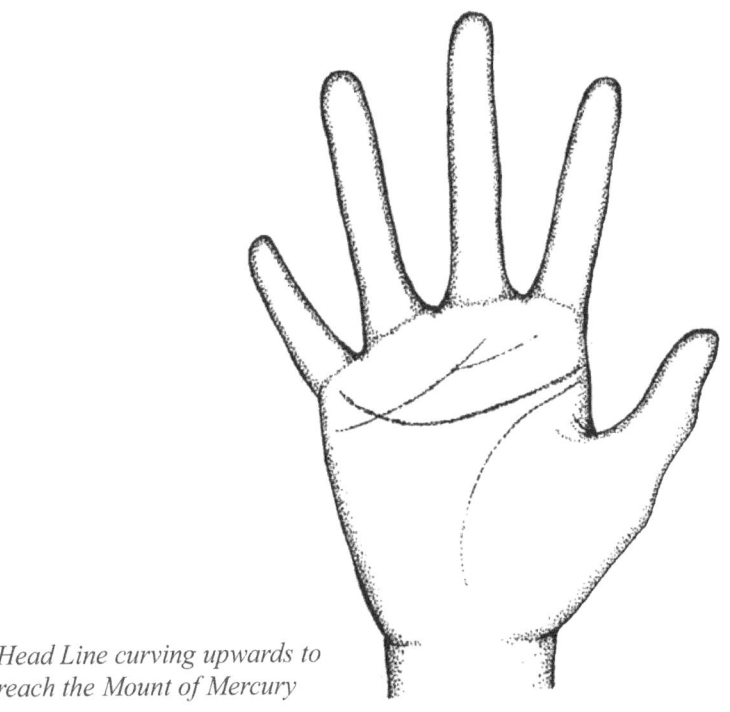

Head Line curving upwards to reach the Mount of Mercury

readily relate. They will be confident, independent people, yet they will feel the need for support and sympathy. While others may be happy in their own little dream world, this is not the case here. On the contrary, these individuals need something solid in which to believe, a reason for being, otherwise their relationships all seem in vain. To be isolated and rootless for them would represent hell on earth.

Head Liners of this type are great organizers. They love to be in thick of it. Given a worthwhile cause to pursue such people are capable of bringing out the best in others and, while by no means to be described as rabble-rousers, often display considerable talent for swaying public opinion. They make good teachers, and excellent politicians of the sincere kind – and therefore, their opponents would no doubt say, of the most dangerous kind!

An upwards curve towards the end of the Head Line is comparatively uncommon, and when it occurs it suggests an outstanding ability to organize the lives and direct the wills of others. When combined, perhaps, with a long thumb and evenly

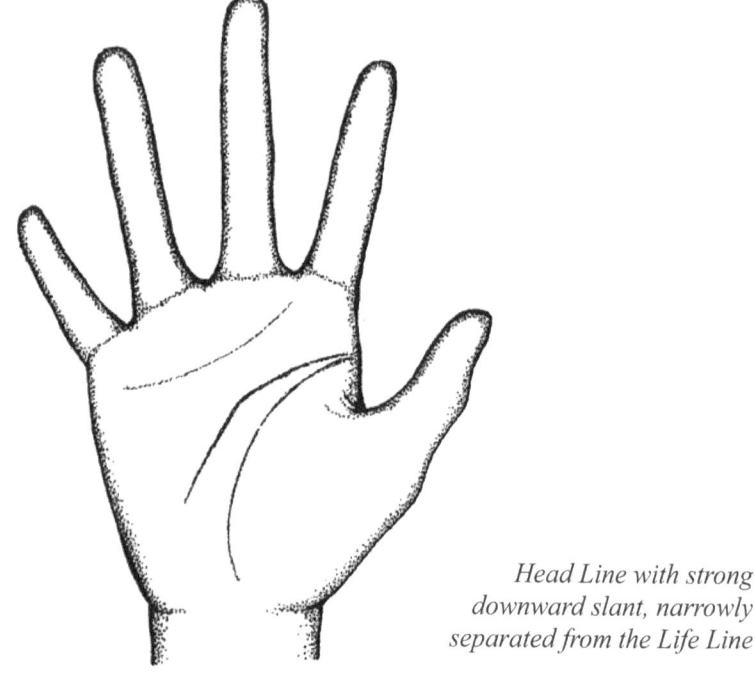

Head Line with strong downward slant, narrowly separated from the Life Line

disposed fingers, it represents the ruthless driving force that characterizes the mind of a tycoon, the successful businessman who strides the corridors of power, buying, selling, bullying, hiring and firing.

Occasionally this upward curve at the end of the Head Line is very pronounced, even reaching to the Mount of Mercury beneath the little finger. Traditionally, this is said to be one of the signs of a money maker. But whether truly wealthy in the normal sense or not, owners of this sign will certainly be most unusual characters. Their penetrating minds will exert a powerful influence on everyone with whom they come into contact. They will seem to emanate a special charisma that has people skipping to obey their every whim – while quite likely emptying their own pockets for the privilege of doing so.

Most people, as we have seen, have a Head Line that curves slightly downwards. A more strongly downward-curving course than average does not really associate well with a fairly narrow but distinct separation at the commencement of the Life Line. Purely

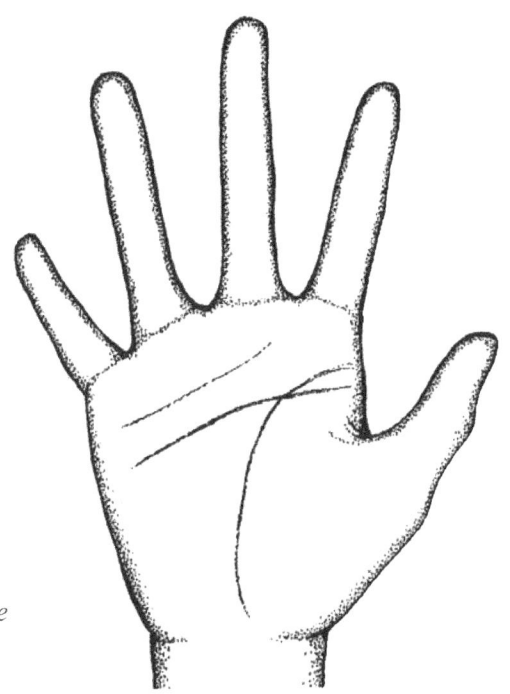

A straight Head Line commencing below the Life Line

abstract qualities, the intuitive, creative impulses associated with the Mount of the Moon – without at least a balancing fork leading part of the Head Line into more materialistic, more aggressive, Martian realms – mean that the subject will always feel a frustrating lack of solidity. In the fields of work and social relationships, this trait may show itself as well-meaning unreliability.

Firmness of mind, determination, decisiveness – when these characteristics are lacking, there will be a corresponding lack of achievement. A strongly downward-curving Head Line symbolizes just such a shortage and portends a life that may frequently be clouded with dark pessimistic moods and bouts of depression. Opportunities may seem never to arise. But when the bearers of such a line also show that narrow gap between the Life Line and the Head Line at their commencement, and where they are fortunate enough to find a driving purpose that fits their potentially bold, independent nature and is also in tune with the intuitively abstract direction of their thoughts – symbolized by the downward slant – they can shine as creative geniuses.

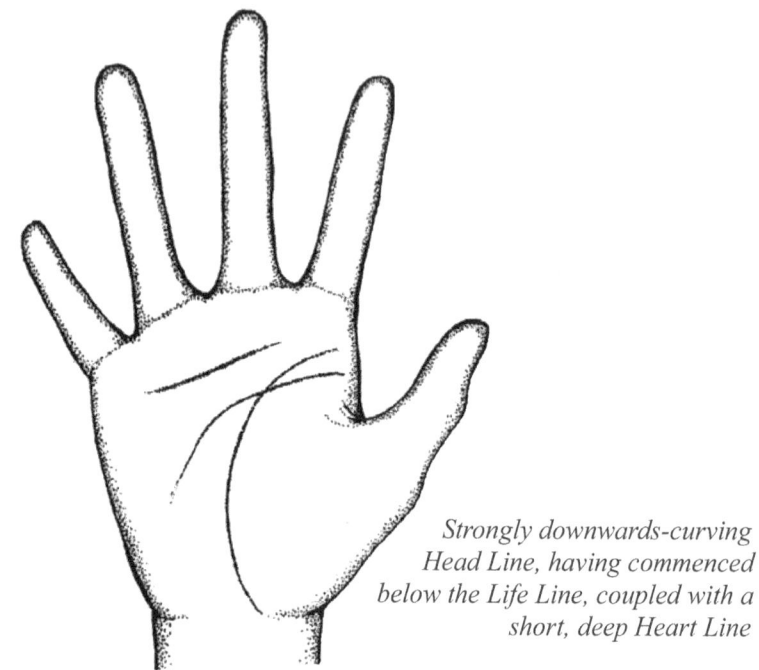

Strongly downwards-curving Head Line, having commenced below the Life Line, coupled with a short, deep Heart Line

In cases where the Head Line is only just barely connected with the Life Line at its commencement, it can be surmised that the bearer's approach to life – the course he or she has found between dependence and independence, diffidence and confidence, caution and recklessness – will be average and unremarkable. To put it in another and more tactful way, it will be just right, always reasonable, never approaching anything too extreme; in other words – at the very centre of all possibilities and ready for anything. He or she is sure to remain reliably prudent when the situation calls for prudence, but will never be too timidly unadventurous, neither too shy nor too brash.

Naturally, this social reliability will be modified by the habitual type of thought patterns, as registered by the Head Line's direction across the palm. Whether this course suggests such people find their niche in commerce and impersonal science on the high route, or in art and personal, social welfare on the low route, you can be sure that they will be moderately successful in their career, moderately regarded by their colleagues, moderately popular with their friends, and moderately contented with their personal life.

Sometimes you meet people whose instinctive reaction to each encounter seems to be one of suspicion and aggression. Such people seem to act as though offended by the very fact of living on earth. Bad temper and irritability truly seem to cloud their lives, and though their mothers may love them, it is difficult for outsiders even to speak to them without causing offence.

If you are rash enough to risk reading their hands, the chances are that you will discover their Head Line rises *below* the Life Line, on the Lower Mount of Mars, the seat of physical aggression. In this case, ultimately the aggressor is the sufferer, and nobody would willingly choose such a fate. The situation is sometimes mitigated if the Head Line, on emerging from its encircling Life Line, runs straight across the palm, bringing at least the flavour of common sense into everyday relationships. They will then be able to set their irritability at least temporarily on one side, or put it to practical use in the hard-headed world of business. If the Head Line curves strongly downwards, however, as though rejecting the influence of logic and the saving grace of self-control, the signs are not optimistic.

Purely abstract thought sits ill on an aggressive nature. This negative brand of sensitivity is the 'artistic temperament' at its worst and unlike the hard-headed variety, abstract aggression is unlikely even to be channelled into useful directions. It is more likely to result in ever-increasing bad-tempered isolation and social withdrawal.

16 Attitudes and Obsessions:
Head and Heart Line Links

ANY SPECIAL SIGNS that may be visible along the Head Line should be interpreted according to where they appear, always relating them to the fleshy background of the mounts, whichever one is directly above. In this manner, a fork or branch-line which connects the Head Line with the Heart Line can gain significance in two ways, depending on its point of departure and its point of arrival. Where a fork or branch-line leaves the Head Line early, beneath the Mount of Jupiter, and if this connecting line joins the Heart Line beneath the Mount of the Sun, for instance, it will relate to matters of ambition as perceived by the brain. But it will imply that, where these are associated with matters of culture, the heart will take over this function from the brain.

This would be someone who prefers to stick to what he or she knows rather than launch out on risky enterprises which do not have their roots in safety and calculated reason. But as a parent, he or she will encourage growing children to aim for all the marvellous but illogical goals that they have denied themselves! They will enjoy the idea of their offspring 'reaching for the skies', or taking up 'the jobs they like doing' rather than those which provide unadventurous security.

Whichever mounts are involved, when connections of this sort occur, it is almost as if that particular concern were being pushed from the mental into the emotional sphere. It is not necessarily an odd or unbalanced situation, though sometimes it seems that something akin to a split personality can arise as a result. At all events, there will be a certain amount of inner turmoil, an argument between heart and mind. The brain may seem to care little for personal advancement; though the emotional feelings may wish fervently for great things to happen, and dream of glory, the stolid brain will have none of it, dismissing all such hopes as illusion.

On a personal basis, the pipedream ambitions of a Head Line Jupiter to Heart Line Sun branch-liner will rarely come to substantial reality. In truly spiritual as distinct from 'religious' matters, though the feelings of the heart will be cherished as something precious, in circumstances wherein the brain should perhaps take charge and

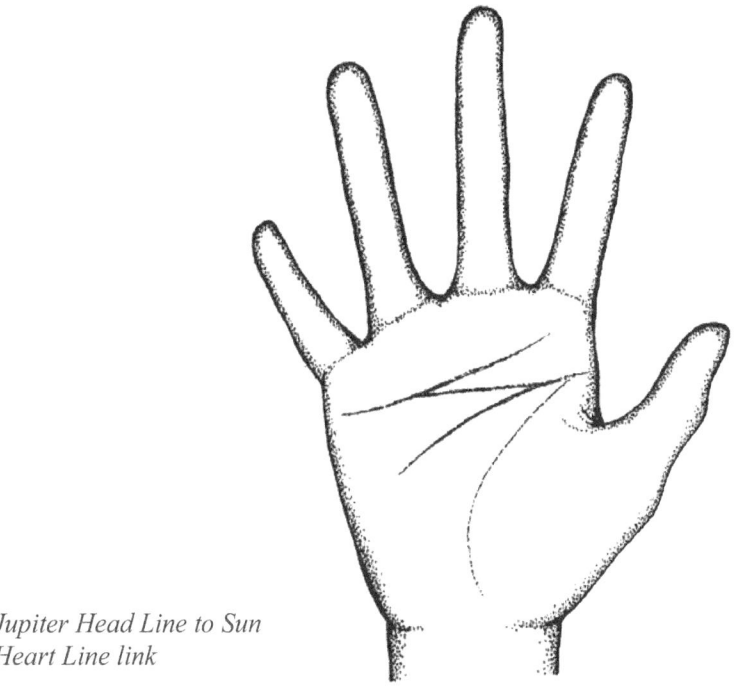

*Jupiter Head Line to Sun
Heart Line link*

dictate the time or the place, because of this 'untouchable' emotional flavour about it, such matters will be left in the air. Without positive encouragement, the wearer of this early Head to Heart Line branch will be fated to reject the direct whisper of the soul along with the sentimental slogans of the heart. The brain, having surrendered its interest in the subject, will have no suggestions to offer.

A linking branch-line from the Head Line, rising to join the Heart Line beneath the second finger and the Mount of Saturn, suggests that the subject's mental processes will tend to delegate matters of material well-being to the heart. Wearers may seldom take the matter of money very seriously. They will probably be the bane of the 'tradesman's' life, because bills will tend to lie unopened on the sideboard. Neither malice not meanness is involved. It is simply that money matters are a nuisance.

Such subjects would *like* to be wealthy, of course; indeed, they may even *be* wealthy. But for them money is not a matter for polite discussion. The heart may dwell on riches to the point of

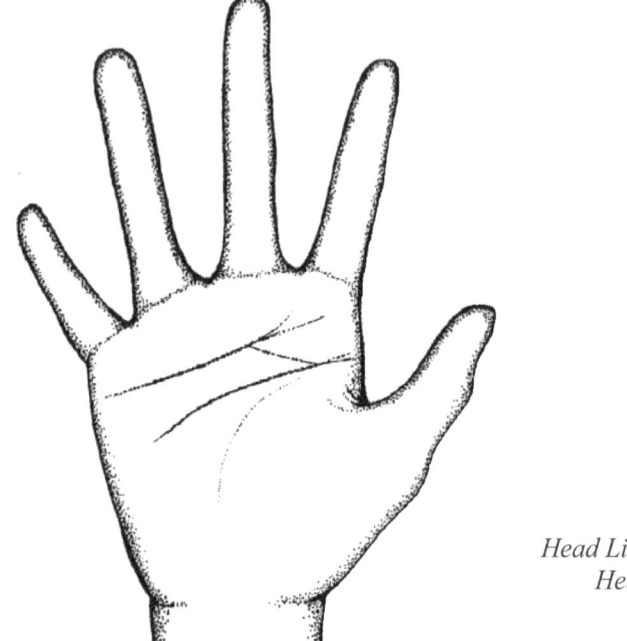

*Head Line to Saturn
Heart Line link*

sadness, but the brain will see this interest as a vice best kept hidden. Instead, they will perhaps insist on an occupation that brings peace of mind rather than material gain, or social contacts that bring dividends in friendship rather than finance. I have seen this link in the hands of teachers and men of religion – people who have seemed to reverse the usual division of responsibilities between thoughts and feelings.

A line rising from the 'Saturn-point' of the Head Line to link with the Heart Line beneath the Mount of the Sun, in its traditional interpretation, indicates personalities who will delegate matters of prestige and public acclaim to the emotional sphere, where they are liable to remain a dream. There is no lack of confidence in such people's own ability to achieve success, but, though their heart would love it, their brain will simply have no wish to win a laurel wreath or a place in history.

These Head Line Saturn to Sun linkers may seem to have all the ingredients for worldly success – knowledge, talent, tenacity and opportunity – and yet when the reality of this success seems to be within grasp, they will shy away from it, turn aside and go off on another mental tack entirely, seeming to lose interest in the winner's

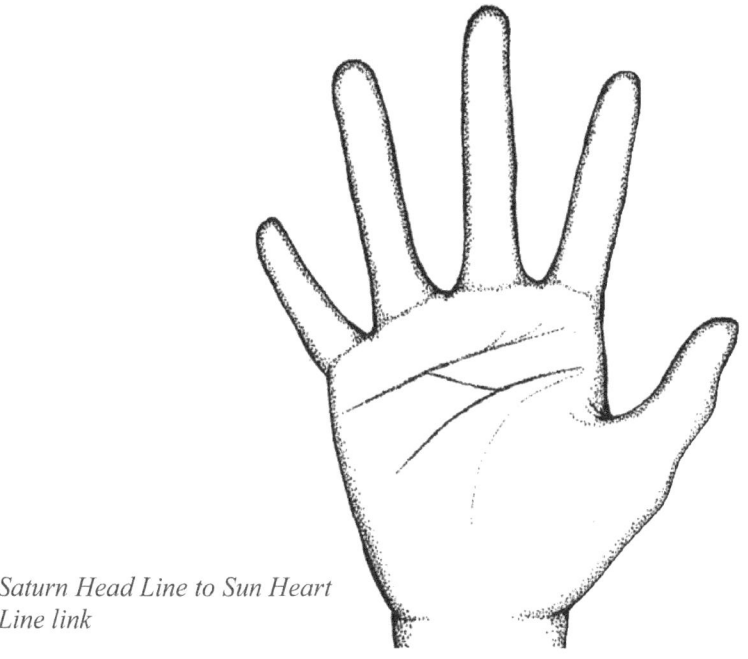

Saturn Head Line to Sun Heart Line link

crown. To the outsider they will seem to have fluffed their chance of success, to have tried and failed, though they personally will not see it like this at all. And the palmist may wonder if success ever was their actual goal. Do not think of these subjects as born failures – not at all! They may very well have produced some fine achievements of which their hearts are rightly proud, and yet their intellects will seem to place little value on them. They will speak of their successes disparagingly, as though they were failures – and are only being sincere when they do so.

      A similar link rising from the Head Line around the 'Saturn-point' to meet the Heart Line somewhere beneath the Mount of Mercury will indicate the sorts of people to whom communication is a solid matter of work and wealth. Their hearts will be allowed to rule only when the welfare of others is at stake. Such people will work unsparingly for some worthy cause, particularly where they consider that innocent people are suffering – perhaps because of famine, or civil war, or an earthquake in some far-off land. They are all for the underdog, for the loser. Compassion for the outsider will override any ideas they may have had to amass wealth for their own family,

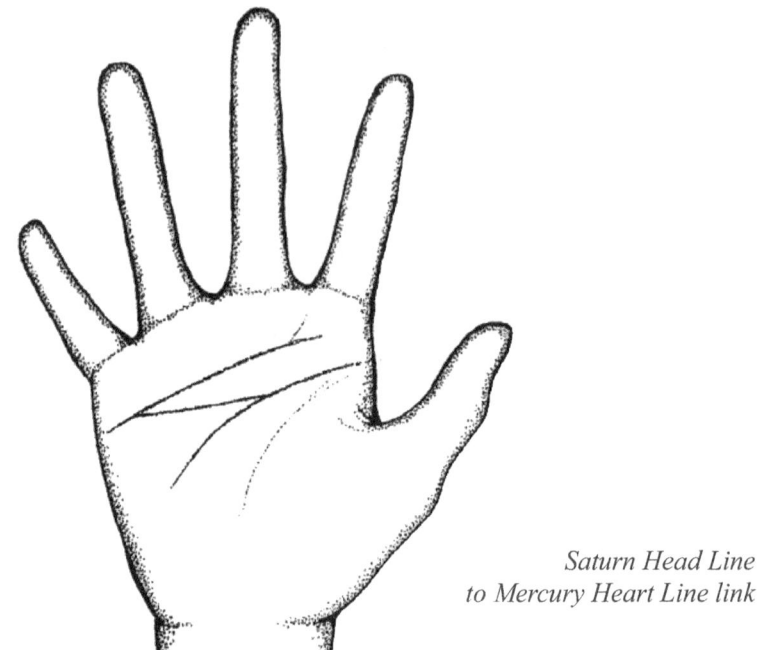

*Saturn Head Line
to Mercury Heart Line link*

and there are times when they will be generous to a fault. It is no use advising such people that charity begins at home: they know with emotional certainty where their priorities lie, and nothing can shake that view.

Any of these matters could be interpreted equally accurately in terms of marriage. Indeed, when the one having his or her palm read seems to be experiencing marriage doubts or difficulties, many traditional palmists slant all the available information in that direction. The Head Line now will represent the subject personally; the Heart Line will represent the marriage; and the linking lines will represent habitual attitudes that may be at the root of the trouble. The ambitious spouse may well be continually thwarted because the main breadwinner persists in plodding along in a safe but low-paid job, instead of taking a chance and launching out on some money-making but risky scheme.

A Saturn-Mercury link husband may be only too ready to send flowers or chocolates to some 'poor old dear', completely overlooking the fact that his long-suffering wife would also appreciate some small token. Or the wife with a similar sign may be

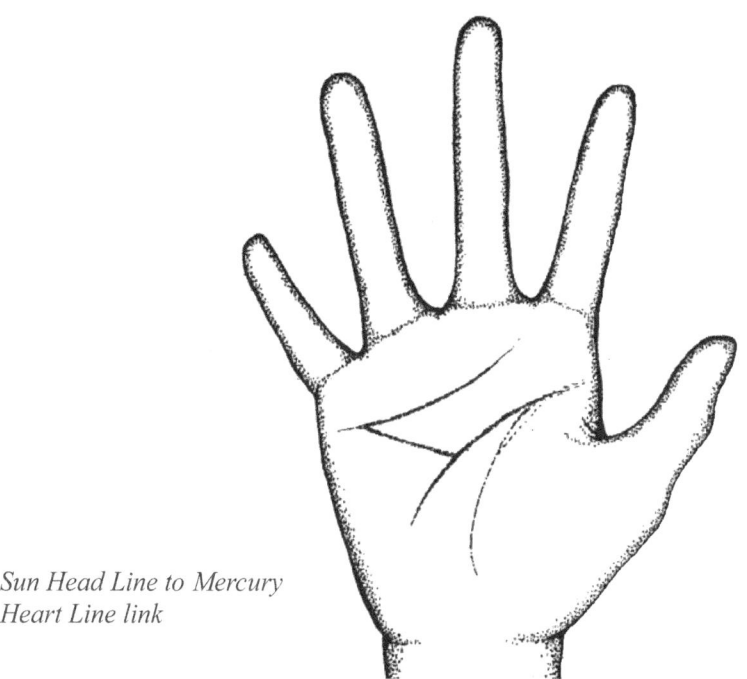

Sun Head Line to Mercury Heart Line link

quick to bestow favours on some under-privileged young chap, while her jealous husband broods darkly in the background. Interpreting along similar lines, a Saturn Head Line link to a Sun Heart Line will, if a woman, be supremely content to leave all the public and social achievements to her husband, or *vice versa*. A Sun Head Line link to a Mercury Heart Line will be content to leave all the social entertaining and the party talk to his or her spouse.

The long and short of it is that, to a palmist, the lines of thehand are symbols of the subject's habits and fortunes. They never indicate a hard-and-fast fate. They are no less significant in the case of a confirmed bachelor or spinster than with a much-married person, or a wild chaser after every available partner. All the signs of the hand need to be interpreted according to the lifestyle of the subject. Plainly, it is no use talking about marriage difficulties to a happy bachelor, though his lines may be similar to those of a married man. They should be seen as a pattern of influences rather than a set of concrete meanings. The broader the pattern, the more palmistry can relate to the whole person — to the human soul rather than merely the surface personality.

17 Common Sense and Uncommon Sense:
Branch Lines and the Supernal Zone

IN GENERAL TERMS, as we have seen, a branch line which links Head and Heart Lines suggests that one or other of these two major functions – thinking and feeling – will tend to dominate the other when decisions are to be made. Remember which way the line is 'going', and that the Heart and Head Lines rise above the thumb and strike out from there across the palm. A branch represents a divergence from the main flow of one line or the other – of one function or the other.

Having commenced near the Mount of Jupiter, a branch line that forks from the Heart Line and strikes down and outwards to join the Head Line characterizes somebody for whom thinking is the chief function. It implies that logic, or common sense, will be allowed to rule the heart, and 'mere feelings' will be dismissed as sentimental nonsense. There will be no great emotional attachments in this person's life. Conversely, the line that strikes out and upwards from the Head Line to link with the Heart Line above it suggests that the subject's heart will rule their head in certain compartments of life, depending on the 'human attributes' associated with the nearest mount.

A linking branch line can be one of the most strikingly significant signs in the palm. Owing to the basic division of the psyche into heart and mind, a simple branch line portrays a very definite psychological trait, an emphasis that will always be evident in the subject's life.

A branch line running from the Heart Line to meet the Head Line is often to be seen in the hand of dedicated entrepreneurs who seem to use their feelings only to augment their own business convictions. They will not care much for the feelings of people who seem to be standing in the way of their career, or any important business deal. Even when their successes do not seem to be particularly outstanding, they will certainly love their job. They tend to have one goal, though this goal may be multifaceted: to achieve success in the material sphere. The symbolism will probably hold good when looked at with regard to this person's marriage too,

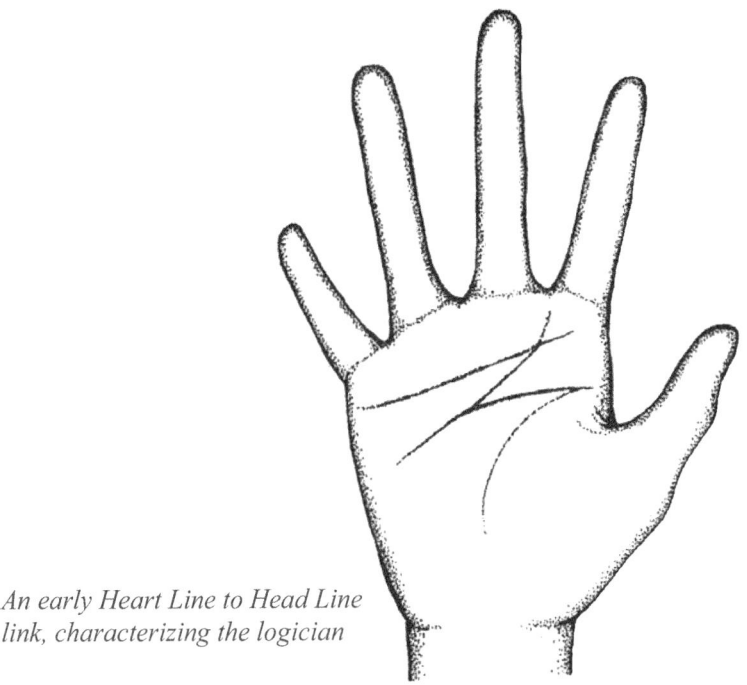

An early Heart Line to Head Line link, characterizing the logician

and this is particularly true when the branch line has its origin or its destination beneath the Saturnian mount of resources.

Even where no business deals are involved, the sign has often been linked with marriage, as has the reverse link, from Head Line to Heart Line. Traditionalists have it that the former in particular implies a marriage of convenience – for money, for prestige, or perhaps purely as a business arrangement. It may apply equally to the woman who marries with the full intention of leaving all money matters – buying, selling, insuring, paying the bills – to her husband. The couple who jointly run a successful business, whether under the guise of marriage or not, will probably both wear this sign. Responsibilities for money-making and management will then be split evenly. It does not necessarily imply a barren relationship, devoid of love or affection. It merely points towards areas of priority: the compartmentalization of cold logic having extricated itself from warm sentiment.

Where a branch line from the Head Line carries straight across the palm to meet the Heart Line, like an extra-large fork which augments the Heart Line, running on to skirt the Mount of Mercury

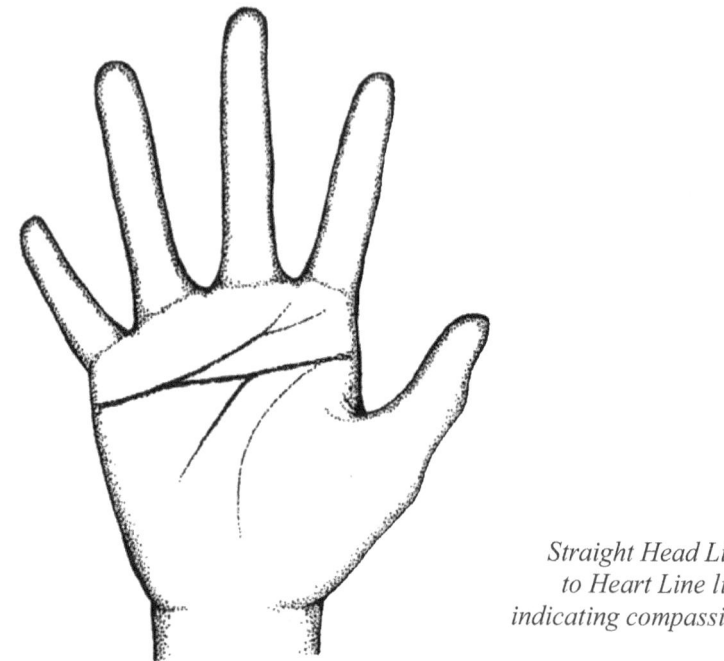

Straight Head Line to Heart Line link indicating compassion

while the Head Line itself – or what appears to be its lower fork – dips downwards towards the intuitive, creative area of the palm, the Mount of the Moon, compassion will be a noticeable feature – not so much a virtue as a recurring theme in the subject's life. If this branch line joining Head to Heart Lines appears on both hands, augmenting the Heart Line and carrying it, growing in depth and clarity, across to the edge of the palm, it will denote a quite extreme type of personality. Such people will certainly be outstandingly compassionate; emotional arguments will always win the day. Certainly they will give their all to any cause that appeals to their heart, and their heart will always seem large enough to accommodate numerous causes.

However, boundless compassion is not always a blessing in everyday life, particularly when coupled with material generosity. Taken to extremes, it can prove a hindrance, a handicap even. It can be rather like interfering in another's affairs, or spreading the gospel indiscriminately from door to door, where it may not be appreciated. Applying compassion where it is neither justified nor required can not

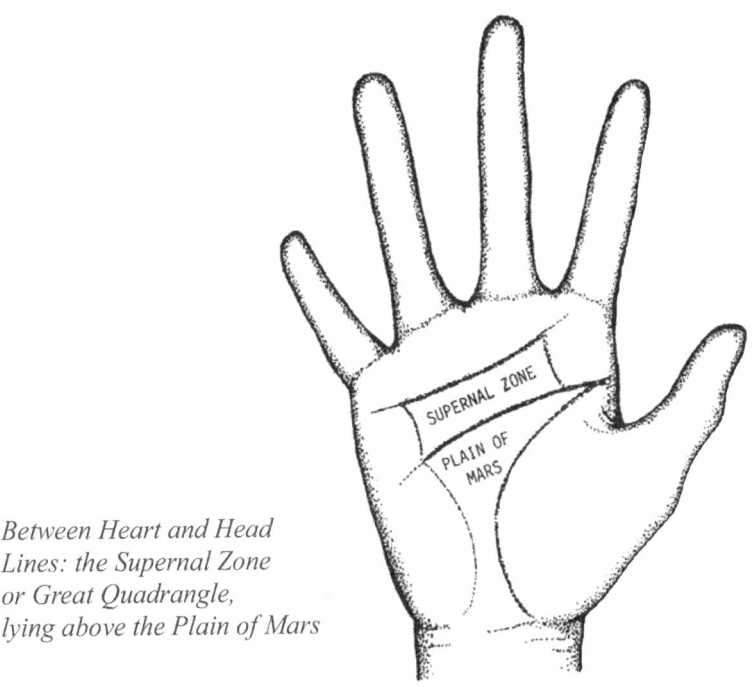

Between Heart and Head Lines: the Supernal Zone or Great Quadrangle, lying above the Plain of Mars

only stretch your own resources too far but also cause strained relationships. It can even introduce undesirable elements into the soul, a 'throwing away of virtue', and really can be the cause of unnecessary suffering for the individual so afflicted. When well regulated, however, a modicum of compassion carries spiritual dividends, and it is an essential adjunct of personal integrity.

When trying to read the palm not only as a means of disclosing personality but also as an aid to understanding the soul, minor lines linking the Head Line with the Heart Line are particularly important, for as a rule they start and finish within the Supernal Zone. This is a particularly 'spiritual' area of the hand, also known as the Great Quadrangle, overlooking the so-called Plain of Mars. It is the field of the karmic pendulum, the great void between thinking and feeling, and, according to the cosmology of palmistry, is directly linked with the soul. The area it represents is central to the whole human psyche, abstract and concrete, conscious and unconscious, and any lines which arise there are bound to carry deep significance.

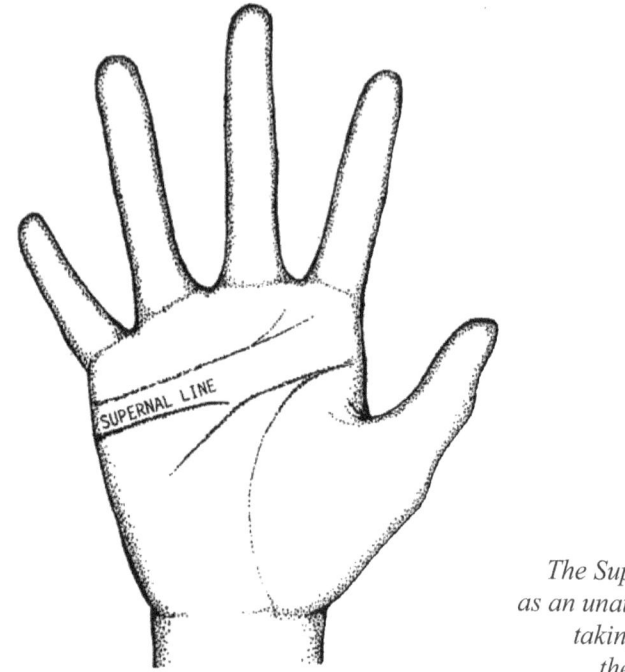

*The Supernal Line,
as an unattached fork
taking over from
the Head Line*

A line of this nature is to be seen in the sample analysis in chapter 40. Here the right hand differs markedly from the left, and the upper fork on the left-hand Head Line seems to have taken on a life and individuality of its own. Not really attached to the Head Line and rising so clearly within the mystical Supernal Zone, it carries on as a line of the first magnitude to the edge of the palm and even beyond. In palmistry it is the inner self that is represented by this Great Quadrangle.

In some hands the Supernal Line may begin as an unattached fork from the Heart Line rather than the Head Line: the one represents an intellectual approach to spiritual matters; the other, an emotional one. But neither the intellect nor the emotions have any part to play in the life of the soul and the awareness that this zone implies. When the soul makes its presence known, the mind is made to move, as it were, to one side, the heart or emotions to the other, where they can be witnesses to the event that unfolds and not partakers in it.

Nothing, of course, is dependent upon the lines of the hand;

they are only the symbols of a situation and not its cause, not its reality. But you can be sure that when the Supernal Line appears, clear and true, the inner life – the human soul – will indeed be brought to full awareness during the subject's physical life here on earth.

I hope I have made it clear that the absence of this line by no means precludes so thrilling an event. But its presence, its rising within the Supernal Zone, does imply a foregone conclusion. Karmic contents, perhaps from ancient times, have led towards this eventuality, this awakening. Sometimes the potentiality for the event can be seen in the left hand of inheritance, but other events may have prevented it from reaching its goal – the attainment of true spiritual awareness, which is far and away the most valuable form of uncommon sense.

18 Mental Instability: Islands, Chains and Breaks in the Head Line

AN ISLAND on the Head Line, a circular interruption or, on a much smaller scale, a chained formation, is something of a warning sign. In the Heart Line it portends some sort of emotional disturbance. Here in the Head Line it suggests some kind of mental disturbance. It symbolizes the flow of psychic energy having met a mental obstruction and running in circles, seemingly unable either to ignore or to disperse the interruption.

An extensive chained formation suggests some protracted disturbance, a continuing mental condition, depending on its length and location. A distinct island points to an isolated event, though one that may be traumatic and protracted in its consequences.

There is no traditional way to measure time on the Head or Heart Lines directly and thus put an approximate date to the trouble, but note can be taken of the relative points of intersection of the Lines of Fate and Fortune, which can bear a timescale, and which dissect the Head Line at the age of thirty-five and the Heart Line at the age of forty-nine. There may too be other clues in the hand that will give some indication of when such mental disturbances are likely to occur, or to have occurred. There may be link lines running upwards from any point along the Life Line, which by its own age scale will have the effect of fixing in time the point on the other lines that they dissect.

As we know, soul impulses are envisaged in the hand as flowing outwards from the base of the index finger, and we should watch out for signs which may symbolize some sort of barrier to this free flow. Some traumatic event that caused the confusion represented by an island will often be symbolized by a clear, short line crossing the Head Line close to this island, on the index finger side. Such a mark, the 'actual barrier', may indicate a physical injury to the head or some other particularly traumatic accident. A clear break in the Head Line beneath the Mount of Saturn is sometimes given the same meaning.

As with branch lines, islands are usually best read and interpreted as relating in some way to the mounts above them. They will usually then give some indication in which sphere of mental

Head Line with a clean break beneath the Mount of Saturn, and a chained formation beneath the Mount of the Sun

activity problems are liable to arise, or to have most effect – in the field of ambition, communication, general well-being, money or possessions. The problem may consist of obsessive ideas. Power and success, or the lack of them, can readily become obsessions in this competitive age.

Many an overwrought business person wears a clearly defined island in their Head Line beneath the Mount of Jupiter or, equally likely, beneath the Mount of the Sun. These islands can appear and fade away, strengthen and weaken, as circumstances change. The minor signs of the hand at least are not always fixed for life!

The onset of depression, typified by brooding or excessive introspection, can be foretold by an island beneath the Mount of Saturn. Such a sign often betokens social isolation. Beneath the Mount of Mercury, the seat of restless thoughts, an island in the Head Line can mean mental strain brought about through an excess of work, studying too hard or worrying over complicated issues. The very fact of its placing beneath the Mount of Mercury indicates an unusually long Head Line: the subject has a very busy and, perhaps,

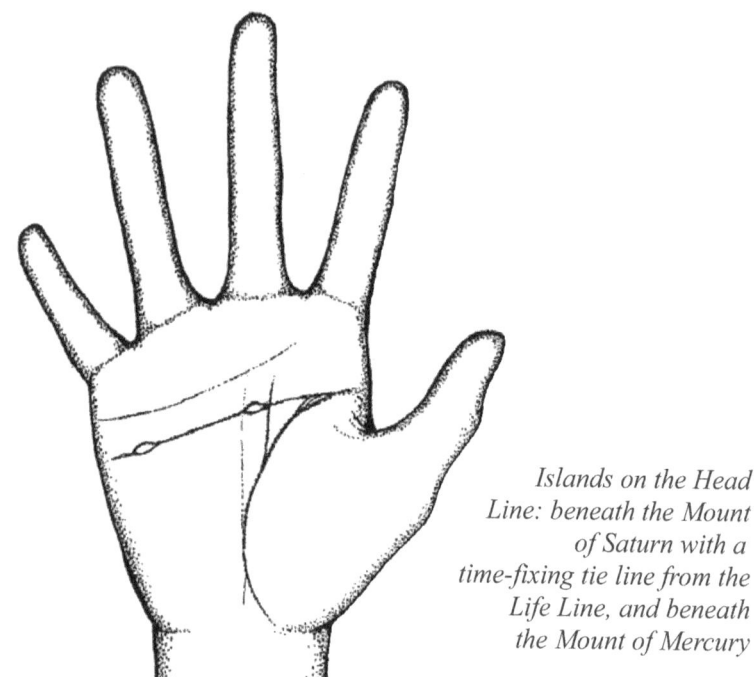

Islands on the Head Line: beneath the Mount of Saturn with a time-fixing tie line from the Life Line, and beneath the Mount of Mercury

an obsessive mind.

Whenever disturbances are indicated along the Head Line, the Heart Line too should be consulted. The root cause of many problems is more often emotional than mental. But as with the Heart Line, a chained Head Line formation symbolizes a continual and confused chasing of one's own tail. It implies, if not outright and obvious instability of a serious nature, as least a difficulty in concentrating, an essential woolly-mindedness, as worried thoughts cycle endlessly, never reaching any constructive conclusion.

19 The Life Line:
Energy, Time, Travel and Health

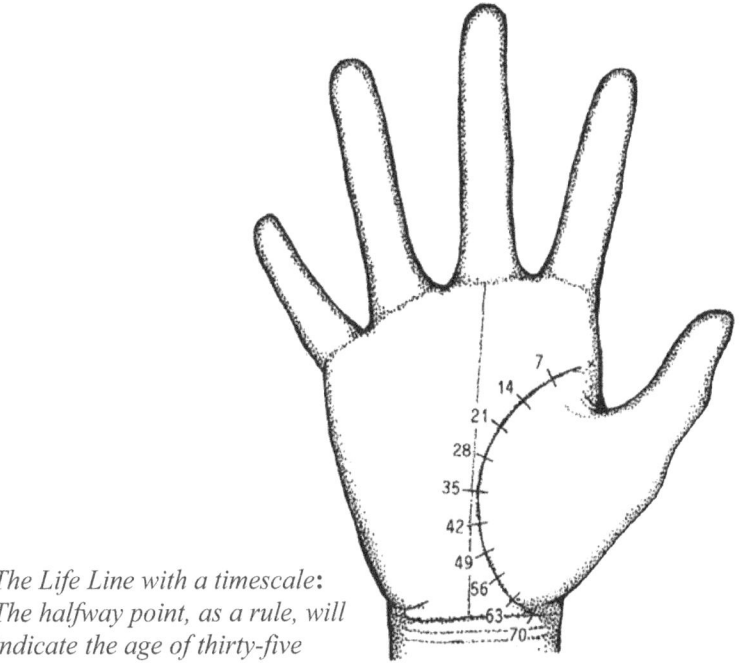

The Life Line with a timescale: *The halfway point, as a rule, will indicate the age of thirty-five*

THE LIFE LINE charts the basic course of physical well-being. As we can deduce mental and emotional stability from the Head and Heart Lines, so from the Life Line we can trace physical stability, vigour and general condition. But unlike the other two lines, which tend to be once-for-all indicators, the Life Line can be set to a time-scale and can conveniently be seen as a chronometer of events.

A long, strong and clear Life Line usually betokens a long, strong and vigorous life. A short, faint and shallow formation suggests a troubled life, characterized by physical weakness and health problems. But of course this is only an outward symbol of inner strength or weakness. By no means does anyone's life depend on the clarity of their Life Line. The tendency is there, however, and when read intelligently, along with all the other signs, it will sketch out a reasonably accurate picture of the subject's general health.

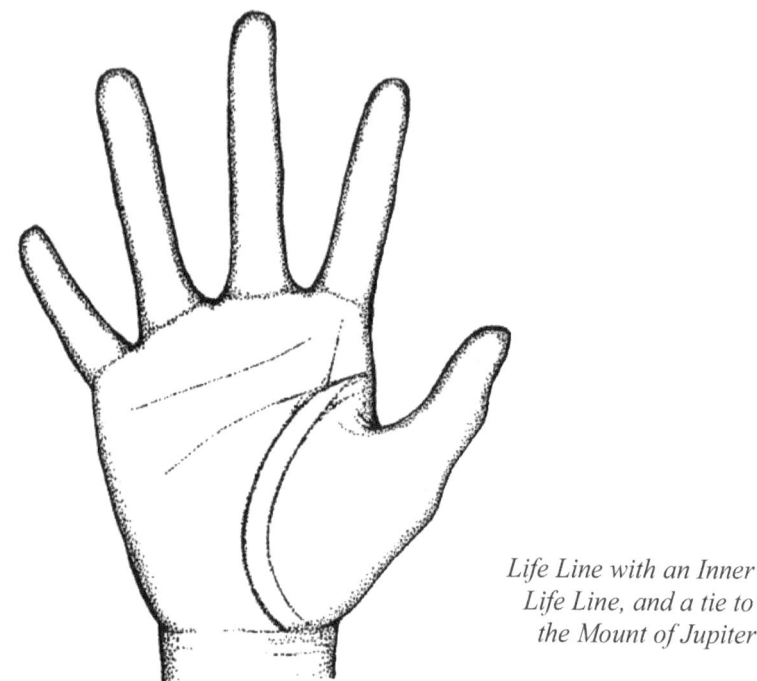

Life Line with an Inner Life Line, and a tie to the Mount of Jupiter

There are other factors besides physical strength and freedom from accident and disease that affect vigour and thence longevity: mental health, emotional security, happiness, contentment and sheer stubbornness all add up to the ingredients for a long and happy life. Hope is the key. We have all heard of characters who give up hope and 'turn their face to the wall'. They lose the will to live, though they may still possess the physical capacity to struggle along for many years to come.

On the other hand, patients given a poor outlook by their doctor often rally, turn away from their own problems and, instead of moping, spend their time spreading light and hope around the world, with the result that they may confound medical opinion and outlive all the rest.

The point is, somebody's Life Line may 'end at fifty-six'. and if you are reading your own hand – well, some folk seem to enjoy a modicum of doom and gloom, and you may well belong to that category. But if it is another's palm being read, for goodness' sake

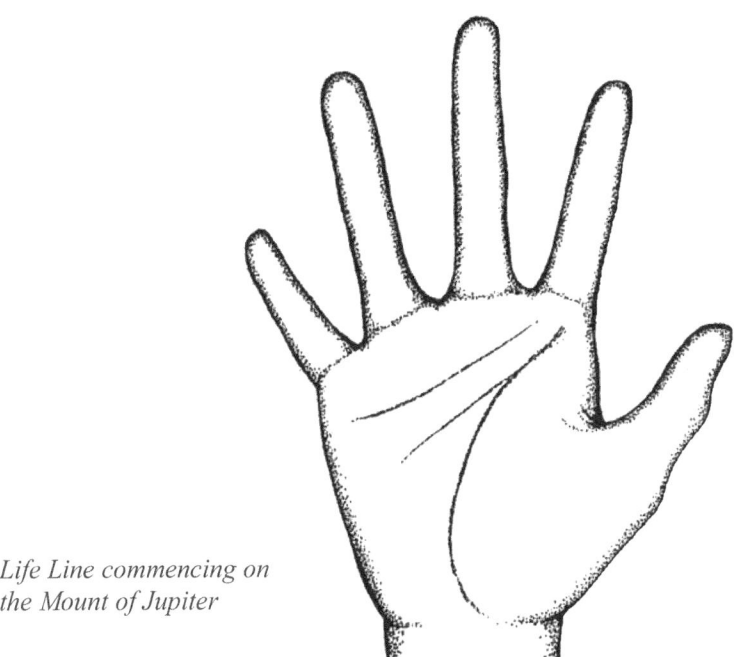

Life Line commencing on the Mount of Jupiter

don't be like the naive 'palmist' at the fête and say cheerfully: 'You'll die at fifty-six!' It *can* cause *a* great deal of alarm and unnecessary worry. It can even prove fatal – in which case the awful prediction will have come true: it will be what is known as a self-fulfilling prophecy. So I am stating unequivocally now, the lines of your hand cannot predict the time of your death, and it would be very unwise to assume otherwise.

You will sometimes find an extra, duplicate Life Line, the two together resembling a tramline curving around the Mount of Venus. In the race for well-being and longevity, this inner Life Line – the clearer the better – is a bonus. If a cat has nine lives, it would presumably possess eight inner Life Lines, because they each seem to act as a 'second chance', a physical guiding force, an ever-present guardian angel who can protect the bearer against the worst of illnesses and accidents that would flatten others. It is also known as the Line of Mars. Very old but still vigorous people are often found to bear this line. They may appear to have aged physically, as far as wrinkles are concerned, but their health and strength will still be youthful and they will be able to boast the staying power of a youngster.

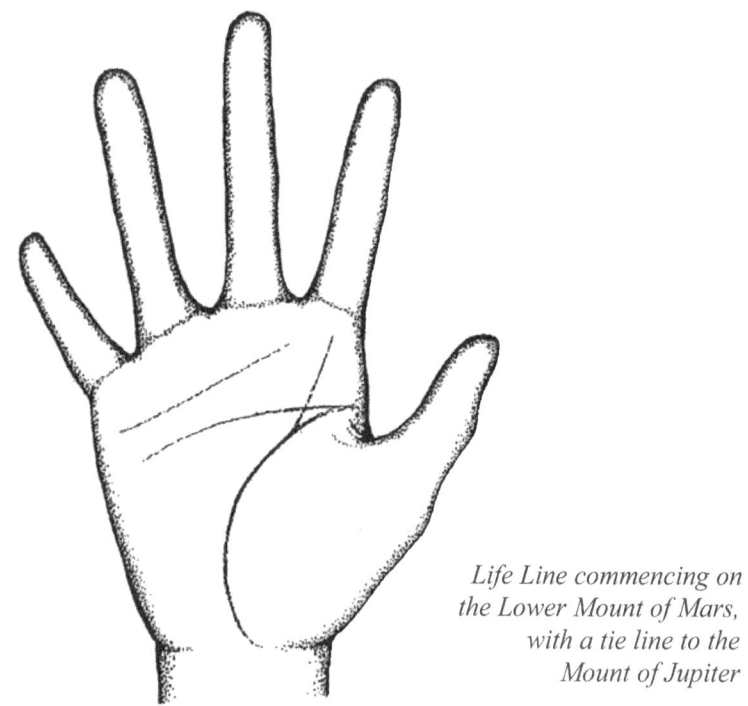

Life Line commencing on the Lower Mount of Mars, with a tie line to the Mount of Jupiter

Since, in traditional palmistry, the Mount of Jupiter is considered to be the 'seat of ambition', it follows that the closer the ties which the Life Line displays with this mount, the more ambitious and physically outgoing the lifestyle is likely to be. Sometimes the Life Line starts near to or actually on the Mount of Jupiter itself, but this is not such a good sign, as it implies disruption to the mental and emotional functions. Furthermore, if the Life Line rises above the Head Line, you can expect a case of 'bad-tempered isolation'.

Usually, however, an association with the Mount of Jupiter comes about merely through a linking branch line, though the Life Line itself may have started quite low down – perhaps in the lower Martian region, denoting physical aggression. A lifestyle thus coloured by both a dynamic, thrusting nature, physically orientated, and an inborn tie with ambition could belong only to a forceful personality possessing enormous impetus towards success.

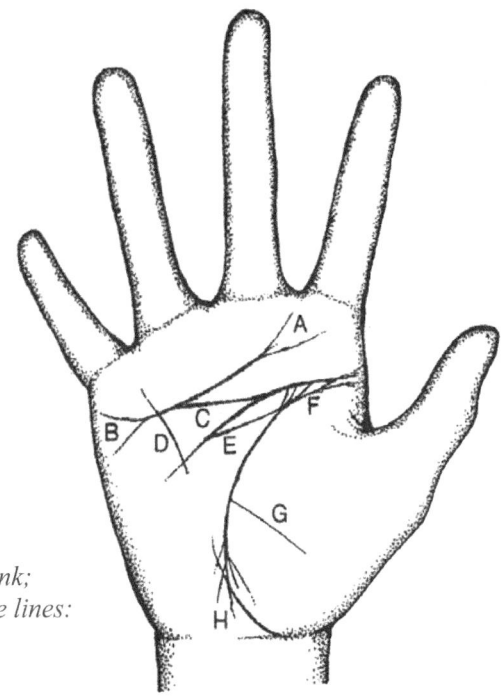

A) Tributaries; B) fork;
C) Branch or tie; D) Link;
E) Backwards tie; F) tie lines:
G) Line of Influence;
H) fragmented fork

The difference between branch lines, tie lines and link lines is not always obvious. A branch is a clear line forking out from a major line which, following the same general direction, joins on to another major line. A tie is a minor line tying two major lines together without overlapping. A link is a minor line that crosses more than one major line, thus incidentally linking them. A fork from a major line does not form a link with another major line; if it does, it becomes a branch! These link-ups can be complicated, but they always offer a clue to the various influences which involuntarily enter every person's life.

A Line of Influence generally takes the form of a tie line. When lines like this tie the Life Line to the Head Line, they usually represent family support that is freely available, especially at an early age. In this case, they sweep down from the Head Line along the course of the Life Line, eventually to touch it. Money is said to be involved when, in addition to the more commonly seen flowing lines

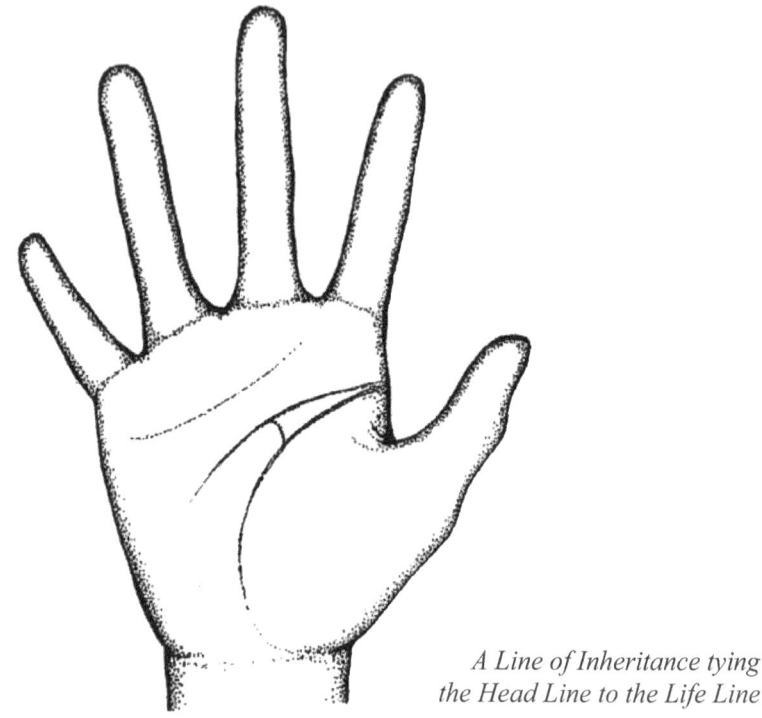

A Line of Inheritance tying the Head Line to the Life Line

linking the two, a distinct backwards tie from the Head Line runs in the opposing direction, against the flow of the Life Line.

A Line of Inheritance rarely (and only coincidentally) indicates the actual receipt of money from the family; a precise date cannot be set for the event and other indications must be sought here. Tradition has it that there is no time or time limit for inheritance to be found in the hand, and if you consider all the factors involved, it is fairly obvious why this must be so. An inheritance is simply something to look forward to in due course.

A contrary-flow tie line of this sort can really be meaningful only when at least a small gap exists between the commencement of these two main lines. The average Head Line is tied to the Life Line for a very short distance; when these two lines are firmly tied for some distance – traditionally taken as an indication of a cautious nature – a contrary link with the Head Line does have significance of a related but slightly different nature. It indicates that subjects will receive all the blessings that a happy family environment can bring as a child, but

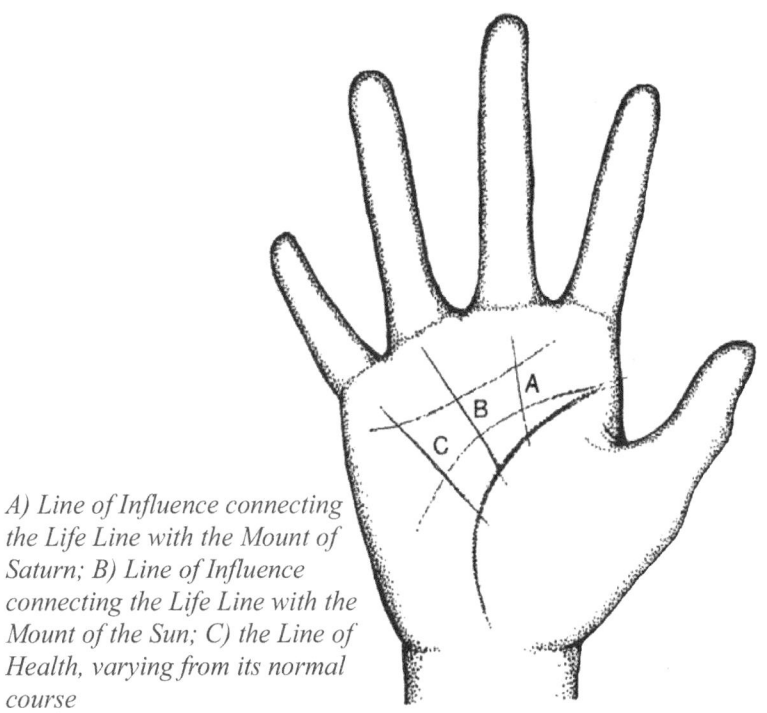

A) Line of Influence connecting the Life Line with the Mount of Saturn; B) Line of Influence connecting the Life Line with the Mount of the Sun; C) the Line of Health, varying from its normal course

the natural independence of their nature will begin to assert itself when they reach teenage years, leading them to 'go it alone' in the psychological sense and break away smoothly from parental restraint.

Long ties and links which touch or cross the Life Line carry special significance depending on where they start and finish. For instance, we have already seen that a line connecting the Mount of Jupiter to the Life Line indicates ambition, or a certain physically operative driving force. A similar line reaching the neighbouring Mount of Saturn has a sterner meaning, but here again it relates to the whole life-style rather than to any particular point on the timescale. Such a link is said to predict a marked lack of financial luck. There are unlikely to be any significant inheritances or winnings, and life may prove a financial uphill struggle.

A connecting Line of Influence running from the Life Line to the Mount of the Sun is usually considered to signify success, in the sense of public achievement. It speaks of outstanding talent being put

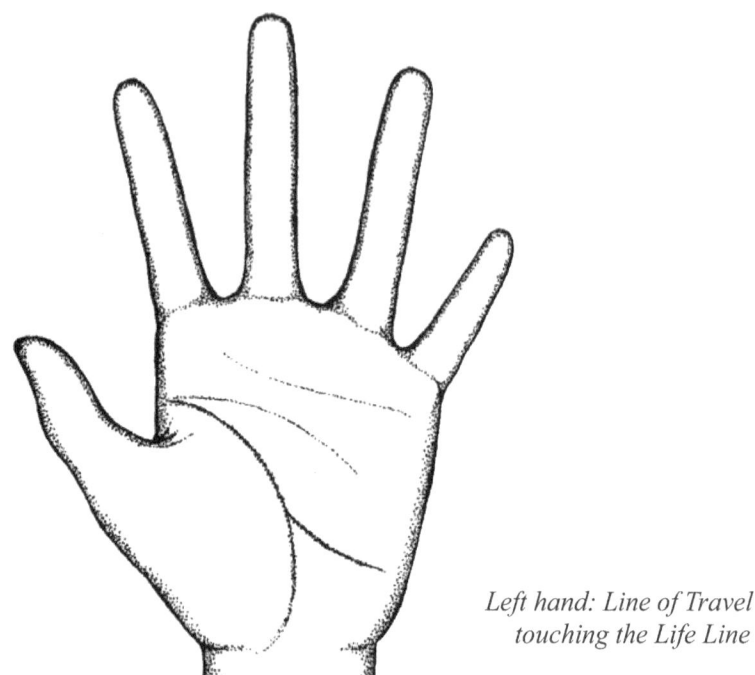

Left hand: Line of Travel touching the Life Line

to good and profitable use. What may appear to be a lengthy link line or Line of Influence leading from the Life Line to the Mount of Mercury is usually considered to be a line in its own right and is given a separate name: the Line of Health. In fact, it is a variation from the normal course of the Line of Health, which usually runs between the Mount of Mercury and the lower part of the Mount of the Moon. It betokens not robust but poor health, or rather a 'concern' with health, and therefore is not a very welcome sign. The basic Marriage Line too will sometimes extend from its proper place on the Mount of Mercury to reach the Life Line, and when it does so it usually suggests an unhappy marriage.

    Some hands show a confusing network of lines. They may denote an interestingly complex personality, but it is not really reasonable to expect numerous minor lines such as these to fitprecisely into any identifiable timescale. The influences they represent are ongoing ones, making their presence felt throughout the subject's life. But the places at which they meet or cross the Life Line are usually the 'trigger points' for various other significant though

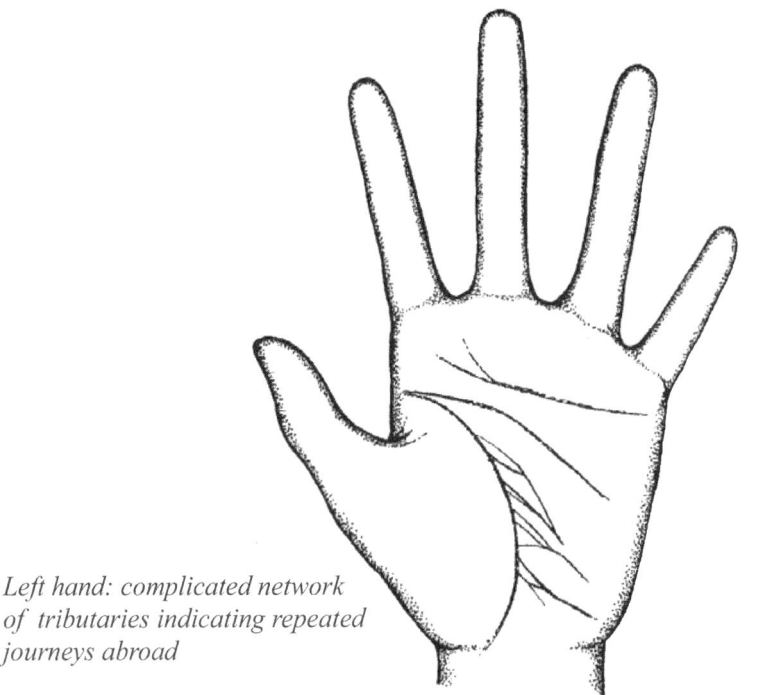

Left hand: complicated network of tributaries indicating repeated journeys abroad

seemingly unconnected occurrences. There is always more than one significance waiting to be attached to any one line or minor sign; it depends largely on the interpreter's train of thought and the subject's expectations. After all, a symbol is not a fixed entity; there is nothing to suggest that it cannot symbolize more than one thing at once.

    A fork on the Life Line, the lower prong curving downwards to end on the Mount of the Moon, is traditionally taken to signify travel abroad, and in the past, at least if you lived in the British Isles, that had to mean 'a sea voyage'. Nowadays, of course, journeys abroad are almost invariably by air, so the phrase 'a journey across the water' has replaced the old interpretation and covers most eventualities. Lines of Travel such as this cannot be relied upon to lead off the Life Line at the precise time of the journey according to the Life Line timescale, though they frequently do. As the left hand deals with concrete, events and the right hand with abstract, spiritual ones, it often happens that physical travel is recorded in the left-hand Travel Lines only. The right hand may chart significant spiritual

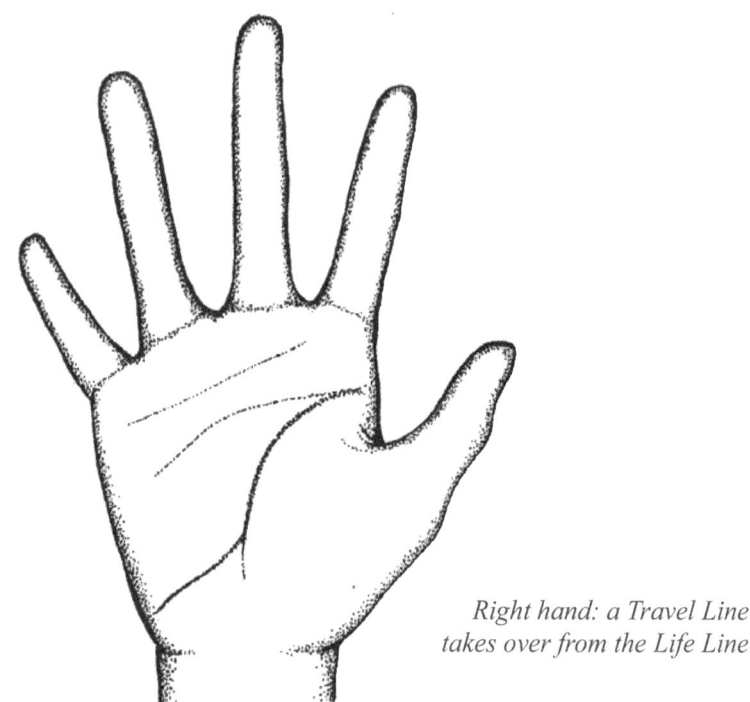

Right hand: a Travel Line takes over from the Life Line

journeys, however – those involving the soul rather than the body – and have no doubt that such journeys of inner discovery do take place and are very real.

It is normal and very common for the Life Line to fork or to become fragmented to a greater or lesser degree near the base of the palm, at the point where it begins to curve beneath the bulky Mount of Venus. This type of configuration is more commonly seen in the hands of men than women, and usually corresponds with the 'forties' on the Life Line timescale. Well, men are at 'a funny age' then, and it is normal for them to branch out, physically, morally and spiritually, during this age range. Even if they do not actually change their careers, 'changing horses in midstream', they will, consciously or unconsciously, be working for the future, and for their own inner welfare and that of their dependants.

Sometimes a complicated network of tributaries to a Travel Line fits precisely in synchronization with repeated journeys and spells of residence abroad. In cases where the years of particularly significant travel are already known, as they will be when reading

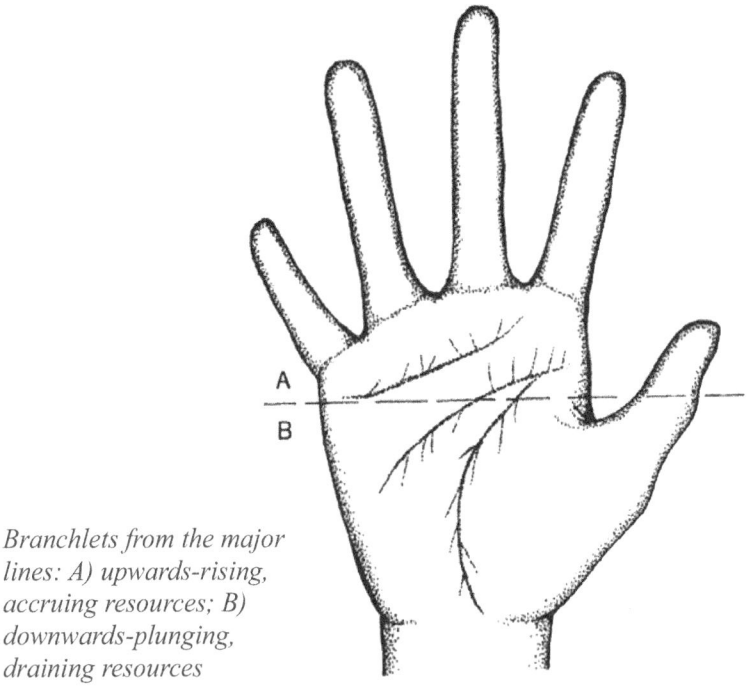

Branchlets from the major lines: A) upwards-rising, accruing resources; B) downwards-plunging, draining resources

your own hand, they can often form the basis of an accurate timescale to be superimposed on the palm print. At all events, the presence of at least one noticeable line of this nature is a fairly accurate indication that a long period of the subject's life has been or is to be spent abroad.

So we can be fairly certain that when a fork breaking away from the Life Line and ending on the Mount of the Moon is as clearly defined as the Life Line itself, the inference is foreign travel with a prolonged spell of residence abroad. On some palms, such a Line of Travel may seem to have 'taken over' from the Life Line altogether, becoming deeper and clearer, while the Life Line proper fades out. In such cases subjects are unlikely either to return or to wish to return to their country of origin, particularly if this feature appears on both hands.

On 'simple', straightforward palms even quite tiny lines crossing or leaving the Life Line may be taken as significant, depending on where they end, what other lines are associated with them, whether they have any minor signs along their own length and,

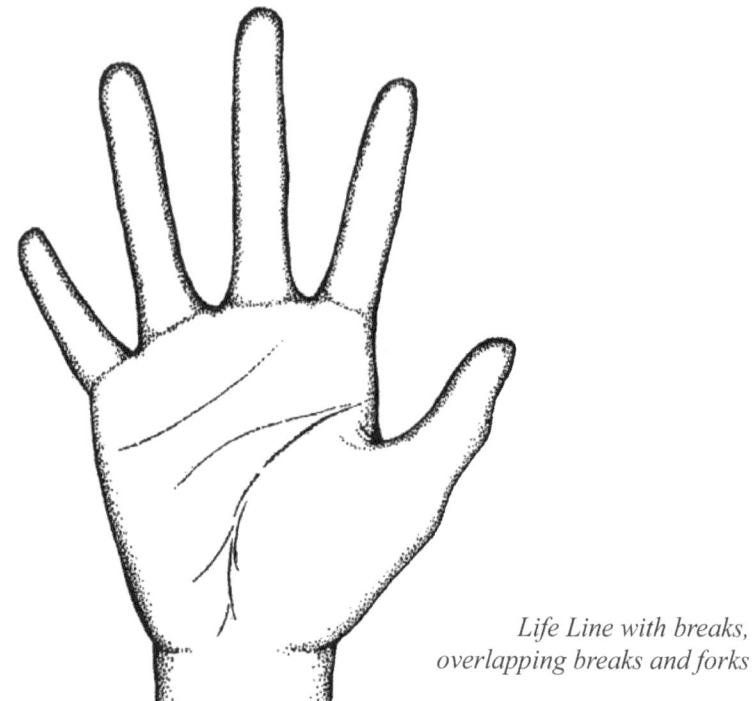

Life Line with breaks, overlapping breaks and forks

of course, at what point on the timescale they leave or cut the Life Line. On more complicated palms which may have a great many fine or short lines leaving the Life Line and running out a short distance, though a precise meaning can scarcely be applied to each one, they may be interpreted collectively according to whether their course is upwards or downwards, inwards or outwards.

    The same principle also holds good where the Head and Heart Line are concerned. Tiny 'branchlets' plunging downwards towards the wrist are looked upon as in some way draining the energy, squandering resources. But those rising upwards towards the fingers are looked upon in a more favourable light, as bonus points, as 'good' occurrences, adding psychic strength perhaps to the primary function expressed by their source line – the physical lifestyle, mental health or emotional welfare.

    Bearing in mind what has already been said about the 'change of life direction' fork that commonly occurs near the base of the Life Line, and making the distinction between these forks and lines of travel, a fork from the Life Line where one prong terminates after a short distance, or a marked change of direction in the Life Line itself, betokens an equally distinct and abrupt change of orientation in the subject's lifestyle at that point along the timescale. This is particularly significant if the sign appears in both hands. It may refer to the onset of a disability of some sort – or the opposite, a breaking away from some kind of conventional restriction, the finding of a new freedom. If the change of direction is clear and clean, you can be sure that the subject has made best use of it, though the change may have been quite involuntary.

Traditionally, a break in the Life Line is said to refer to an illness or an accident. To bring out the full significance of this, it can certainly be timed on the Life Line timescale. But if we are looking at the hand with a view to assessing *spiritual* possibilities, the outward and visible signs of the workings of the soul, we must see breaks, and forks too, as breaks and forks in the flow of base passions. We depend on them for life on earth, but these base passions form a lurid cloud of impulses, instincts, actions and reactions, desire in all its forms, self-will, which conceals the human soul from the direct awareness of our own hearts and minds. In short, they consist of all that stands between a man and his maker. It is these passions, these lower life forces, that are dented, broken and changed during the period indicated by the corresponding break or fork in the Life Line. Like breaks in the Heart Line, these signs are indicative of 'inner turmoil', but there is no constructive rebuilding without corresponding demolition and, taken together as a whole, such signs can add up to spiritual turmoil of the most productive kind.

20   The Line of Fate:
Timescale of Fate

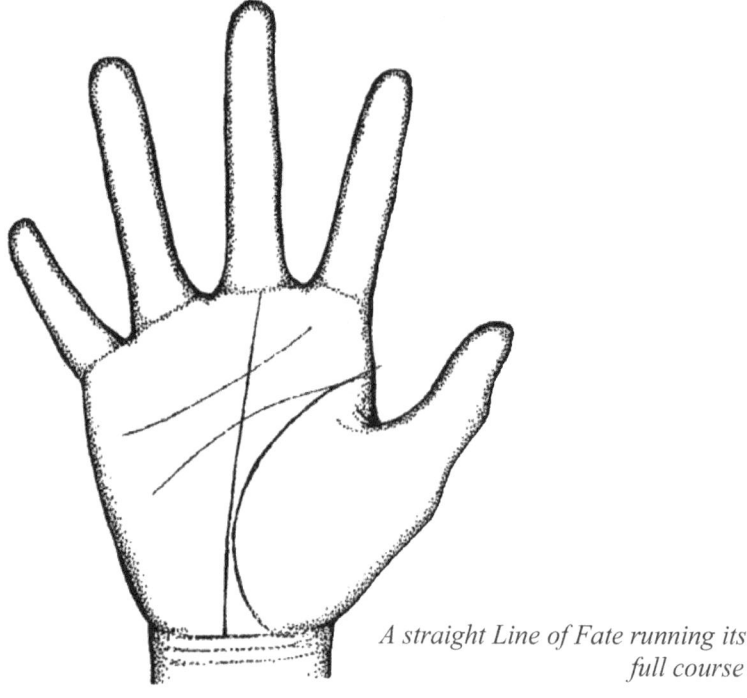

A straight Line of Fate running its full course

THE KARMIC SIGNIFICANCE of the Line of Fate was mentioned earlier in the book, as was the fact that it is not necessarily a particularly welcome line to possess. Along with the adjacent Line of Fortune, it is a line of secondary importance. People who are truly free, in spiritual terms, have no 'need' for either of these lines, and usually have neither in fact. The lines occur only when, in symbolic terms, there is some inbuilt intrusive fate, some long-term cause and effect, some resistance, indeed, to karmic freedom.

This is not to say that the absence of these lines implies that such karmic freedom already exists; it implies no such thing. Their absence is more likely to imply that karmic retribution, or atonement, has not begun to take place. Every act, and in particular every wrong

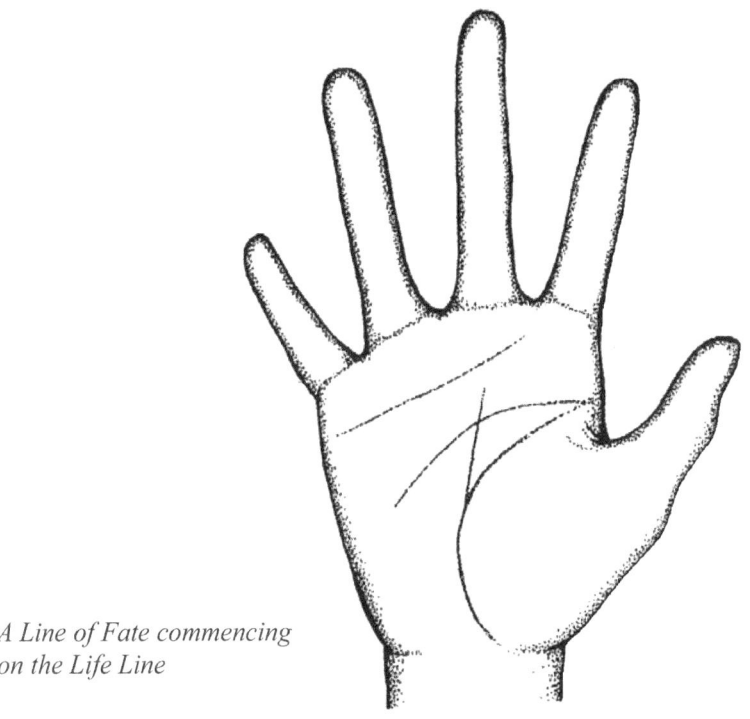

A Line of Fate commencing on the Life Line

done to others, has to find its balance sooner or later. It has to be atoned and, I suppose, sooner is better than later.

This has a religious flavour about it, but really neither the Line of Fate nor the Line of Fortune is connected with religious ideas. But a parallel can perhaps be drawn with religion and a person's relationship with it. It would be fair to say in this sense that there are 'pre-religious people', 'religious people', and 'post-religious people'. That is, there are those who have never given such matters a thought and would as soon fly to the moon as 'turn to God': these are our pre-religious or 'pre-fate people'. Then there are those who 'believe in some power', or who would consider themselves reasonably religious, or who may even be rather superstitiously devout people addicted to ritual, holy books and mystic signs: these are our 'fate people' proper. And finally there are those fortunate ones who see the truth behind all religions, who feel equally 'close to God' whether they are in a special place of worship or a bustling marketplace: these very few are our 'post-fate' people.

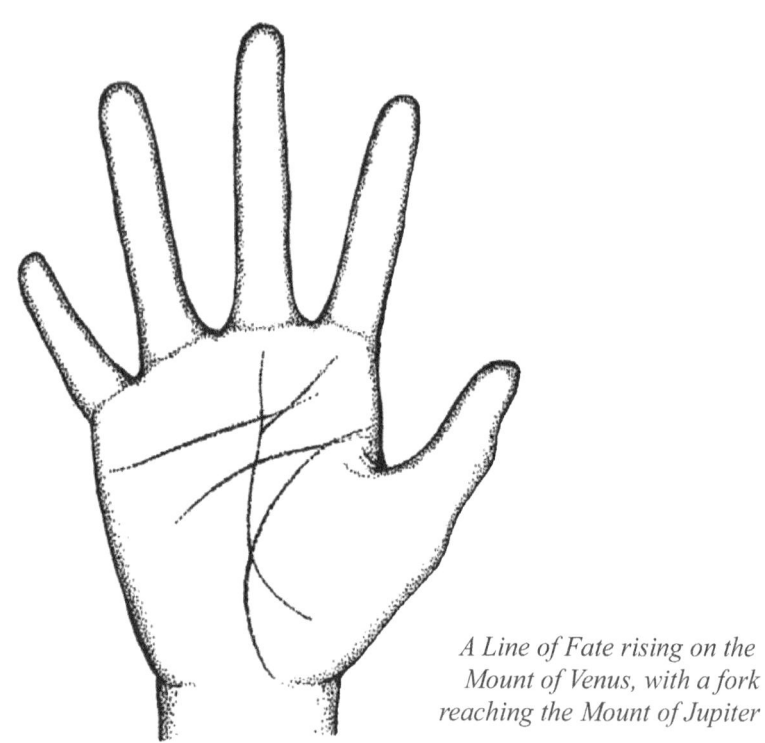

A Line of Fate rising on the Mount of Venus, with a fork reaching the Mount of Jupiter

Firmly traced Lines of Fate and Fortune will normally be found on hands belonging to the middle category. Such people are apparently not left to muddle their way through a chaotic world or vegetate without hope. But neither are they 'attached' to their own soul, in the way that ensures divine guidance is freely available to them from this inbuilt source, without need for outside intervention. No, indeed, children of fate and fortune are firmly attached to the pendulum of karma. They have grown out of the chaotic state of sheer chance and have arrived at a condition of life that has been preordained for them. They are travelling, as it were, between the Rascette and the Mount of Jupiter, between the common undercurrent of life and their own personal destiny.

The full, normal course of the Line of Fate stretches from the topmost bracelet of the wrist to the Mount of Saturn. A clear line running this full course, free from adverse signs, predicts that its wearer will enjoy a happy and successful life. The career of 'fate'

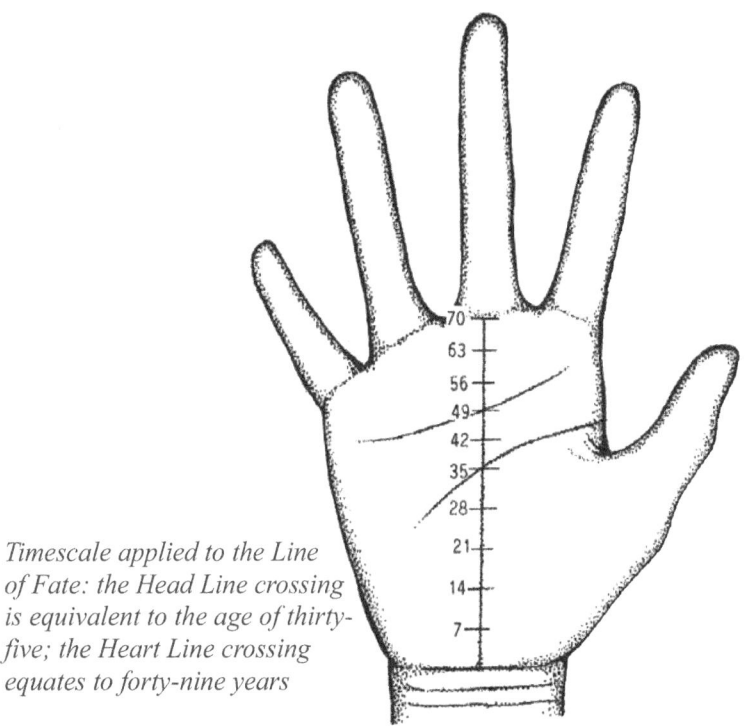

Timescale applied to the Line of Fate: the Head Line crossing is equivalent to the age of thirty-five; the Heart Line crossing equates to forty-nine years

people such as this will seem to have been mapped out at everystage, and they will take justifiable pride in their achievements and in their wide circle of influential friends.

It frequently happens that the Line of Fate is seen tocommence, not at the wrist, but at some point along the Life Line. This implies that the subject's youth was or will be very much withinthe influence of home and family background, to the extent that hisor her natural independence of spirit is hampered. This is also the case when the Line of Fate crosses or emerges from the Life Line,having risen somewhere on the Mount of Venus. But in the latter case, the early influence of family life will ultimately have a beneficial rather than a stultifying effect. It will seem to have provided the subject with the wherewithal for a happy, successful life, according to the predictions of his or her Line of Fate, and only happy memories of childhood days will be retained. The timescale will show the age at which the subject becomes free from parental influences.

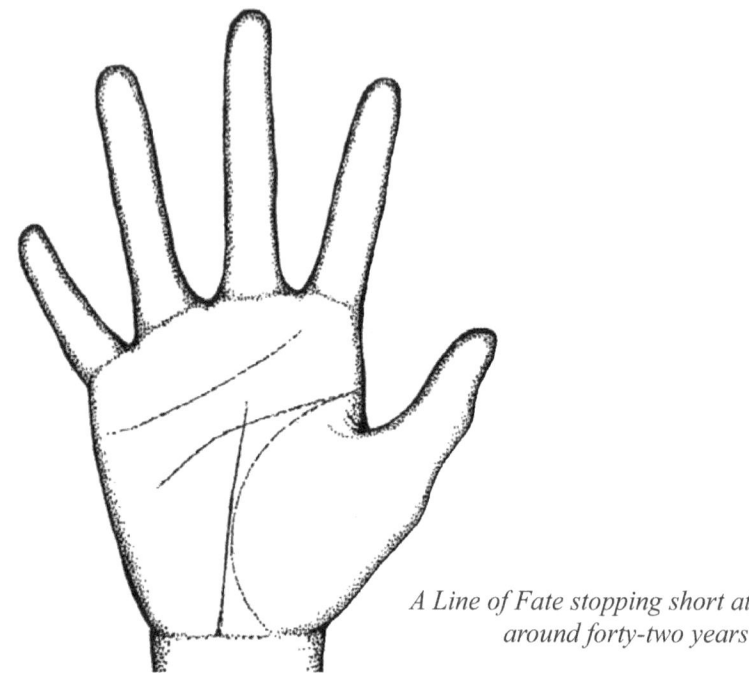

A Line of Fate stopping short at around forty-two years

Occasionally the Line of Fate will commence at its usual on or close to the Rascette, only to merge with the Life Line for a time, or even to cross it and travel some way before re-emerging. The implication of this is that an otherwise normal childhood with early independence has encountered hampering circumstances which forced the subject to enter a state of dependence. The Line of Fate that merely merges with the Life Line for a while may well indicate that the subject is fated to live with a substitute family, *in loco parentis,* for the period indicated by the timescale. Where the Line of Fate actually penetrates the Life Line, and runs for a while actually on the Mount of Venus, the implication is that the family itself has altered in some way, either in structure or in attitude.

On its own timescale, the Line of Fate is said to register the age of thirty-five as it touches the Head Line and age of forty-nine when it reaches the Heart Line above it. A Line of Fate that rises at any point along this scale suggests that fate will have begun to take a hand at that point in the subject's life. Conversely, at the point where a Line of Fate ends short, fate will seem to have flown out of the

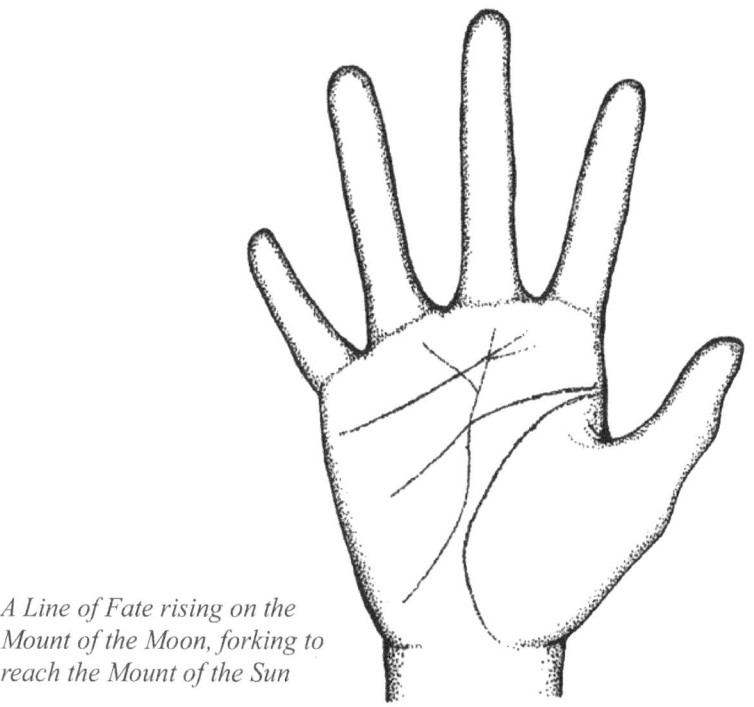

A Line of Fate rising on the Mount of the Moon, forking to reach the Mount of the Sun

window. It can have a 'good' connotation or a 'bad' one. It all depends on your own level of perception, on the type of person to whom the hand belongs and on the kind of information you are trying to uncover.

By and large the Line of Fate, with its natural goal on the Mount of Saturn, bears a material significance: this is the fate of material benefits, of possessions and finance. It is probably within the ranks if the middle 'fate' category, and especially among the possessors of a strongly marked Line of Fate, that the millionaires of this world are to be found; then again, they may experience a lifelong fate that is not so good. Whichever it is will be clearly mapped out for them. The pre-fate people do not have their careers mapped out for them. They may have a hard struggle to make a living, or perhaps they are more likely to earn a steady wage in regular employment, like millions of others. The post-fate people do not know what awaits them, but they often discover that no matter how hard they work, whether they do much or little, whether their family's needs are modest or great, they will always seem to have *enough* to meet those needs, but never a surplus. The Line of Fate is a mixed blessing, and so is its absence.

On the theme of family influence, wealth and success – and we have seen that the Line of Fate which rises on the Mount of Venus has family influence at its root – a Line of Fate rising on the opposite side of the palm, on the Mount of the Moon, has non-family influences at its root. Such a rising point for this line has to be a favourable sign when found in the hands of those who seek or depend upon public acclaim: actors, entertainers, politicians. In this case it will be outsiders, the public – and in particular members of the opposite sex – who will supply the necessary boost towards fame and fortune.

The natural ending point for the Line of Fate – the Mount of Saturn – is the seat of time-bound fate and materiality. The Line of Fate that curves or forks to provide an alternative ending for itself also needs to be interpreted in material terms. Thus a connection with the Mount of Jupiter implies success in the sense of worldly ambition achieved, the sign of the powerful individual whose word is law. A connection with the Mount of the Sun, in the other direction, implies success in the form of public acclaim and popularity. An even wider divergence connecting with the Mount of Mercury implies success in the sphere of communication and knowledge, science, medicine and public relations.

Such connections should always be interpreted as having positive value. Without these, a successful Line of Fate in itself should be clear and straight, with no obvious kinks. One that veers from side to side, aiming first at one point and then another, implies negativity. It predicts that the subject's ambitions too will vacillate, and they are liable to dissipate their energy in wasted efforts throughout their life.

21 The Ups and Downs of Fate: Dominance, Islands, Chains and Breaks

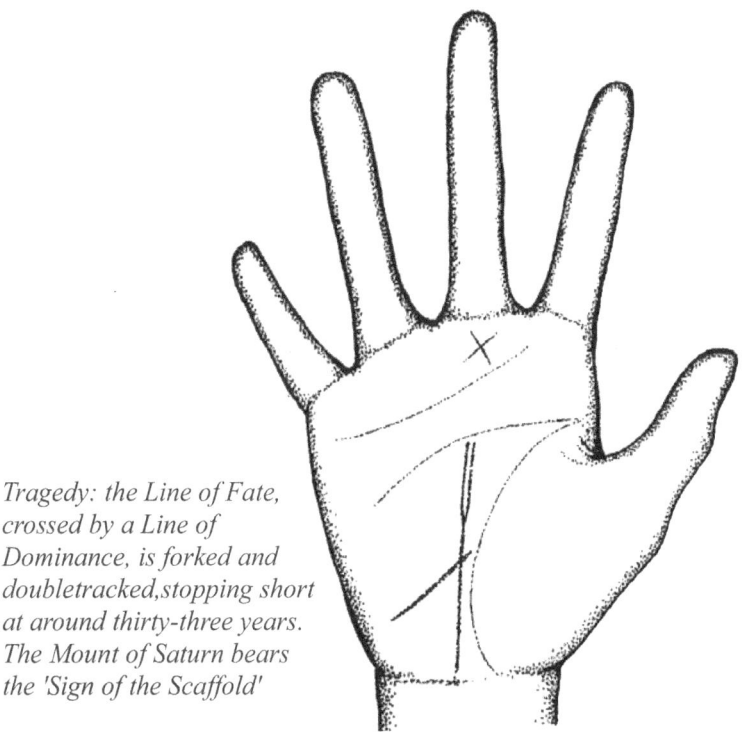

Tragedy: the Line of Fate, crossed by a Line of Dominance, is forked and doubletracked, stopping short at around thirty-three years. The Mount of Saturn bears the 'Sign of the Scaffold'

YOU WILL QUITE OFTEN find a minor line which, having risen at some point on the Mount of the Moon, joins or cuts across the Line of Fate. This has been called the Line of Dominance. Normally it is a right-hand line only, and rather similar to a shortened version of the Travel Lines, which are usually limited to the left hand. As a rule, the Line of Dominance may be taken to represent the influence of one particular individual of the opposite sex – usually the marriage partner – and illustrates something of the quality of the relationship. In ideal circumstances this line should barely touch the Line of Fate and should be of similar or slightly less intensity. This will imply just enough 'dominance' for the partner to be ever uppermost in the

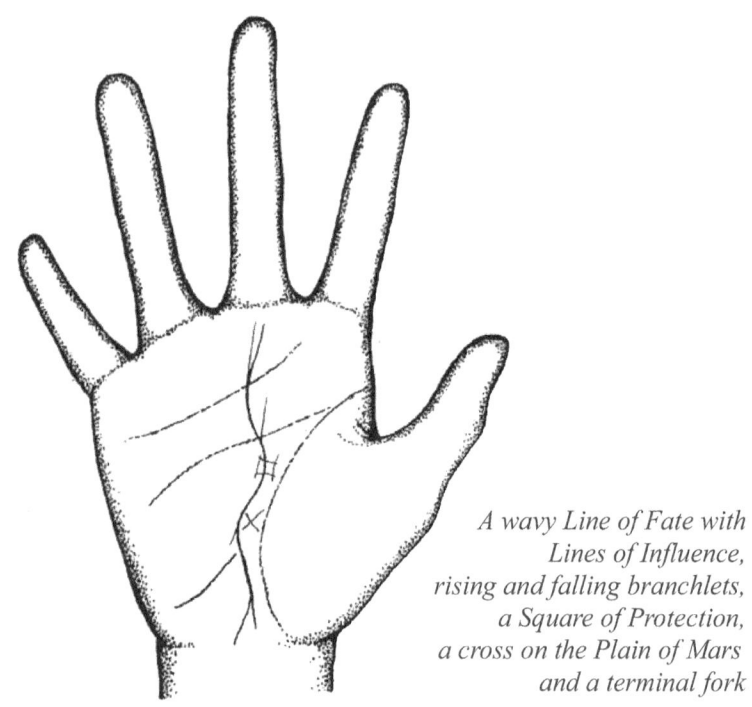

A wavy Line of Fate with Lines of Influence, rising and falling branchlets, a Square of Protection, a cross on the Plain of Mars and a terminal fork

subject's thoughts and portends a faithful relationship. A Line of Dominance that is stronger than the Line of Fate itself, however, implies that the subject will indeed be dominated in a rather unpleasant way by his or her marriage partner.

When such a line stops just short of the Line of Fate, it implies that actual marriage is fated not to take place. A short Line of Dominance is to be found in cases where one partner of an engaged couple keeps the other guessing and waiting for years on end, and the promised match never occurs. When the Line of Dominance actually cuts through the Line of Fate, the union will probably take place with all due ceremony, but everything will not be well and the match is almost certain to end in separation. The timing of this event can be placed fairly accurately on the Line of Fate timescale.

Islands and sections of chained formation occurring along the Line of Fate may be given an interpretation similar to those relating to the three main lines, but in this case they will be connected with the gains and losses and uncertainties of material fate. Either a cross or a star marking the Line of Fate is traditionally said to be a 'bad' sign connected adversely with the subject's career and financial prospects. But when these occur *alongside* the Line of Fate rather than actually on it, they predict a favourable event in this respect.

Although by tradition not measurable on the time-scale, a cross occurring at the very tip of the Line of Fate, on the Mount of Saturn itself, is said to foretell a violent and ignominious death, brought about by the subject's wrong-doing. It has been called the 'Sign of the Scaffold'. No doubt this interpretation arose as a sort of parody of the Christian cross on the mount and certainly it should not be taken too literally, but it *can* serve as a timely warning. Truly violent, dangerous people are probably unlikely to have their hand read, but relatively non-violent people can sometimes seem to be heading towards trouble of some sort, or some kind of unpleasant showdown, through their own reckless or ill-conceived actions, when there is sure to be a much safer and more pleasant alternative course that can be pointed out to them.

A square formation of tiny lines occurring at any point along the Line of Fate is said to act as a safeguard against misfortune, and this holds true for the other lines too, particularly if the square actually surrounds a break or other less propitious sign. The square is a natural symbol of security and this Square of Protection is always welcomed by palmists, wherever it is found in the hand.

One of the most significant formations to be seen on the Line of Fate is a narrow fork leading into two distinct and separate channels, like a tramway running up the palm. Often these join up again after some distance. They cannot really be described as islands; they are not disruptions in that sense, but they always represent duality of some kind. Often, the subject is found to be leading a double life, or perhaps he or she has some dire secret to conceal. This double-tracked formation may be timed fairly accurately in its duration along the timescale, and particular significance may be attached to whether it appears in the left hand of material inheritance, in the right hand of personal fate, or both. The nature of such a split in the lifestyle will usually be well known to the subject, once its existence has been pointed out. Its origin, however, may not be quite so clear.

A break in the Line of Fate, as with the three major lines, implies a break in the flow of material *passions* rather than possessions. Often enough, it records a change of occupation or a general upheaval in lifestyle. If the break overlaps, the change of

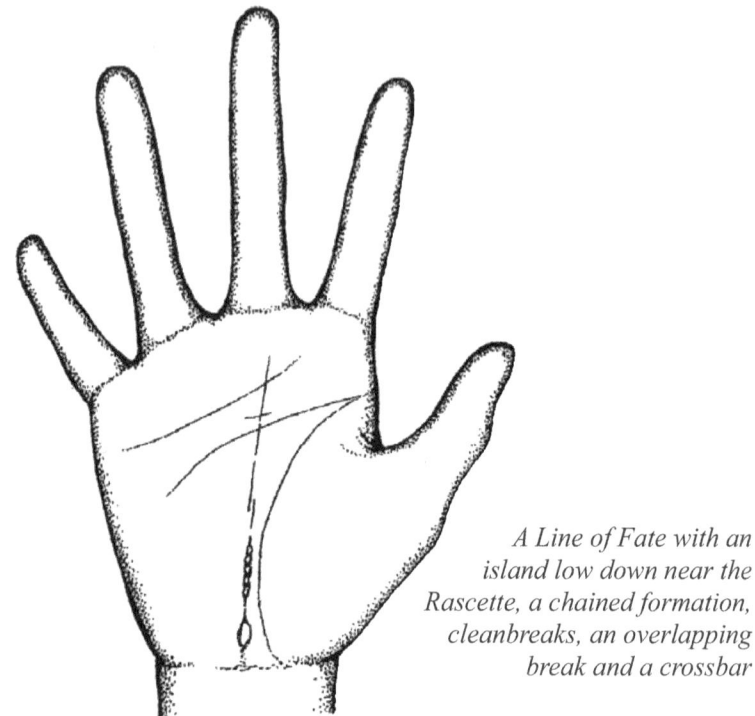

A Line of Fate with an island low down near the Rascette, a chained formation, cleanbreaks, an overlapping break and a crossbar

circumstances is likely to be desirable and, indeed, hoped for. A clean break implies some unexpected change, though not necessarily one for the worse. A similar effect is hinted at by the presence of a crossbar, a short line cutting across the Line of Fate, but this is more likely to refer to matters of repute than to material losses; it sometimes indicates a period of depression.

    Again as with the three major lines, several short lines or branchlets running either upwards or downwards from the Line of Fate imply, respectively, a gain or a loss of resources – normally material ones, and these small lines may be interpreted accordingly. But at their most subtle they apply to the psychic *weight* of materiality – that is, when the lines run downwards they betoken depression and when they run upwards, elation. But in neither case are they really propitious, and they can indicate periods of 'possession' by material life forces; even the upwards-tending material gains may be of such a nature as to be viewed with horror by others with whom the subject comes into contact.

22 The Line of Fortune:
Timescale and the Seven-year Cycle

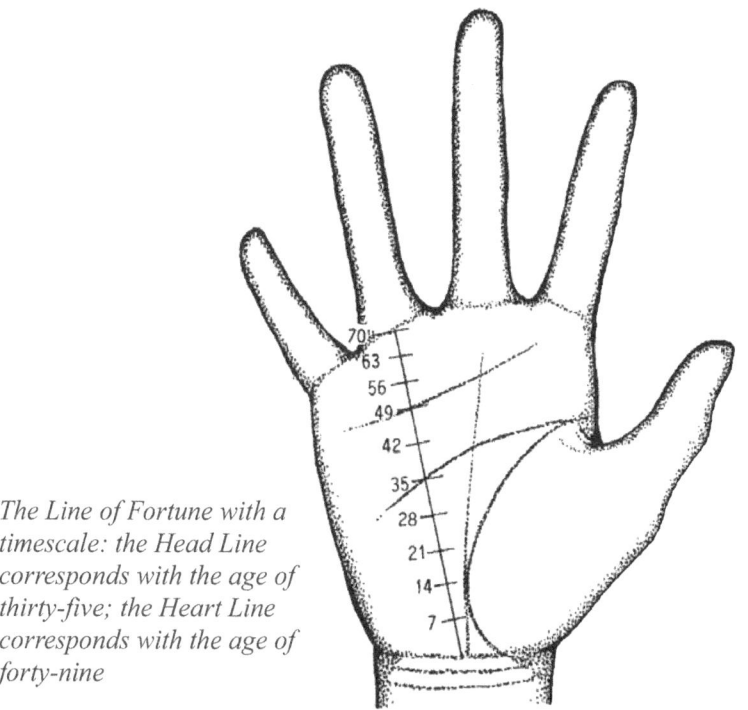

The Line of Fortune with a timescale: the Head Line corresponds with the age of thirty-five; the Heart Line corresponds with the age of forty-nine

A COMPANION to the Line of Fate, when it follows its full course the Line of Fortune runs from the topmost wrist bracelet to the Mount of the Sun. It is often called the Line of the Sun. Those in whose hand this line appears, entire and clearly traced, when compared with the rest of us will seem to have more than their fair share of good fortune.

Bearing in mind what has already been said about these two lines and their intermediate, transitory nature, this may seem a remarkable thing. But this kind of fortune – fame, prestige and success for the individual – is certainly not what we have in mind when we talk about 'spiritual blessings'. Spirituality, or mankind's true state in the universe, is necessarily based upon collectivity. It cannot be a wholly personal state, because all are one in spirit. The truly human

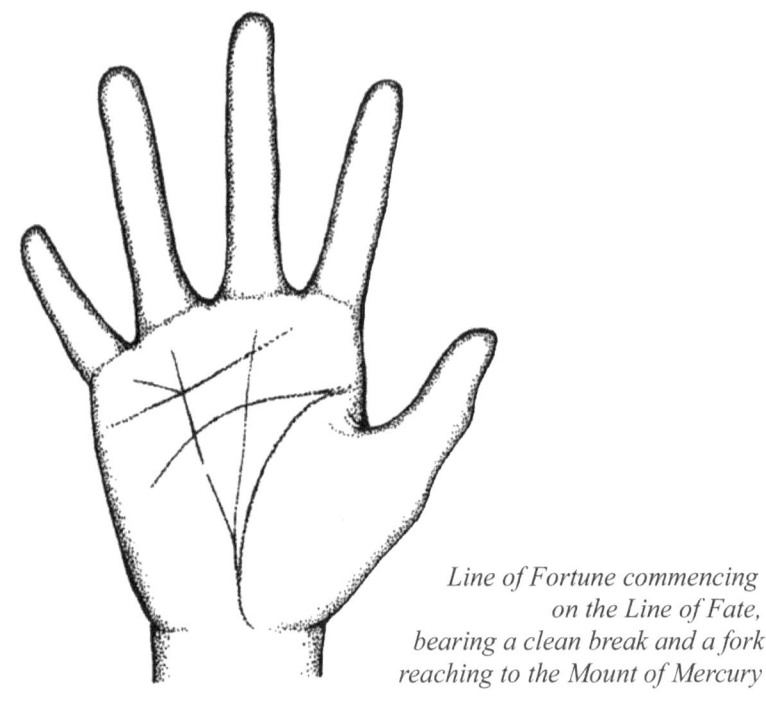

Line of Fortune commencing on the Line of Fate, bearing a clean break and a fork reaching to the Mount of Mercury

collective state of mankind does not really 'possess' these two central lines; they symbolize the passionate 'self' of the outward personality. When the brand of good fortune represented by these lines makes its appearance it will function equally well whether its lucky possessor is a good person or not, a religious person or not, an intelligent person or not, a moral person or not.

To have such a line is to affirm that your individual culture is in tune with the principle of personal integration. When you have it, it is a splendid line to have. When you do not have it, it is not really something to be envied. It is frequently to be seen in the hands of successful business people, but it can just as well represent the sort of success that comes to the effective racketeer, the efficient gangster or the really proficient bank robber. It is all sunshine, fame and fortune, but only on the material level – the lowest level in the subtle world of universal spirit. Nevertheless, the owner of a clear, straight Line of Fortune is a truly fortunate person, and usually a completely likeable one too.

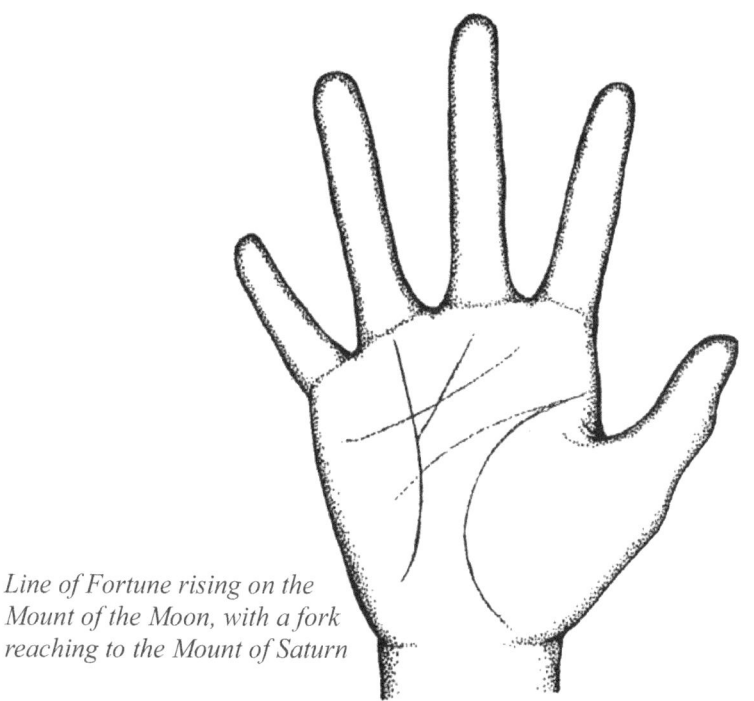

Line of Fortune rising on the Mount of the Moon, with a fork reaching to the Mount of Saturn

More often than not, the Line of Fortune rises short, at some point between the Rascette and the Head Line, and frequently on the Line of Fate itself. In the latter case, it implies much the same as the Line of Fate that springs from the Life Line: it registers the birth of independence in the worldly pursuit of wealth and cultural assets. For example, a person who is in employment in his early years but becomes self-employed, say in midlife, is likely to possess a Line of Fortune that rises from the Line of Fate at the appropriate point on the timescale. In effect, it means that from then on the subject has only himself to thank or blame for his 'good fortune'. He will not be a truly free agent: he cannot decide how clever his brain will be, how keen his nose for business or how useful his talents. But, unlike the average employee, he will no longer be able to blame 'them' when things go wrong.

The part of the hand on which the Line of Fortune rises should be noted with care as it will have great significance. This rising point frequently differs from its normal source on the Rascette, and when this happens it says a lot about the wearer's motivations and

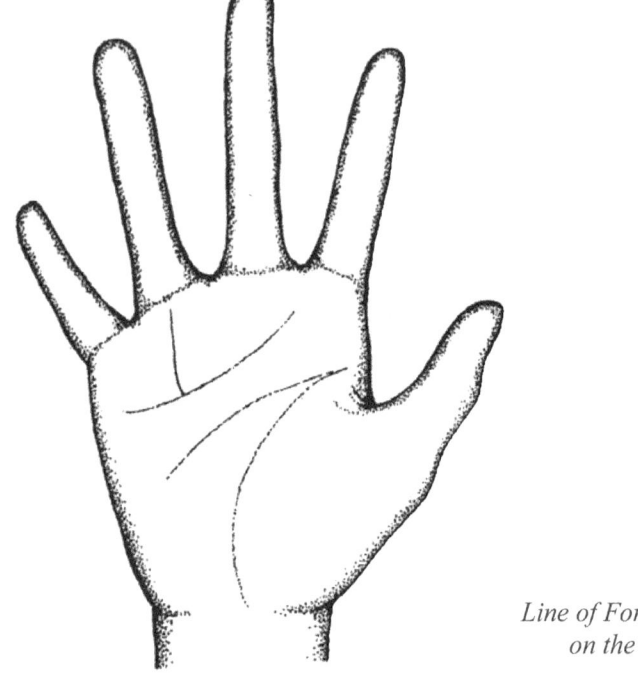

Line of Fortune rising on the Heart Line

basic personality. As with the Line of Fate, the Mount of Venus as a rising point represents the caring parental background, the loving childhood home that provides or has provided support and assistance for its dependants. Equally the Mount of the Moon represents the affectionate non-family background, and in particular the helpful and perhaps admiring attention of the opposite sex, as a spur to individual success.

There may come a time in a person's life when success or acclaim begins to appear – though it may be in very small measure compared with the truly successful and famous – a time when it seems that past efforts have at last begun to be rewarded. In this case, it will often be found that the Line of Fortune rises or commences at this point along its own timescale. (Don't forget that, even when the lower parts of the Lines of Fate and Fortune are missing, as they often are, the timescales of both should be measured from the uppermost bracelet, even when they actually rise on one of the adjoining mounts).

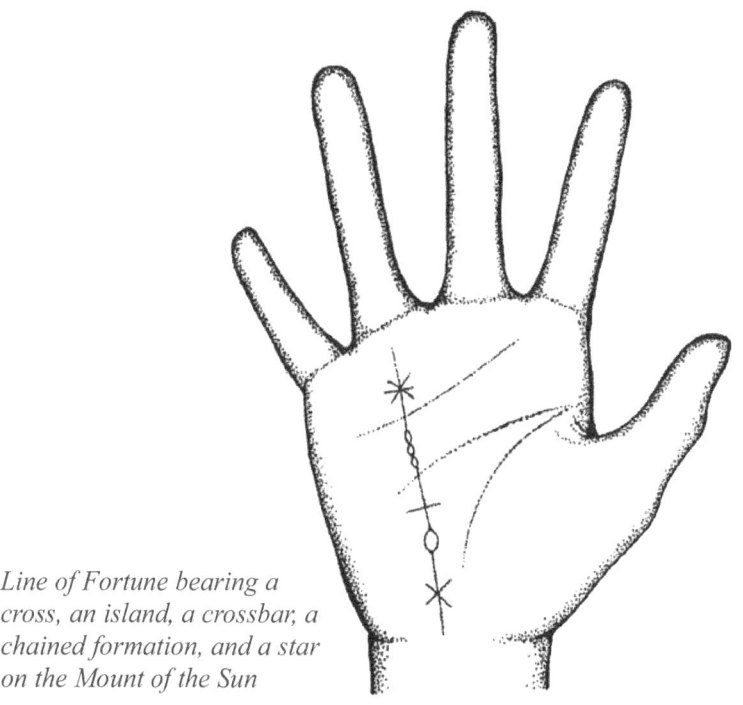

Line of Fortune bearing a cross, an island, a crossbar, a chained formation, and a star on the Mount of the Sun

It frequently happens that the Line of Fortune rises later in life, on or around the Head Line (registering the age of thirty-five), or the Heart Line (registering the age of forty-nine). Happenings that are particularly significant, changes in lifestyle, even the proverbial 'seven-year itch', are usually governed by the human seven-year cycle. Whether you find evidence of this in palmistry, or astrology, or through plain observation, it is a fact. Fourteen, twenty-one, twenty-eight, thirty-five, forty-two, forty-nine, fifty-six – these are the years of greatest significance, when things happen psychologically, when personalities change course, and it is always useful to remember this when reading the palm.

A fork at the end of the Line of Fortune indicates a division of success and usually a corresponding lessening of benefits, a diluting of fame rather than a loss of prestige. Certainly it suggests a division of interest, and the more fork prongs that appear, the more diverse one's interests, the less likely one is to be truly successful in any.

Perhaps it reflects that fact that virtuosity after all depends upon specialization and concentration in one particular field of endeavour.

When a clear fork is broad and long enough to reach the adjacent mounts, the implications are more positive. A connection with the Mount of Mercury speaks of communication through clever brainwork and strengthens the business aspect. And as always, a connection with the Mount of Saturn implies materiality, solidity, and in this case the placing of success and good fortune into hard financial terms.

Breaks and obstructions along the Line of Fortune seem chiefly to refer to matters of prestige, though traditionalists usually insist on stressing monetary loss or gain. But never forget that this line, like the other lines of the hand, symbolizes a flow of energy. In the case of the Line of Fortune, the passionate drive is towards personal culture, towards becoming a whole and much-admired person. The better to understand the principles involved, remember that it should feature strongly, without breaks, in the hand of a professional 'personality' whose whole lifestyle depends upon his or her prestige.

As I have already hinted, the same principle applies when 'fame' becomes 'infamy'. International confidence tricksters too depend entirely on 'what others think' of them, and so do vicious protection racketeers. It is very much a case of exaggerating the old familiar neurosis, 'What will the neighbours think?' This is the base passion represented by the Line of Fortune and it follows that breaks in the line, as registered on its own timescale, will signify breaks in the flow of 'prestige' of the appropriate kind.

Such a 'break' in real life can come about in a multitude of ways: an enterprise may go wrong, the hoped-for support for some project may not be forthcoming. But it may also come about because the subject no longer wants to pursue a particular course – in which case the corresponding break in the line will not be a 'bad' sign at all.

Short crossbars have a somewhat similar meaning, but these are obstructions rather than actual gaps. Traditionally they are taken to mean interference by a rival, some outside event or person who seems intent on robbing the subject of his or her good name. These are stumbling blocks or barriers to the flow of good fortune, whether placed there maliciously or not. Malign influences such as these are said to be surmountable when the Line of Fortune continues beyond the obstruction as strongly as before, but where it starts to fade above a crossbar, the implication is that some malicious outsider has wrought some mischief only too effectively.

An island in the Line of Fortune is said always to represent a major scandal in the subject's life. It is as though his or her prestige is running in circles by the introduction of a negative influence, causing a conflicting 'yes-no' chorus from the onlookers. But after flowing around the island, the Line of Fortune may keep going as strong as before, and the subject's success may be undiminished – and of course, for a celebrity, they say that even bad publicity is better than none.

A star along the line is said to denote good fortune, a cross is said to portend the opposite. They will usually be found to have significant parallels in real life when placed on the timescale. A chained formation in the Line of Fortune is not a good sign. Its owner will probably be successful in the broadest sense of the word, but in all the 'wrong' things. He or she may be well known indeed, but for all the wrong reasons, and this is a marred Line of Fortune it would be far better not to have.

23 Characters and Predictions
Simple and Complicated Patterns

THERE IS NEVER any need to give someone bad news about the indications of their hand. We never know the damage we might do. An individual's fate is exclusive to him or her, and everyone has to suffer the 'downs' as well as the 'ups'. It only makes matters worse for someone to be told that there is no escape from an unpleasant fate. This is a piece of information that could have only negative results. If someone does seem to be worried about their future, tell them that the road ahead is bright and clear if they adopt a positive attitude. 'Never forget that every cloud has a silver lining!' This is a positive message that should lift anybody's spirits. Remember to be the bringer of good tidings.

What everybody needs is a glimmer of hope – an alternative way through when the door seems to be closed. For instance, if a person is hopeless at sport he will already be well aware of the fact. He doesn't need to be told so. It is much better to use a bit of soft soap and say, 'You have an astute brain with tremendous potential for academic work ... for planning ... for research ... for organization ...' Or perhaps it might be, 'You have an artistic turn of mind, a great talent for selecting those things and ideas that are of real value in the world. You don't waste your time and energy in dead-end pursuits ...' I am sure everyone will recognize their own description there!

And if someone really seems to be no use at anything, they are still left with – the great golden gift of versatility! Jack of all trades, master of none maybe; but they have a marvellous opportunity to try a little of everything, to play the entire field and to gain the sort of wide experience that is quite unavailable to more talented folk. And so, don't let us make ourselves unpopular by saying, 'You seem to be pretty useless at everything!' Let's spread a little sunshine instead by saying, 'You have an amazing gift for versatility ... you never waste time concentrating on just one thing ... the world is your oyster!'

Young people always think that fun and romance are exclusively for the young, and every generation seems to think that they have invented sex! But for the palmist it is always a mistake to go along with ideas like that. If you are reading the palm of an

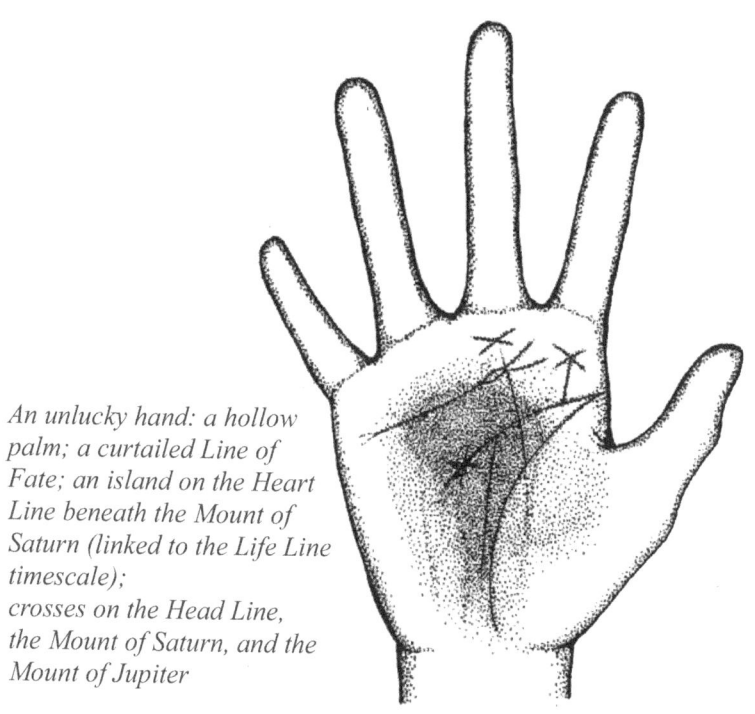

An unlucky hand: a hollow palm; a curtailed Line of Fate; an island on the Heart Line beneath the Mount of Saturn (linked to the Life Line timescale);
crosses on the Head Line, the Mount of Saturn, and the Mount of Jupiter

elderly person, they will not think you are talking through your hat if you predict a stunning romance for them in the near future. If all the signs are there, don't think, 'Oh, it's no use mentioning anything like *that*!' On the contrary, a person's sense of romance often increases and strengthens with the years. Romantic feelings go on and on... right up to the end of the longest Life Line, and the intensity of those feelings is recorded faithfully in the palm.

    A palmist starts with an advantage when he or she believes in the basic goodness of the human race. Besides, I think really bad people seldom consider 'having their hand read'. So let's always assume that someone is a *good* person – unless they are devious enough to enjoy being told otherwise! Being told how good you are always makes you *feel* good, and then, hopefully, you will go on to *be* a better person too. Goodness brings good fortune in its wake.

    So, the three basic lines are the Heart Line, the Head Line and the Life Line, and some people have a very simple pattern of just these three, without any extras. One may assume they will probably have simple, basic thoughts and feelings too, so perhaps it is little use talking to them about high-flown ideas. But we should never imply by our manner that we believe them to be stodgy, dull, unoriginal or stupid. They probably have an honest and wholly reliable character, without any nasty hidden faults, so let's not hesitate to tell them so.

At the opposite extreme, people whose palms show a complicated pattern of fine lines in addition to the major ones will tend to be over-sensitive and very self-aware. It is not the slightest use telling *them* that they are free from hidden faults. They will not be taken in by flattery and probably agonize daily over their numerous shortcomings, glaring or hidden. But they will love being told how bafflingly complex they are, and take it as a great compliment. The moral of the story is, a bit of soft soap works wonders!

When there seem really to be no significant signs in the hand, apart from a fairly basic set of lines, and provided the subject is a reasonably sensitive, perceptive sort of person, we can concentrate instead on the 'background information' of the palm. Early in the book we analysed the lines and mounts according to their subtle 'spiritual' meanings. Now we can put this to direct use and describe the subject's hand in more general terms, as a picture of psychic energy. This by itself can give a very satisfying reading of the hand and pave the way for further revelations.

Well-developed mounts may give the so-called Plain of Mars a hollow appearance. But In cases where the mounts are not very well developed and the palm of the hand is distinctly hollow, this has been taken as a sign of persistent bad luck by traditional palmists. If the subject's hand has absolutely no hint of good fortune to come, here again the general plan of psychic energy can be called into play. Tactfully done, it can lead to an uplift in spirits.

Then there are also the shape and size of the hands and fingers and thumbs, and the fingerprints, which should give you some information to impart. And if subjects want to talk about themselves this is something to be encouraged. Apart from gleaning solid facts, you will quickly find out how their mind works, what their interests and hopes for the future are, what their likes and dislikes – and all this forms a marvellous foundation on which to build and give a convincing reading.

24 Romance: Stars of Venus and Lines of Influence

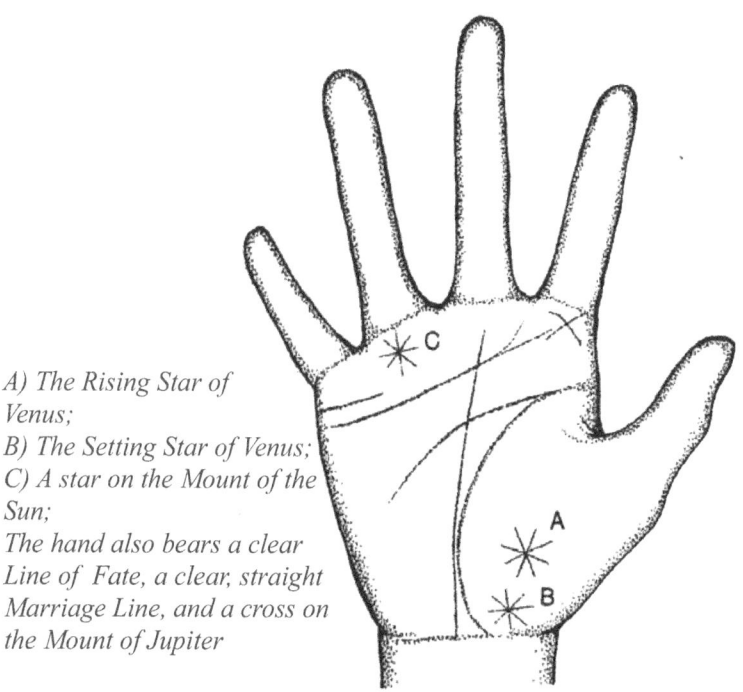

A) *The Rising Star of Venus;*
B) *The Setting Star of Venus;*
C) *A star on the Mount of the Sun;*
The hand also bears a clear Line of Fate, a clear, straight Marriage Line, and a cross on the Mount of Jupiter

THIS IS REALLY the fortune-teller's section, and most people who 'have their hand read' will have romantic ideas, dreams, hopes and ambitions at the back of their mind. They will want to know, in brief, whether they will be lucky in love.

So, after assessing the general size and shape of their hands, fingers and thumbs, and after a glimpse at the pattern of lines, to gain an overall sketch of the personality, look for the Rising Star of Venus; this is the clinching sign of one destined to be lucky in love. It takes the form of a large, well-formed star right in the *centre* of the Mount of Venus, below the thumb. This is a marvellous omen, and if the same hand displays another star, particularly one on the Mount of the Sun, below the third finger, that person can scarcely fail to find happiness in love and romance.

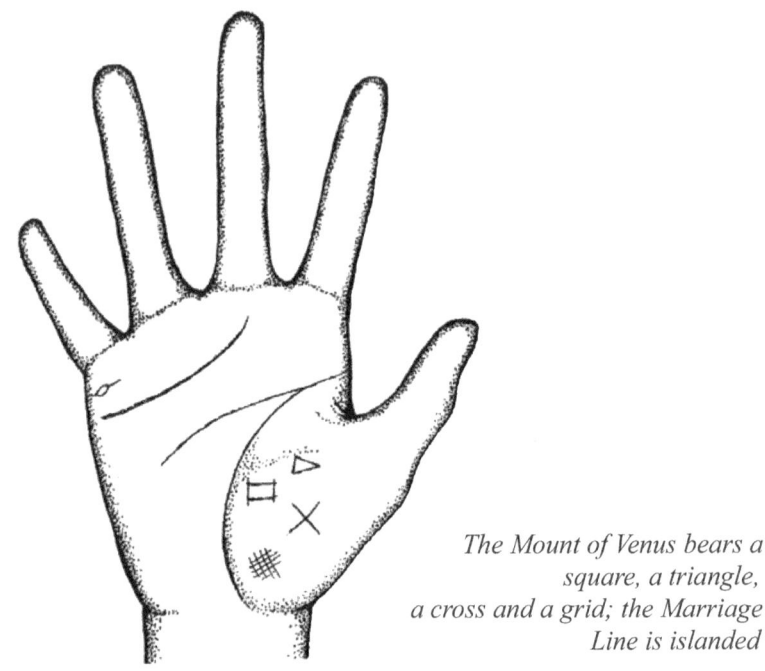

The Mount of Venus bears a square, a triangle, a cross and a grid; the Marriage Line is islanded

The Marriage Lines, as we have already seen, are not very reliable guides, but a good long straight one is never a bad sign. It is only when it curves downwards, especially if it then meets the Line of Fortune, that luck in love and marriage runs away. But when the Marriage Line, or one prong of a fork running from the Marriage Line, meets the Line of Fortune by route of an upwards curve as it runs into the Mount of the Sun, the signs are excellent for a long, happy marriage with more 'ups' than 'downs'.

The luckiest people in love will have a particularly clear, cleanly drawn Line of Fate rising at the top bracelet and running all the way to the Mount of Saturn. But very few hands actually have such a clear Line of Fate, and some people just never seem to have any luck in their romantic relationships. When this unfortunate state of affairs is suspected, the first diagnostic sign to look for on the hand is the Setting Star of Venus – again a clear, large star on the Mount of Venus, but this time low down near the wrist.

A star in the hand is usually a portent of good luck and

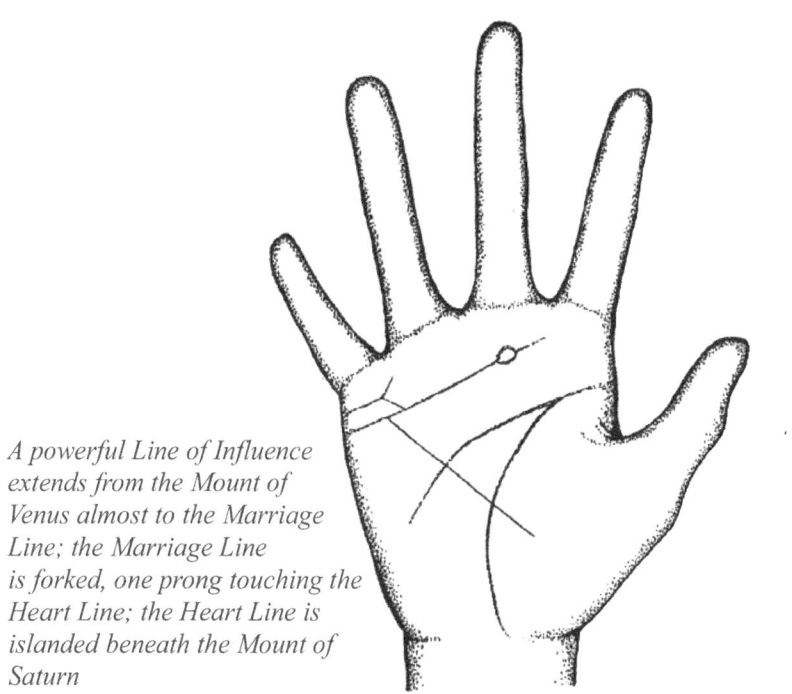

A powerful Line of Influence extends from the Mount of Venus almost to the Marriage Line; the Marriage Line is forked, one prong touching the Heart Line; the Heart Line is islanded beneath the Mount of Saturn

happiness, and the Rising Star of Venus means just that, but in this lowly position near the wrist it always seems to signal just the opposite. Or perhaps in a contradictory way it does indicate happiness – in the form of a certain contentment with the subject's own company, or more likely with their own flesh and blood. Many people find themselves preoccupied with the need to look after ageing parents, or perhaps brothers and sisters, *in loco parentis*. The Setting Star of Venus may signal a situation like this, with too many commitments at home to think about getting married until, eventually, it seems too late in life to take the plunge, and the chance evaporates.

The course of the emotions, as we know, is symbolized by the Heart Line, and this is where your attention will turn next. A Heart Line that starts on the Mount of Saturn, beneath the second finger, suggests that its owner will never really want to give himself or herself emotionally to a marriage partner. Something similar applies when a Heart Line starts on the Mount of Jupiter or between the mounts, and then shows a break where it passes beneath the second

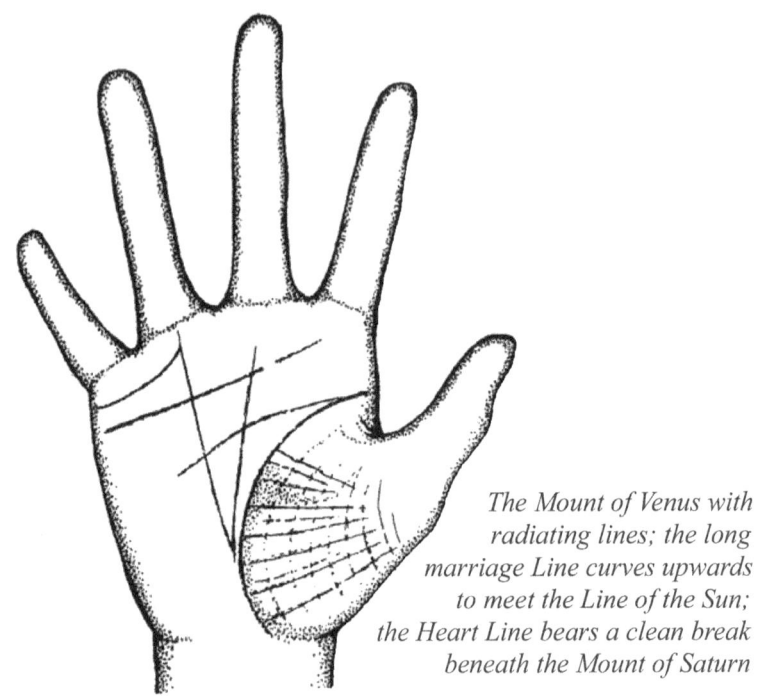

The Mount of Venus with radiating lines; the long marriage Line curves upwards to meet the Line of the Sun; the Heart Line bears a clean break beneath the Mount of Saturn

finger. The flow of soft feelings will have become interrupted through the influence of hard materiality, as symbolized by the Mount of Saturn. In this case it is not 'emotional' so much as material shortcomings that will put paid to any romantic ventures. An island rather than a break in this part of the Heart Line, beneath the Mount of Saturn, speaks very clearly of financial loss – of poverty, even – brought about by a close partner. The subject may well continue to cling to the partner, however, despite this setback. A cross on the Mount of Jupiter, incidentally, is always a welcome sign, denoting a secure and happy marriage.

When a marriage Line, having started out well, runs into the Heart Line, it is said to symbolize separation or divorce, and, as we have already noted, in cases where a particularly long Marriage Line continues across the palm to end on the Mount of Venus, it speaks of family interference – not from the partner's but from the subject's own family – persistent enough to prove the undoing of any romantic

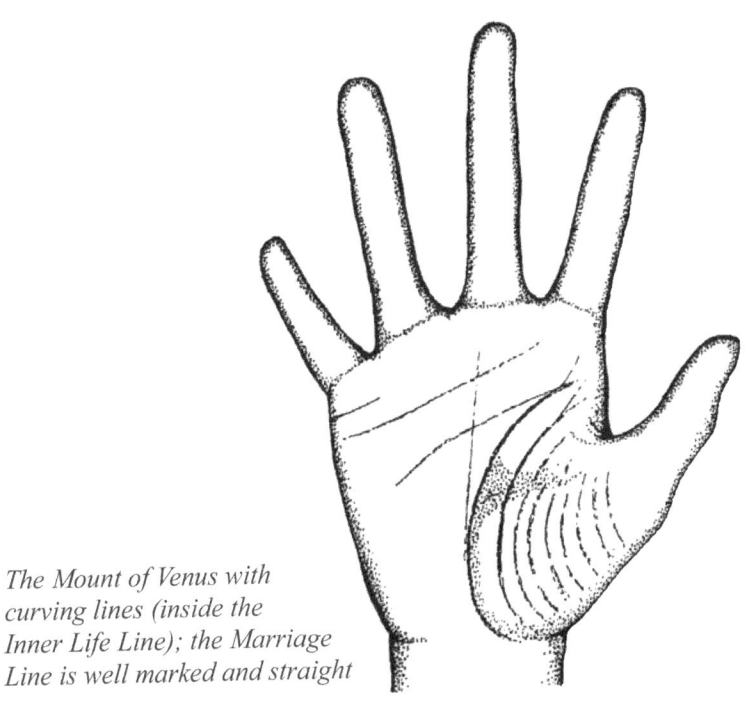

The Mount of Venus with curving lines (inside the Inner Life Line); the Marriage Line is well marked and straight

attachment. Independence is the key here. It may well be that the subject is loath to sever the final apron string that would put an end to the interference.

A similar interpretation applies when a Marriage Line seems to be good – short and clear – but a minor Line of Influence, starting on the Mount of Venus, crosses the Life Line and the Head Line to reach the Heart Line, as though on a collision course with the Marriage Line itself. This suggests direct and uncalled-for interference by the subject's parents. The omens are worse if there is a distinct island somewhere along this secondary line. It implies deliberate deception by the subject's family. They certainly do not want this partnership to work!

Islands connected with romance (apart from the palm-fringed variety!) usually suggest deception of some kind. An island on the Marriage Line itself implies that something rather shocking is being kept secret from the other partner. As the Marriage Line or Lines indicate their wearer's own personal behaviour as it affects the partnership, disappointments in the subject's love life can sometimes be better seen on the partner's, or intended partner's hand, if they are available. Where their Marriage Line forks widely, and particularly if the lower prong runs downwards to touch the Heart Line, you can assume that another romantic interest in *that* person's life will have a devastating effect on the partnership, and probably on the partner too.

The Mount of Venus is the seat of romance with a physical slant, and we have already seen the twin significances that a star on this mount can have – in the Rising and Setting Stars of Venus. A cross on this mount is also very significant, for it tells of a single-track romance; its wearer will be faithful and true to one great love in his or her life. A square of fine lines on any mount is always a fortunate sign, as it signifies protection; on the Mount of Venus it means that its owner will escape the worst effects of any broken romance. A cross and a square together point to the type of classical love affair that outlasts history.

Not such good signs found on the Mount of Venus are the grid and the triangle. You cannot really have a coldly calculating love affair – the two terms are plainly contradictory – but this is the implication of a Venus triangle. It is the sign of someone who is liable to marry or seek a liaison for the sake of money or social prestige, rather than romance. A small grid-shaped arrangement of fine lines (not to be confused with the large criss-crossing Lines of Influence) on an otherwise clear Mount of Venus suggests that its wearer is an extremely awkward person to fall in love with. He or she will seem to set out to make things difficult, and to place quite unnecessary obstacles in the path of true love. They will not see it quite like that, of course. They will be 'cautious', 'playing hard to get', 'testing' their lover, holding out the opportunity to 'prove that you love me'. But what they are far more likely to succeed in doing is to cause sorrow and exasperation. A real heart-breaker, this!

Strong lines radiating more or less from a central point at the base of the thumb, and reaching out to the Life Line, can each signify a 'string-along' lover (see chapter 26). There is really nothing very romantic in the associations that these lines represent. Their implication is likely to involve infidelity, and bigamists will probably be found wearing them. If these Lines of Influence do escape the confines of the Life Line and extend into the Plain of Mars, even reaching and cutting across other lines, they can represent your family's influences, your parents and relations reacting with disapproval to your romantic associations.

It is quite a different matter where the surface of the Mount of Venus is covered with curving lines running roughly on a course parallel with the Life Line. These romantic Lines of Influence should not be mistaken for an Inner Life Line. They appear within the confines of the Inner Life Line, if there is one. In effect, they are contained within the subject's heart – quite unlike the radiating lines of casual liaison which cross the mount directly and reach the Life Line, only to disappear and be soon forgotten. These curving lines each represent a passionate love to the person on whose hand they appear. They may turn out to be ephemeral loves, but this is not the mutual intention at the time. They may not work out, or sometimes they were plainly never 'meant to be'. They are each one *felt* to be the perfect romance, but for one reason or another they just do not prove to be permanent. In later life, we remember those youthful affairs with a warm feeling of fondness and nostalgia. They are enshrined in these curving lines, safely held and treasured in the memory.

25 Jealousy:
Negative Relationships

WHERE ELSE would you expect to look for signs of a jealous heart but along the Heart Line? Envy may be a product of the mind, but jealousy stems largely from the emotions, and the exceptionally jealous personality is sure to be highly emotional. Reflecting this, a jealous Heart Line is sure to be well developed – long and straight, running high across the palm near the base of the fingers, constricting the mounts as though to overrule their influence. Other aims in life – financial, material, cultural – all have to take second place to this strong emotion, this 'all-consuming fire'.

Jealousy usually by definition involves thinking about somebody else. But there is bound to be a strong element of selfishness in it, as though the jealous person is taking himself or herself a mite too seriously. You can certainly suspect that this is the case when the Heart Line rises on the Mount of Saturn. The flow of emotions then will have a possessive, material nature.

The Mount of Venus too is sure to carry some clues about jealousy. It will certainly be well developed, prominent and quite firm – signs of a passionate nature. But the heat of passion is not the same as the warmth of affection, and this will be distinctly cooled if the Mount of Venus displays a clear triangle of fine lines. This sign implies that whenever the emotions become attached to another person, cold, accusing thoughts will interfere, casting suspicion on anything and anybody that happen to be involved.

Jealousy has nothing to do with intelligence. It can happen to anybody, whether dull or brilliant. Some are more inclined towards it than others, but in either case it is an inborn feature of the personality. An habitually jealous person will seldom be able to relax emotionally; there will always be a sharp edge of tension. It can really take the pleasure away from what should be a trusting relationship, and can easily have negative results. A criss-cross grid of fine lines on the Mount of Jupiter will confirm your suspicions of this negative emotion, and if the same sign appears on the Mount of Saturn too, you can be certain that the green-eyed monster is fated to rule any heartfelt relationship.

On the surface, there may be several different apparent reasons for jealousy. It makes sense to suppose that unpleasant

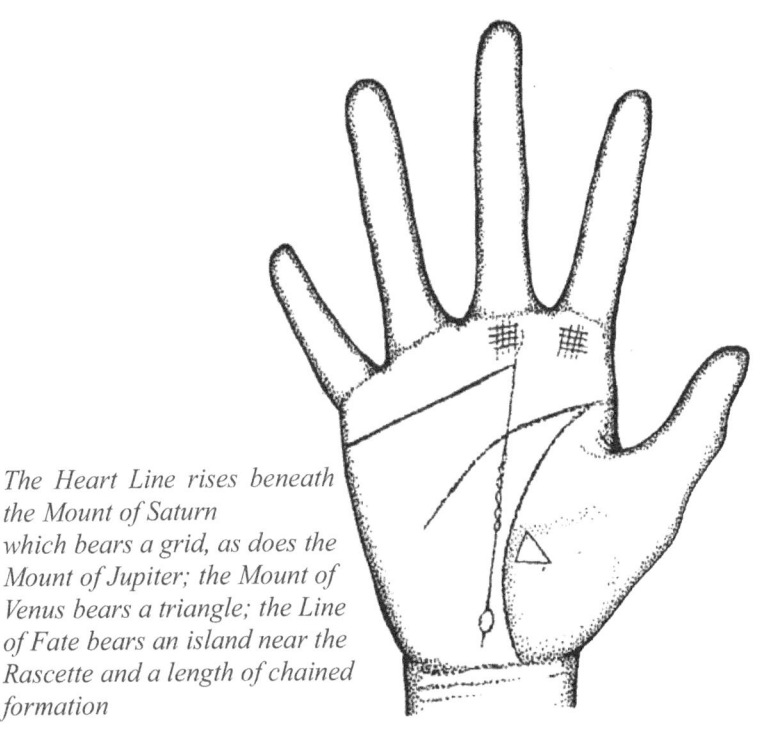

The Heart Line rises beneath the Mount of Saturn which bears a grid, as does the Mount of Jupiter; the Mount of Venus bears a triangle; the Line of Fate bears an island near the Rascette and a length of chained formation

feelings such as this are liable to come about through a basic sense of insecurity, and for signs of this we need to study the Line of Fate, if one is present. When the Line of Fate starts on the Life Line, we can assume that its owner's early life and experiences tended not to provide the self-confidence necessary to ensure a trouble-free emotional relationship later in life.

    The Line of Fate may be seen to be chained along some of its length, and if so the timescale will record periods of anguished uncertainty – disruptions which, if this is what you suspect, may be interpreted as blindly suspicious jealousy operating against a partner. Significantly, the Line of Fate may rise close above the wrist but not actually on the topmost bracelet. Normally, this will symbolize early freedom from the sort of stifling over-protection that a too-close family relationship may inflict on a child. But look closely at the base of this line. When it is marked with a clear island near its commencement, we may assume a negative connotation. The probability is that some unfortunate experience during childhood robbed the subject of the basic sense of security that everybody needs if they are to trust and be trusted later in life and if they are to form loving, sharing relationships.

There is really no good advice that can be given to a person suffering from acute partnership jealousy. No one is perfect, and the jealous feelings of husband or wife, boyfriend or girlfriend, may all too often prove to be justified. The trouble is, jealousy can often precipitate unfaithfulness by its own unreasonable assumptions. At best, they can cause hurt feelings; at worst, they can give rise to the attitude of, 'Well, if *that's* what you think, I'll give you something to be jealous about!' But at least we can console such sufferers and ourselves with the thought that, if the worst comes to the worst, there are plenty more fish in the sea. Some are born to trust, others are not; some are born to be faithful, others are not. We should be compassionate enough to understand such very human characteristics.

26 Infidelity and Separation:
Elongated Islands and the Line of Dominance

SO FAR, we have considered the hands of only either steadfast lovers, sufferers of jealousy or those people who are likely to be crossed in love – doomed, perhaps, to be forever unlucky in their romantic experiences. The really unlucky ones feel themselves to be long-suffering victims and may become soured, as their trust has been betrayed – maybe over and over again. The chances are that they contributed to their own problems in various ways, if only by falling for the charms of plausible rogues and persistent deceivers. It is just as important for us to learn some of the tell-tale signs of the fickle-hearted – the guilty parties in romantic tangles.

The Mount of Venus is the home territory of romance, the foundation every person has on which they can build relationships based ultimately on sex. In the fickle lover's palm, this large mound of flesh near the base of the thumb will be prominent and well developed, but soft, yielding to the slightest pressure. There will be several minor lines running across the mount from near the thumb to the Life Line, each minor line, as far as the palmist is concerned, representing the 'third party' in a succession of eternal triangles.

The Heart Line, as might be expected, is highly significant here. It will probably have a dual rising point, one tributary flowing from the Mount of Jupiter and the other from the Mount of Saturn. It will very likely have a prominent branch line running from it to the Head Line, implying that the subject is well able to think his or her way out of an emotional entanglement.

Where the Heart Line passes near the little finger, the Mount of Mercury will probably stand out prominently, as though a lookout point for considerations more urgent than the natural direction of this emotional flow. The subject's emotions will be ready to communicate themselves to anyone he or she may find attractive, and the need to remain faithful is sure to be overshadowed before long. There may be breaks on the Heart Line too, demonstrating how this emotional flow may be switched on and off, or redirected without any feeling of guilt. But there are more likely to be islands or sections of chain along

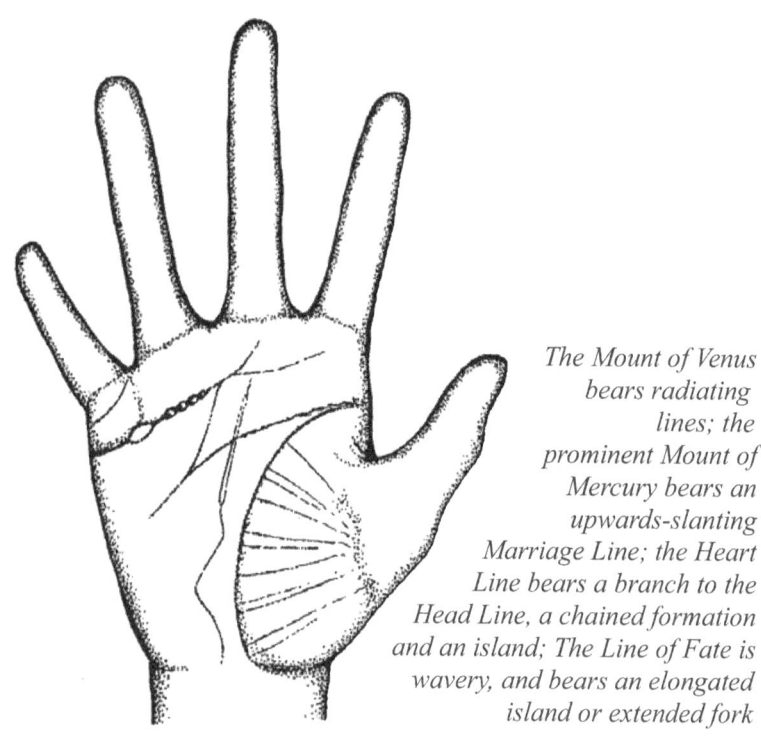

The Mount of Venus bears radiating lines; the prominent Mount of Mercury bears an upwards-slanting Marriage Line; the Heart Line bears a branch to the Head Line, a chained formation and an island; The Line of Fate is wavery, and bears an elongated island or extended fork

the Heart Line if this is the case. Really fickle people, to whom guilty romances are the stuff of life, often have a chained Heart Line, and an island towards the end of the Heart Line is a sure sign of a guilty secret romance – quite possibly a recurring incident.

The doubling of any line is always significant. An 'elongated island' in the Line of Fate often signifies some sort of double life, and if this appears on the same palm as a double Marriage Line, or a Marriage Line that curves sharply upwards as though to seal off the base of the little finger, it will mean that romantic secrets are habitually kept hidden from the official partner of the moment. The true feelings are simply not being communicated in such a case.

People with a strong Line of Fate may well be dishonest in matters concerning their private or business lives, but they are rarely fickle in love and marriage. A fickle person's loyalties and emotions tend to sway this way and that, and if a Line of Fate is present on their palm, it is likely to be equally wavery and uncertain of its true course.

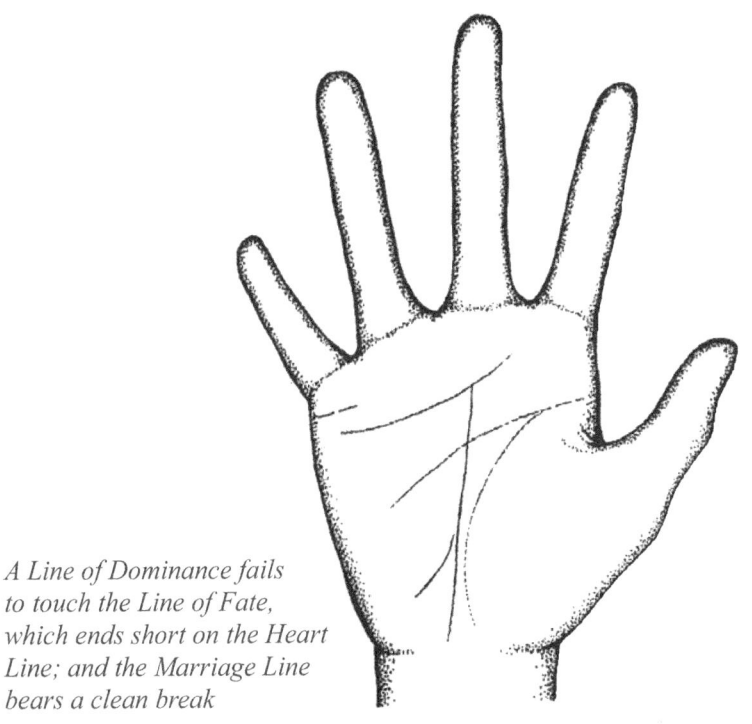

A Line of Dominance fails to touch the Line of Fate, which ends short on the Heart Line; and the Marriage Line bears a clean break

It is not only the cheated who gets hurt; the cheaters can have an unpleasant time of it too. When the hands of people whom you suspect of being unfaithful partners show signs of stress, and their timescales hint at approaching Nemesis, it is not out of place to warn them about the looming consequences of their romantic, and particularly any clandestine, relationships. People 'torn between two lovers' can start to pull apart at the seams. We know that the damage done to others can be considerable, and if the injured party happens to be a faithful and vulnerable soul, the consequences can all too easily be tragic.

We have already seen that the marriage partner, or at least a member of the opposite sex who exerts a powerful influence, may be represented in the subject's hand by the Line of Dominance – a minor line rising on the Mount of the Moon and running upwards, towards the Line of Fate, or roughly parallel with it. This line really applies only in a hand which bears a clear Line of Fate and it should not be confused with the latter or with the Line of Fortune. Where all three lines are present the distinction is clear.

The owner of a Line of Dominance almost inevitably selects a marriage or living-in partner stronger in personality than himself or herself, and the marriage is often unhappy for this reason. But some people enjoy the security of this and seem to need the feeling of being dominated. Where this Line of Dominance and the Line of Fate touch and blend, the chances for a happy marriage are good. But so fine a balance is rarely seen. The Line of Dominance is usually to be found only where there is plainly going to be trouble. If the two lines draw near and do not touch, a broken engagement is symbolized. Where they actually cross, the Line of Dominance cutting through the Line of Fate, a marriage will take place, but it will be violently chaotic, and its unhappy course will finally end in divorce, or worse.

In the majority of hands, especially where the Line of Dominance is missing, the Line of Fate itself can give some indication of a relationship that is destined to be shipwrecked. A Line of Fate that ends on the Heart Line suggests a wrong choice of partner – a choice made on the basis of short-term infatuation rather than long-term prospects for success.

We have already noted in our previous discussion of the Marriage Lines that a break in these may foretell a broken relationship. But the Marriage Lines are frequently so short and relatively obscure that too much reliance cannot be placed upon them. Please don't put ideas of possible infidelity in people's minds. The subject of infidelity should be mentioned only once it has already occurred – when the damage has already been done and the marriage or the subject's confidence is in need of repair. The palmist needs to exercise great tact. It is far better to keep quiet about possibilities than to cast suspicion and possibly be instrumental in bringing about a broken marriage.

27 Money: The Gambler's Cross

MOST PEOPLE want to hear that they are likely to come into easy money instead of having to go on slogging away at the daily grind to earn a crust. If you could please everybody in this respect, now that really *would* be fortune-telling! The chances are, of course, most people will have their fair share of both daily slog and good luck. The most reliable indications in the hand refer to trends and probabilities based on heredity and relationships, and the general flow of passions – whether you have business acumen, the way you relate to others or to the rest of your family, and the likely pattern of inheritance.

The hand can certainly show how much persuasive influence you are likely to have on those with money to give away! Foremost as an indicator in this field is the Line of Fortune. Anyone whose hand displays this line clearly marked from the Rascette all the way to the base of the second finger on the Mount of the Sun, can scarcely avoid financial success.

Any person with a strong Line of Fortune will seem to stand out as a good investment. People will almost queue up to give him or her their money – unless that Line of Fortune also shows negative features that will mar the flow of good luck. And this, of course, is karma too: the eternally dangling carrot of good fortune that the struggling donkey can always see but never quite reach.

Lines of Influence are minor lines that are said to carry the influence of the mounts on which they rise, channelling it in some measure to one or other of the major lines. The Mount of Venus, as we know, represents the area of sensual origin and physical renewal – childhood, home and family. Any Lines of Influence rising on this mount suggest some kind of material advantage flowing from ancestral resources. Minor lines such as this, which cross the Life Line and the Line of Fate to touch the Line of Fortune, suggest that money and property will be transferred in a way very favourable to the wearer. Sometimes, Lines of Influence actually connect two mounts, as though to represent an intermingling of the basic principles concerned. A Line of Influence that runs from the Mount of Venus straight up the palm to reach the Mount of Saturn could be a fortunate example of this, for it is said to foretell a sizeable

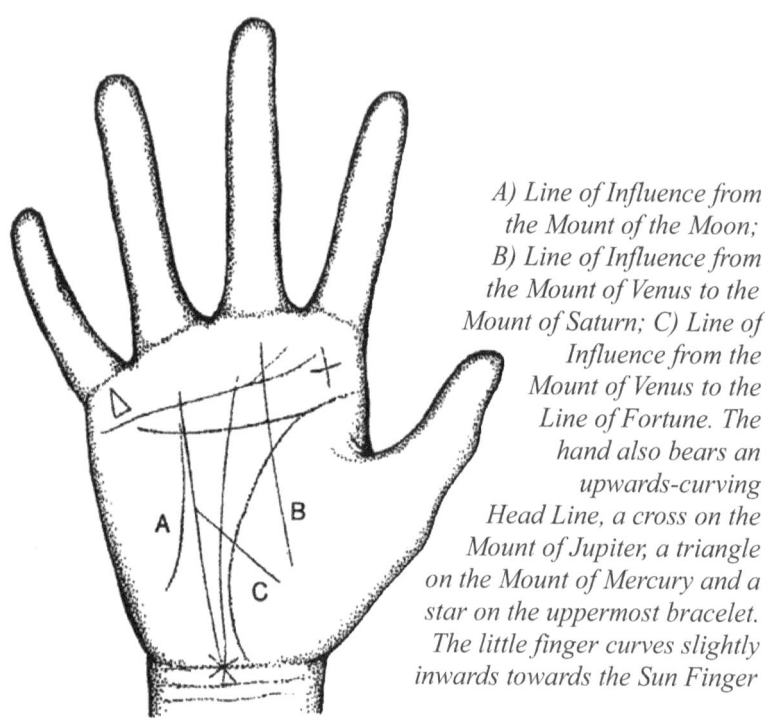

A) Line of Influence from the Mount of the Moon; B) Line of Influence from the Mount of Venus to the Mount of Saturn; C) Line of Influence from the Mount of Venus to the Line of Fortune. The hand also bears an upwards-curving Head Line, a cross on the Mount of Jupiter, a triangle on the Mount of Mercury and a star on the uppermost bracelet. The little finger curves slightly inwards towards the Sun Finger

inheritance to be received through the family. A Line of Influence that runs from the Mount of Venus and then climbs alongside the Line of Fortune suggests that money will be coming in from a relative, but as a gift rather than a legacy.

The Mount of the Moon, looked at from a material point of view, represents non-family background support. It follows that any Lines of Influence that rise on or above the Mount of the Moon and run up the palm, parallel with the Line of Fortune, suggest that money will be coming in from sources outside the family.

These signs relate to gifts and legacies. But, of course, not everyone possesses a Line of Fortune and its absence from the hand does not mean that money will never come your way. Gifts and legacies may still arrive. A clearly marked star or stars, towards the centre of the topmost bracelet at the wrist is traditionally taken as a hopeful sign that money will be coming in when it is needed most.

Another good sign with regard to income, earned or 'unearned', is a Head Line that curves upwards at the end, towards the little finger. Its owner will always have a good head for money-making. An even more positive sign denoting a nose for money is a clearly marked cross beneath the index finger, between the rising of the Head Line and the Heart Line. But this is never connected with the idea of inheritance. It is an 'I did it my way' sign that is traditionally taken to denote an unerring instinct to acquire money through clever business deals or gambles – often known as the Gambler's Cross.

The likelihood of financial success by whatever means always looks much rosier when a distinct triangle is to be seen below the little finger, on the Mount of Mercury. It implies 'intelligent communication', so at least you can be sure that the subject possesses the innate ability to succeed in business. The little finger itself will bear this out and strengthen the trait if it appears to curve inwards towards the adjacent Sun finger.

A strong Line of Fate too can be a positive assurance that the various signs of material success will have real meaning. As we have already seen, it implies that most things which come to pass – and this includes inheritances and business successes – will be already cut and dried, predestined, foregone, in the life of the person who wears it. It is just this kind of 'fixed' luck, good or bad, that the palmist can predict successfully.

28 Ambition: Stars and the Strengthening of Passion

WHEN WE SAY somebody aims for the moon, we mean that they are ambitious. But on the palm of the hand, this carries rather the opposite meaning, and lines that finish up on the Mount of the Moon mean that the person's efforts will probably be wasted in unproductive dreams.

This is where ambition, as expressed by the Head Line, finally runs out of impetus. As a rising point, however, the case is different. A strong Line of Fate that rises on the Mount of the Moon (instead of its usual starting point on or just above the topmost bracelet), and from there climbs towards its goal at the base of the second finger, is taken to mean that fate will guide that person along socially adventurous paths, away from the inward-looking influence of the Mount of the Moon.

The Mount of Jupiter is the traditional seat of ambition, and if someone is more ambitious than the average this mount will faithfully record the fact. If the Life Line actually rises on the Mount of Jupiter, you can be sure that you are reading the palm of a natural-born adventurous go-getter. But almost as ambitious is the person whose Life Line rises lower down, in its usual place, but is connected to the Mount of Jupiter by a clear tributary-like branch line. This could equally well be taken as a Line of Influence running from the Mount of Jupiter. The effect is the same.

A similar criterion may be applied to the Head Line too, while the 'ambitious Heart Line' will certainly rise clearly on the Mount of Jupiter. To strengthen this trait, at its furthest extremity the Heart Line may curve upwards towards the little finger to meet the Mount of Mercury – a sure sign of true Mercurial grit and the determination to succeed.

In the case of a Life Line that starts in its normal place, don't forget that, on the hand of an ambitious person, there will probably be a fairly wide gap between it and the Head Line. Such a person will be self-reliant, financially independent and bold enough to take risks when these seem to be necessary – a person who, in other words, will rise to meet any challenge head on.

In the previous chapter we took note of the Gambler's Cross, below the Mount of Jupiter between the rising points of the

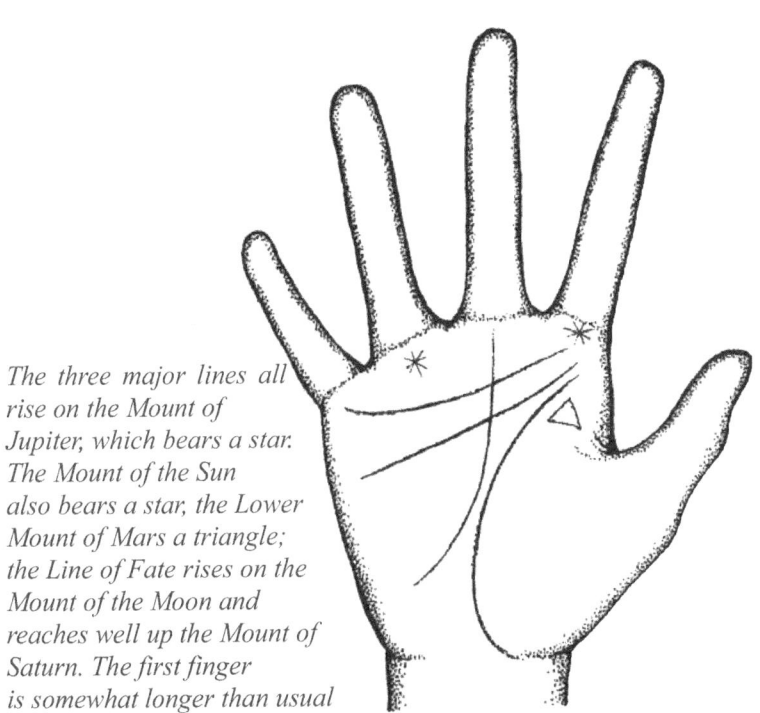

The three major lines all rise on the Mount of Jupiter, which bears a star. The Mount of the Sun also bears a star, the Lower Mount of Mars a triangle; the Line of Fate rises on the Mount of the Moon and reaches well up the Mount of Saturn. The first finger is somewhat longer than usual

Head and Heart Lines. In cases where ambition runs in a particularly materialistic direction, this mark will be clearly defined. Some people are 'financial wizards', able to sniff out the merest chance to make money. They are the proverbial men who broke the bank of Monte Carlo, their money-making instincts developed to an almost supernatural degree.

A triangle is the symbol of constructive thought, and when one is to be seen on the Lower Mount of Mars, near the rising of the Life Line, it means that the aggressive instincts of the wearer will always be well controlled and put to their most profitable use. On the hand of a person bold enough to have a go at almost any adventurous enterprise, and talented enough to succeed in it, you will probably find several clearly marked stars. Stars are nearly always 'lucky'. The only 'unlucky' place for a star to appear in the hand is along the course of the Line of Fate, either between the topmost bracelet and the Head Line, on the Mount of the Moon, or actually on the Mount of Saturn itself.

A star really implies a strengthening of the influence concerned – the particular life force or passion symbolized as flowing along the lines of the hand. In the case of the Line of Fate, as we have already seen, this force is very much a 'material' one, while the Mount of Saturn is of course the seat of materiality. Any strengthening of the material instinct is rather like an increase in gravity (the basic material force), exerting a downwards pull on the body; it will probably result in disablement or an accident.

When assessing ambition, or the lack of it, always remember to examine the shape and set of the hand and fingers. The index finger is the 'finger of ambition'. In most people it will be about the same length as the third finger, but in an ambitious individual it will be noticeably longer. Ambition may be carried to extremes when the index finger is even longer than the second finger – the sign perhaps of a power-crazy tyrant. In general terms, knobbliness of the joints indicates caution, and ambition in that case will probably be limited to the unassuming attainments of the back-room boffin. Smoothness, coupled with broad, supple fingers, demonstrates the adventurous, daring nature of an ambitious person who would like his or her achievements to be shouted from the rooftops.

29 Success: Eminence and Security

SOME PEOPLE seem destined to go right to the top. Everyone likes the idea of success, though not everyone is so keen on the limelight and the loss of privacy that fame brings with it. But really to love the prospect of fame and fortune and actually to succeed in attaining eminence in the world, demands more than the mere wish. It is not merely a case of ambition; a special sort of personality – a sort that may be recorded in the hand – is needed. The attainment of such eminence is normally quite beyond human choosing.

As with more ordinary ambitions, the general shape of a person's hand and fingers can give some idea of his or her chances of megastar success. The great majority of hands show a pattern in which the base of the fingers form a curve around the top of the palm, pushing the second finger forwards so that it may seem longer than it actually is. Natural winners however will tend to have their fingers arranged more or less in a straight line.

In other words, the fingers will appear more nearly to be the same length than is the case with most people. This is not the same as having a long index finger. The fingers themselves will be supple and probably slightly spatulate towards their tips. The little finger, besides appearing longer than usual, will probably have a distinct curve inwards, towards the third finger, while the index finger too will curve slightly inwards towards the second finger.

The three major lines of the palm will probably rise closely grouped and fairly high, on or near the Mount of Jupiter, leaving a small gap between the Head Line and the Life Line. The Head Line will probably curve upwards at the end, as though drawn towards the little finger.

There will probably be a Line of Influence connecting the Mount of Jupiter with the Mount of Venus. There may in fact be several extra lines radiating from this large fleshy area near the thumb, each a minor Line of Influence recording the impulse for this individual to leave his or her parents and childhood home safely behind, having gained all the benefits of inheritance, and venture boldly out into the world. Lines such as these also suggest that

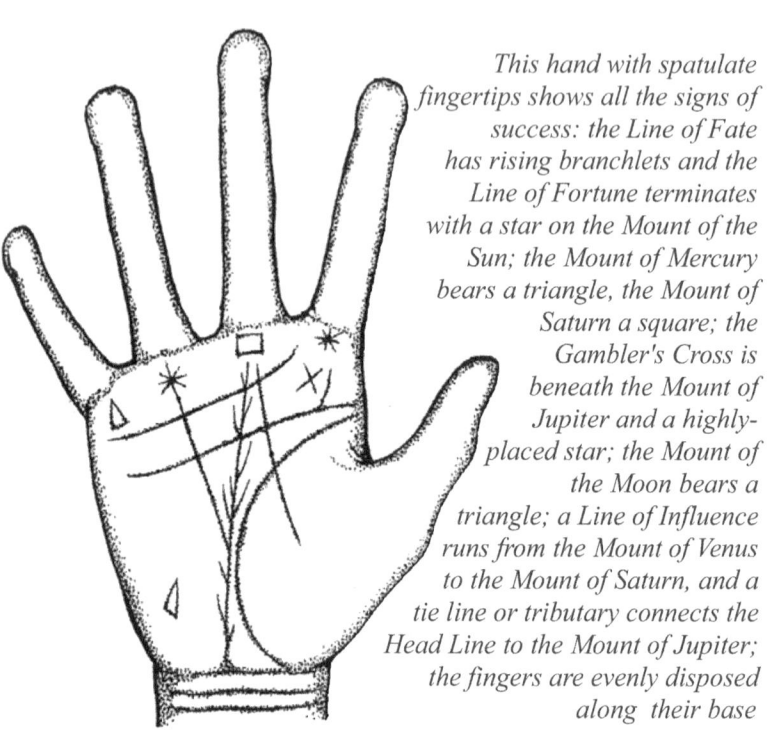

This hand with spatulate fingertips shows all the signs of success: the Line of Fate has rising branchlets and the Line of Fortune terminates with a star on the Mount of the Sun; the Mount of Mercury bears a triangle, the Mount of Saturn a square; the Gambler's Cross is beneath the Mount of Jupiter and a highly-placed star; the Mount of the Moon bears a triangle; a Line of Influence runs from the Mount of Venus to the Mount of Saturn, and a tie line or tributary connects the Head Line to the Mount of Jupiter; the fingers are evenly disposed along their base

their owner's romantic affairs will come under the public gaze, and this is the inference to be placed upon them when the other signs of success are not in evidence. This type of public scrutiny is what usually happens once a person becomes newsworthy.

On the really successful hand, there is sure to be a clearly marked Line of Fate, probably running from the topmost bracelet all the way up to the Mount of Saturn. This line may well fork near the top, with one prong running to the Mount of Jupiter, as though to reinforce the driving power, but the other prong will still end in its appropriate place, on the Mount of Saturn, 'home' of material resources.

On the business tycoon's hand there may be several small branchlets springing from the Line of Fate and running upwards a short way to form a fishbone pattern. This is a fortunate sign, marking a career that is constantly branching out and climbing, sending out feelers in all directions. There will probably also be a well-developed Line of Fortune. It may begin near the wrist or higher up on the

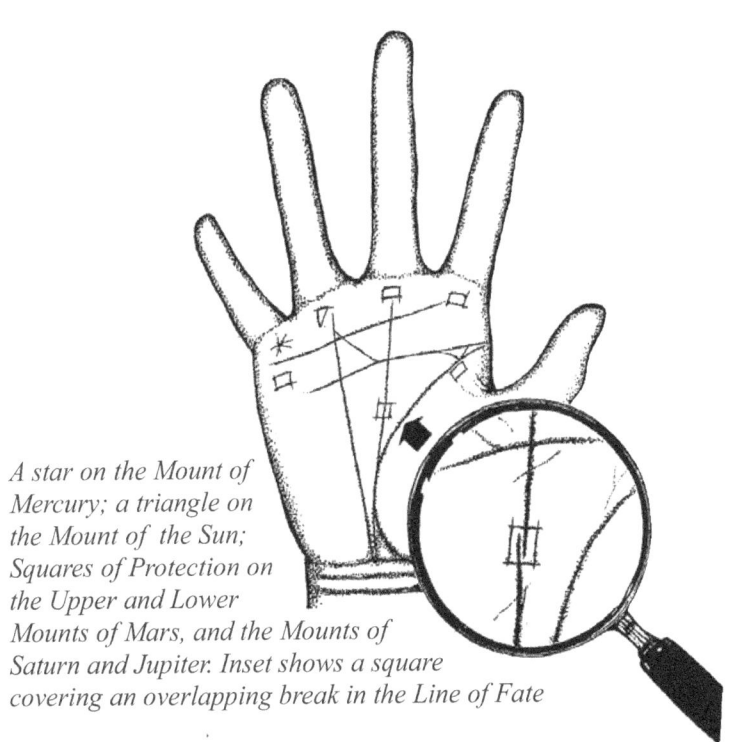

A star on the Mount of Mercury; a triangle on the Mount of the Sun; Squares of Protection on the Upper and Lower Mounts of Mars, and the Mounts of Saturn and Jupiter. Inset shows a square covering an overlapping break in the Line of Fate

Mount of the Moon, and sometimes may spring from the Line of Fate, near its base. But wherever the rising point, in the hands of the most successful people it is certain to reach right into the centre of the Mount of the Sun, beneath the third finger. There may be minor forking lines reaching to the adjacent mounts, as though to clinch the integrating process.

The ultimate clinching symbol to look for on the Line of Fortune is a clearly marked star, especially if it occurs near the top of the line, or actually on the Mount of the Sun. This is the Star of Success. It will be further strengthened if there is also another star on the Mount of Jupiter. This combination marks the sort of 'luck' that cannot drain away, and seems to ensure pre-eminence in the subject's chosen field.

A square is the symbol of security, and there will probably be Squares of Protection too on the hand of this highly successful person. These are clearly marked squares of fine lines – always a good omen, particularly when they appear on any of the mounts, or if they surround another sign that may seem to indicate misfortune of some kind, such as a break in one of the major lines. Their presence implies that their wearer will always seem mysteriously well protected against the slings and arrows of outrageous fortune. With Squares of Protection, he or she will be able to walk unscathed through any traps set by scheming enemies.

30 Vigour: The Competitive Athlete

IF SOMEONE having their hand read happens to be particularly vigorous and good at sports, it is no bad thing to please them by telling them so. They will, of course, know it already, but communication in these circumstances is so much easier once a positive rapport has been established.

Athletic people usually have firm, squarish hands, with a fairly straight thumb and rather stiff, strong fingers. On their palm the two opposite Mounts of Mars will both be strongly developed, indicating physical aggression coupled with a great deal of moral conviction. They like to feel they 'know' they are in the right when opinions are divided.

They will probably have few minor lines, for they are rarely very complicated people, and their character will be openly on show for all to see. They will probably have a fairly straight Head Line, indicating their practical, down to earth nature.

They will almost certainly have a long and deeply marked Life Line, and possibly an Inner Life Line to reinforce it – an inner physical resource, a reservoir of extra energy and stamina that becomes available to them during times of fatigue, protecting them from exhaustion and illness.

The Mount of Jupiter, as the soul base, is the seat not only of ambition but also of competition and social interaction. The more closely the Life Line is connected with this mount, the more powerful the impetus, the will to succeed, the physical driving force. Though there will be few fine lines on the hand, there may be one or two at least, linking the Mount of Jupiter with the Life Line.

Similarly, the Heart Line will very likely rise on the Mount of Jupiter, illustrating the emotional satisfaction drawn from physical competition and displays of strength. But here again there may well be a branch line running from the Heart Line to the Head Line, implying that the feelings often have to give priority to the thought, the idea, of winning. The love of sport has a strongly emotional flavour, of course. But you will find that where thoughts have to yield to feelings (in terms of palmistry, when a branch line runs from the Head Line to the Heart Line) that person is more likely to be a keen supporter or spectator rather than an actual competitor.

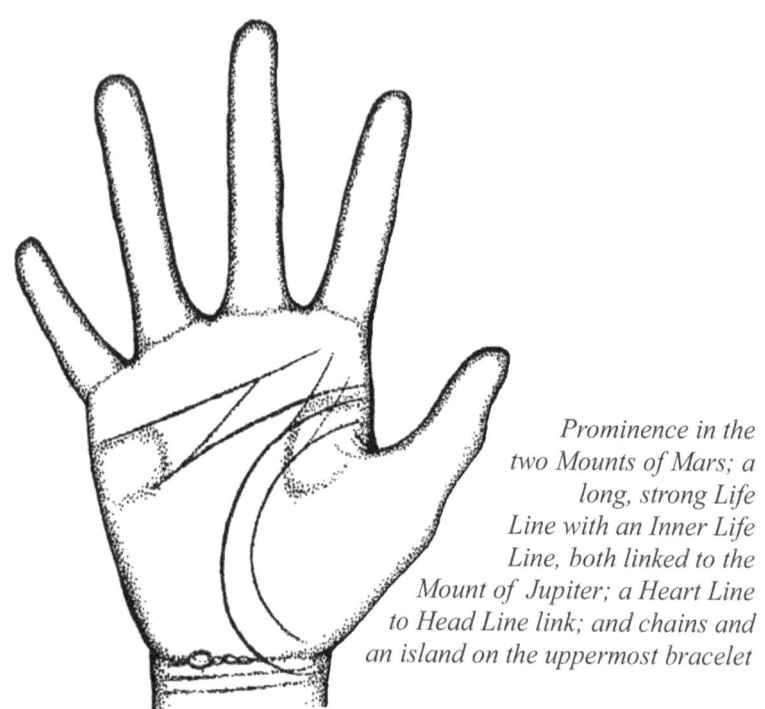

Prominence in the two Mounts of Mars; a long, strong Life Line with an Inner Life Line, both linked to the Mount of Jupiter; a Heart Line to Head Line link; and chains and an island on the uppermost bracelet

There is sure to be a fairly wide gap between the Head Line and the Life Line, suggesting the necessary element of physical bravery. This gap is often a characteristic of someone who leaps before they look, and the act of 'leaping in' successfully without dithering is often the very essence of sport. People who are not keen on strenuous physical activities and sport tend to hang back the longest before leaping into the fray. Athletes have to be ever-ready. Hearts, minds and bodies must be united in a common aim: successful competition.

In the life of a top competing athlete, hardships occur in plenty, but most of them are overcome through sheer grit and determination. This characteristic may be confirmed by the Rascette: the three bracelets will be clearly marked and evenly parallel, and hardships that have to be overcome can be seen as islands along the uppermost bracelet. A chained formation in this topmost bracelet also implies that many comparatively minor difficulties can be overcome during their wearer's life, through effort and perseverance.

31 Stress: Nervous Exhaustion and Guilty Secrets

SOME PEOPLE are more stress-prone than others, and the tendency to suffer from tension is often recorded on the Head Line and the Heart Line. A timescale marked up along the Life Line and the Line of Fate will predict the year, or the subject's approximate age, when particularly difficult patches which have to be lived through can be expected.

If a combination of circumstances in early childhood, or some feature passed on from the parents, is likely to lead to stress later in life, this fact will be recorded in the left hand. The outcome of these problems can be seen in the right hand, but such signs will indicate only a potential. Outcomes can rarely be seen in terms of cut-and-dried fate. So much depends on the subject's personal strength of character as it develops through the growing years.

If stress signs occur in both left and right hands, we can take it that some kind of upheaval is inescapable. But the outcome need not necessarily be bad. Stress is sometimes necessary as a spur to facing up to problems or for overcoming some kind of handicap. Perhaps it is like the surge of adrenalin that is said to push performers on to give their very best.

In palmistry, the warning signs of stress are usually either breaks or islands, and they may occur in any of the basic character lines. A general tendency towards persistent stress is clearly indicated by a chained formation. Broken lines that in fact overlap, or remain faintly connected by little cross-lines, suggest that everything will come right in the end. So does a break that is surrounded by a small square of minor lines – the Square of Protection that is traditionally said to shield its owner from harm.

A break in the Head Line always suggests some kind of mental stress. It may even portend an actual head injury –particularly if its owner is a sporty, physical type, rather than an academic thinker. A Head Line break that occurs beneath the little finger points to the kind of stress brought on by an over-tired brain; it suggests mental fatigue or exhaustion through overwork. It can really affect only particularly intelligent people, for obviously it cannot occur without an unusually long, straight Head Line. Most Head Lines do

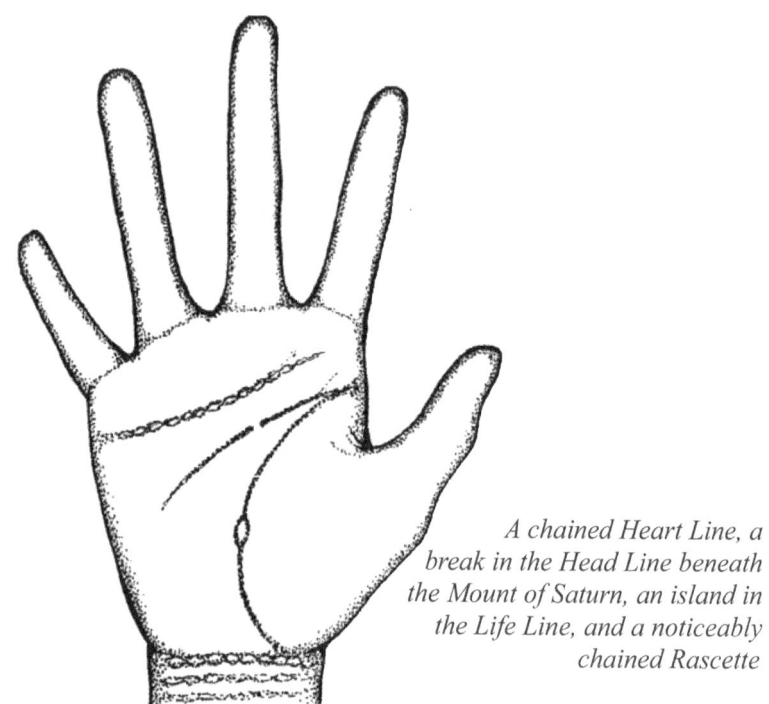

A chained Heart Line, a break in the Head Line beneath the Mount of Saturn, an island in the Life Line, and a noticeably chained Rascette

not extend so far. Perhaps the possessor of a Mercury break such as this is liable to study too hard for exams, or worry too much about his or her career. A chained Head Line is more serious and the results more permanent; it suggests a severe breakdown or even a prolonged spell of mental unbalance.

Isolated islands on the Heart Line suggest that the subject will suffer from some kind of emotional stress. And where the islands, though small, are so continuous that they merge into chain formation – and in some hands the Heart Line is chained throughout its length – this denotes a continual, nagging tension which is quite capable of growing into severe emotional disturbance. The sufferer needs to be advised to seek fresh interests, to take up new hobbies, new friends.

We have already noted that a chained Rascette – particularly along the topmost bracelet – signifies the many small difficulties that most people have to overcome. Such difficulties are usually connected with physical well-being, but this type of underlying stress can be beneficial in providing motivation towards healthy pursuits and a share of dogged persistence. A chained Life Line, however, is more

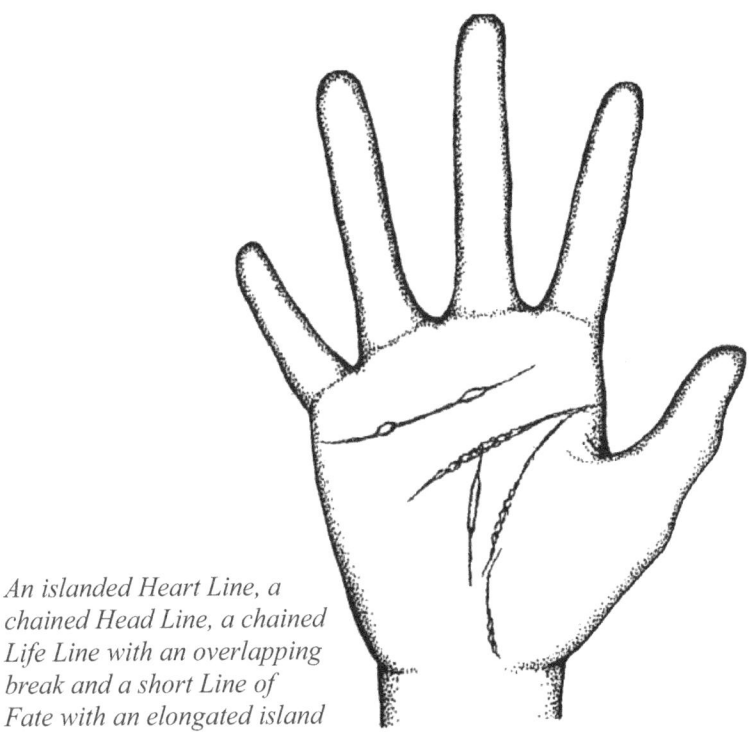

An islanded Heart Line, a chained Head Line, a chained Life Line with an overlapping break and a short Line of Fate with an elongated island

serious. It suggests that poor health is forever causing trouble, to the point of nervous exhaustion. An isolated island or section of chain can be pinpointed on the Life Line timescale and can become a clear warning that its owner must take care of his or her health, avoiding strenuous activities as far as possible, during these vital years. A purplish tinge to the Life Line reinforces this warning.

On the Line of Fate, an island so elongated that it forms a separate parallel line suggests that the person is likely to be leading some kind of double life during that period on the timescale. If this sign appears on the left hand alone, he or she will probably be keeping some part of their life a secret from the family. This situation will certainly lead to unhealthy stress. An elongated island on the right hand alone means that the deception – or concealment – is applied to the general public, not to the family. A doubled-up Line of Fate on both hands implies a real Jekyll and Hyde situation. The only good advice you can offer such a person is, 'If you can't be good, for goodness sake be careful!'

32 Sociability: Mixers, Loners and Timidity

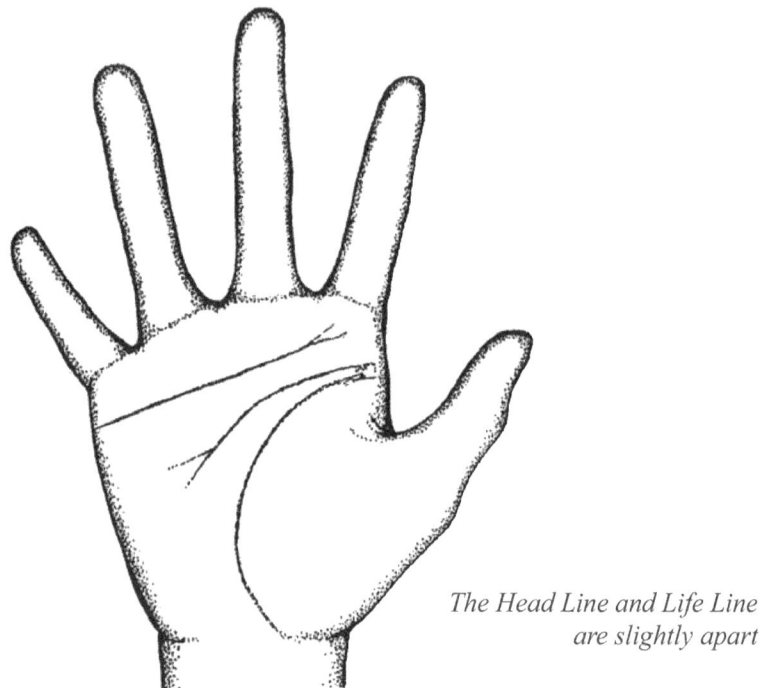

The Head Line and Life Line are slightly apart

IT IS A VERY FUNNY THING, but people who enjoy being in the limelight and are always looking for public attention simply love telling everyone how shy they are. If you as a palmist make a point of telling them they are secretly a shy sort of person, they will positively purr with pleasure. But if you tell that to a *really* shy person, he or she will hate it. They will probably hate you too for mentioning it.

So the golden rule for palmists is, if you see signs in the hand telling what a good mixer a person is, tell them they have a secret shy and retiring side. And if you notice the signs that tell of a very retiring personality, inform them that they prefer their own company, or that they are self-sufficient, or that they are happiest with just one or two good friends rather than a mob – anything, in fact, but the painful truth.

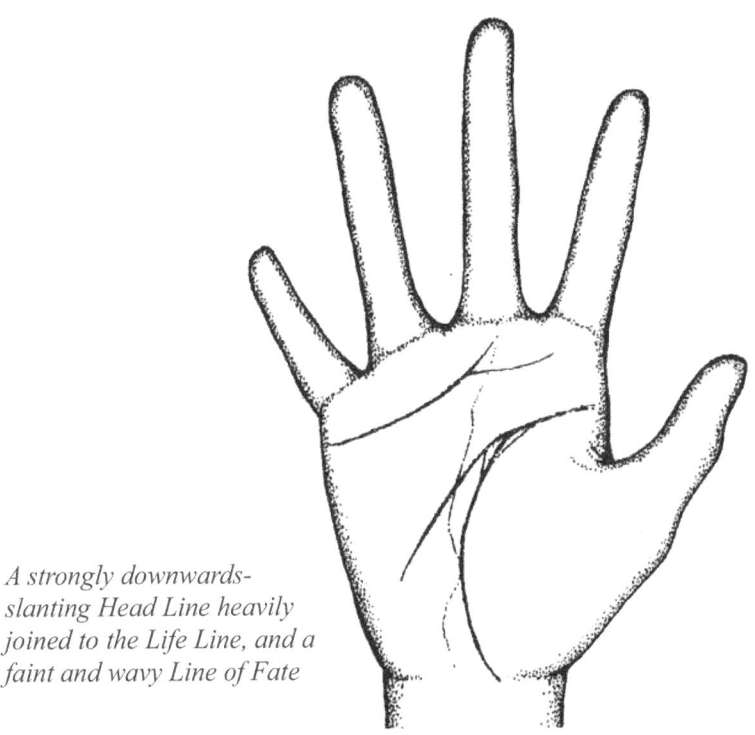

A strongly downwards-slanting Head Line heavily joined to the Life Line, and a faint and wavy Line of Fate

Look first at the point above the thumb where the Life Line and Head Line both start. On a good mixer's hand, the two lines will be slightly apart or barely touching. On a less sociable person, they will be joined together for quite a way – 3 centimetres (1¼ inch) or so. Use the right hand as a guide rather than the left, because this side of a person's character is often brought out or modified through their own personal experiences.

If a very retiring person has a Line of Fate on his or her palm, the chances are it will be faint and rather wavy, neither particularly governed by fate, nor particularly self-governing. Luck may come his or her way, but as often as not the subject will feel unable to take full advantage of it and will certainly miss many opportunities through backing away at the crucial moment. Both personality types may have a long, sloping Head Line, but in the case of the lone wolf it is more certain to reach as far as the Mount of the Moon. A good mixer often has a fork at the very end of the Head Line. The Heart Line will

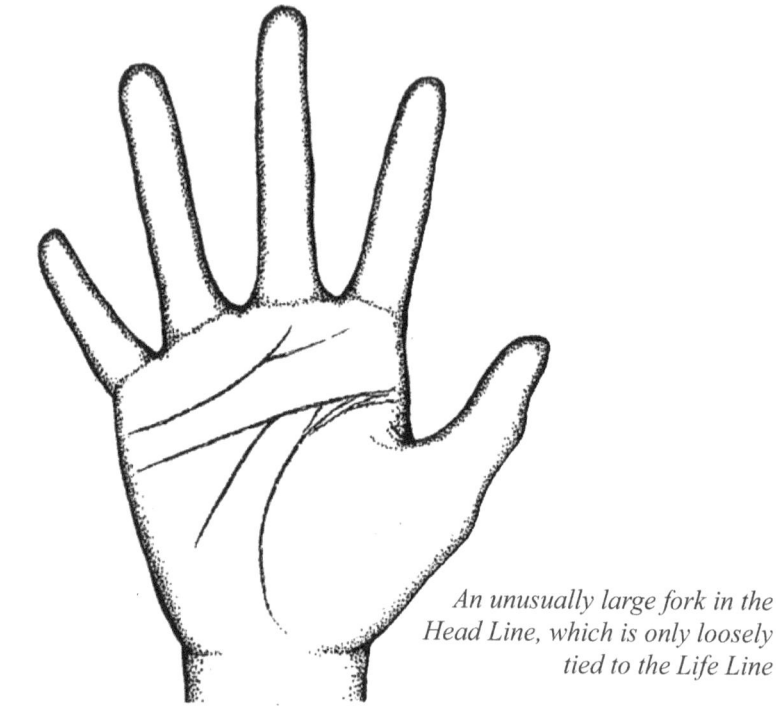

An unusually large fork in the Head Line, which is only loosely tied to the Life Line

usually be long and clear, often with two or more tributaries rising on the Mount of Jupiter.

A few people are very noticeably sometimes shy and sometimes outgoing, but not in the sense of minute-to-minute moods. Sudden mood changes may be symbolized in the hand when the Heart Line rises with two tributaries, one on the Mount of Jupiter and the other on the Mount of Saturn. But these long-term changes of personality may be signalled in the timescales which you will visualize as etched along the Life Line and the Lines of Fate and Fortune.

This periodic personality change runs in seven-year cycles. It happens to everyone but is not as a rule sufficiently pronounced to be remarked upon. In the case of those people in whom the trait is very noticeable indeed, you will usually find they have an unusually large fork in the Head Line. One prong will go straight across the palm, while the other will curve down into the Mount of the Moon.

The naturally 'outward-reaching' years of a person's life are from birth to age seven, from fourteen to twenty-one, from twenty-eight to thirty-five, from forty-two to forty-nine, from fifty-six to sixty-three, and from seventy to seventy-seven. And the naturally 'inward-looking' years of a person's life are from age seven to fourteen, from twenty-one to twenty-eight, from thirty-five to forty-two, from forty-nine to fifty-six, from sixty-three to seventy, and from seventy-seven to eighty-four. Then if he or she lives long enough to experience it, the cycle starts over again!

The natural loner often has quite large hands with rather knobbly fingers. Usually, the second finger is particularly long. The first finger may also be long, but it will still be shorter than its neighbour. If the first finger is very short, this suggests that its owner has a timid nature – which is not at all the same as being shy. Certainly, they will both be 'retiring', but a timid person can be said to lack aggression, and in this way he or she will be easy to get on with. Shy people, however, can be very aggressive indeed. They find that aggression is very useful in keeping unwelcome people away.

33 Assertiveness: Domineering and Submissive Types

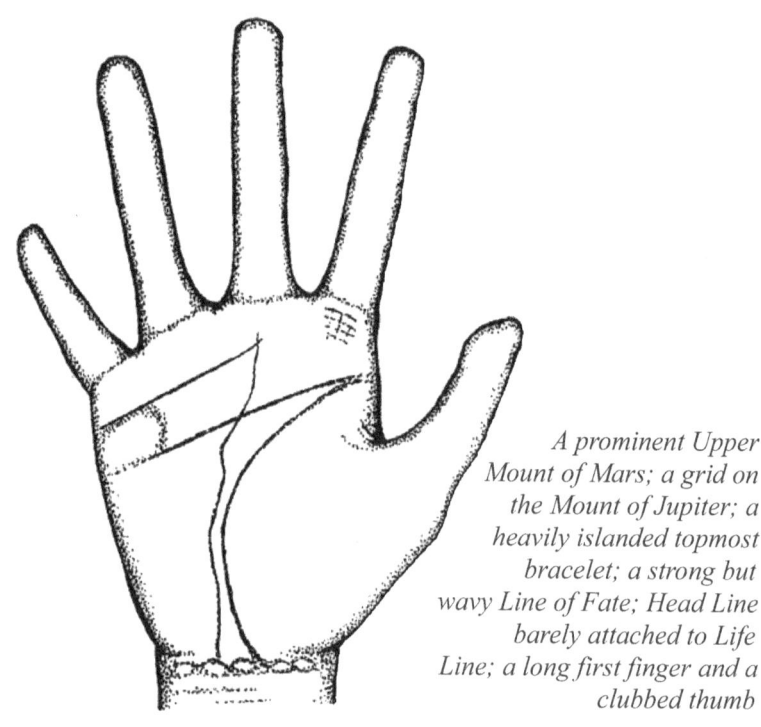

A prominent Upper Mount of Mars; a grid on the Mount of Jupiter; a heavily islanded topmost bracelet; a strong but wavy Line of Fate; Head Line barely attached to Life Line; a long first finger and a clubbed thumb

WE HAVE JUST LOOKED at the type of aggression often displayed by shy people as a defence mechanism, but this is not to be confused with assertiveness. Shyness is not a factor here. People tend to be either assertive or submissive, and we always hear more about the assertive types. They receive most of the attention. But there are some who enjoy being rather submissive; it lets them avoid having to make decisions and thus lessen their chance of making mistakes. So the two opposing types tend to get on quite well together, but put two assertive people together and you have a recipe for trouble.

Usually, it becomes obvious if a person is the domineering type as soon as he or she walks into the room, before you have a chance even to glance at their hands. But it is not always like that. Some innately bossy people like to keep quiet about this characteristic in themselves, and may even pretend to be meek and mild.

The first thing to notice when weighing somebody up is the shape of their hands and fingers. The most assertive people usually have the longest index fingers – their first finger is often equal in length to their second finger. Their thumb will also be longer than usual, and it will tend to be rather stiff and straight. If the thumb is shaped like a cave-man's club, take great care what you say. The symbolism of the club is very apt, for they are liable to club you over the head – verbally at least – if you annoy them.

It is advisable to tread lightly as well if the subject's Head Line starts *below* the Life Line and then crosses it. In effect, such people's thoughts will all be based on aggression, rising on the fierce Lower Mount of Mars, but they will not necessarily be particularly assertive. The 'domineering Head Line' will usually run fairly straight across the palm. The type of aggression symbolized here is usually orientated in an intelligently practical way, and subjects like nothing better than to link up with a meek partner who can be dominated. But if the Head Line curves downwards after leaving the Life Line, though its owners may be spoiling for a fight, they will be less likely to direct their aggression towards domin-ating another person. Ideas, principles, causes – these are the things that will make them take up arms.

The 'domineering Heart Line' is usually rather late in starting – often actually on the Mount of Saturn – and tends to run straight, close to the base of the fingers, as though impatient to reach the actively demonstrative area of the palm, leaving room for a strongly developed Upper Mount of Mars, which it throws into clear relief.

At the wrist, the topmost bracelet will be well islanded or fully chained. This sign has been mentioned before and it is not necessarily indicative of assertiveness in the physical sense. It simply means that subjects will be stubborn enough to fight their way through any opposition, and a bossy person is always stubborn.

There are one or two minor indicators which should clinch the diagnosis. A grid-like arrangement of tiny lines criss-crossing the Mount of Jupiter is always a sign of 'me first'. Its owners will see it as their right to have both the first and the last words whenever decisions are to be made. If some decision is particularly tricky, they can always delegate responsibility and say 'I'll let *you* decide, my dear!'. They like to leave the way open to be wise after the event.

If there is a Line of Fate in the over-assertive hand, it will probably be clearly defined but wavy. And at the top of this line, a clear cross on the Mount of Saturn warns that personal aggression of this assertive kind will be backed up with violence if necessary. The best advice to the palmist is to be very tactful when reading these signs!

34 Physical Problems:
Hypochondria, Illness, Excess and Solomon's Seal

WE HAVE ALREADY come across the Line of Health and considered whether it might not be better named the 'Line of Ill-health'. Its presence on the palm always implies that the subject's health is of ongoing concern; it is one of the factors normally present in his or her awareness. In the case of the healthy majority, health itself is never even considered. As people say, 'You don't value it until you start to lose it.'

The Line of Health runs between the Mount of Mercury and the general area of the lower Life Line. Most palmists consider that it *rises* at the little finger and flows towards the wrist, but this is a moot point. It may be absent early in life, only to appear later. When people start to age and health becomes a problem, this line often begins to develop visibly, commencing usually on the Mount of the Moon, occasionally on the Mount of Venus, and gradually extending up the palm. A Mount of Venus Line of Health will have to cross the Life Line at some point, and where it does it will register on the timescale the age at which precautionary measures should be taken.

Marked clearly and cleanly, the Line of Health usually denotes hypochondria. It is more likely to record actual ill-health when less well defined, wavy or broken. A wavy Line of Health, of whatever length, indicates intestinal problems or chronic indigestion. The Line of Health that ends (or begins) on the Life Line itself denotes a continuous state of nervous tension. This again is a condition that shows itself first and foremost in the abdomen and will indicate poor digestion and an over-acid stomach.

A Line of Health that crosses the Life Line and travels some way across the Mount of Venus suggests that health problems have been or will be brought about in some way through childhood indulgence: perhaps an unsuitable diet. Especially when it is a child's hand that is being read, the higher up the Life Line that the crossing takes place, the more likelihood there is that the subject will suffer from diabetes at some time during their adult life. There is far less risk of this when the crossing happens lower down.

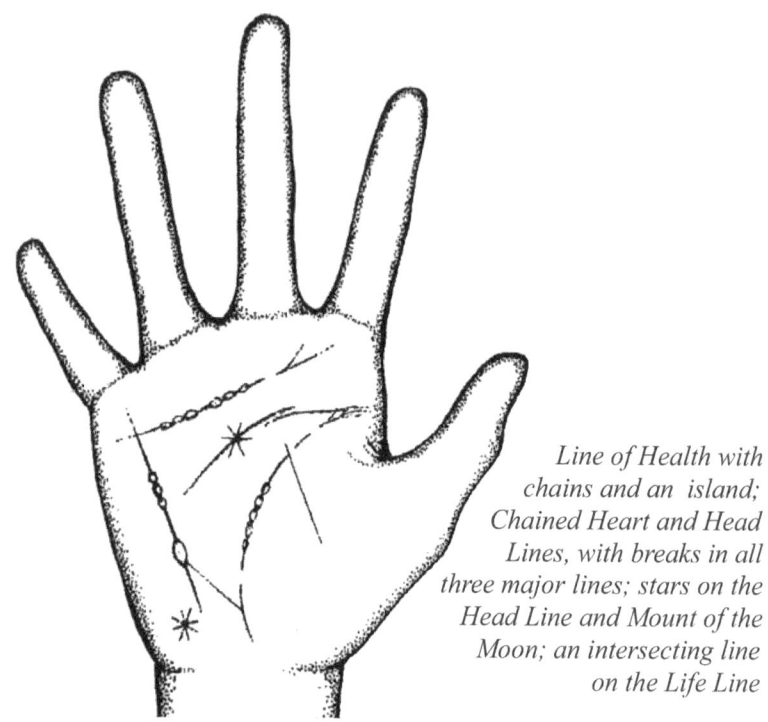

Line of Health with chains and an island; Chained Heart and Head Lines, with breaks in all three major lines; stars on the Head Line and Mount of the Moon; an intersecting line on the Life Line

    A single distinct island on the Line of Health is taken to indicate a serious internal condition, and when this feature appears on the palm you should look for anything — a connecting line or a similar island on the Life Line — that will enable you to put an approximate date on the problem. Many small islands, or a chained formation, along the Line of Health are said to be a fairly reliable indication of a lung condition. Look for confirmation of this from the fingernails: habitually starved of oxygen, their development will be arrested or constricted, and they will appear narrow and distinctly fluted, pale or slightly bluish. A Line of Health broken into small segments points to general weakness and may indicate a liver condition.

    Some palmists ascribe importance to the colour of the hand and to spots of colour along the lines, supposing them to refer to illness or injury. A severe liver condition may be forecast when a wavy Line of Health is tinted darkly yellowish along most of its length. Along the Life Line, black spots are supposed the most dangerous,

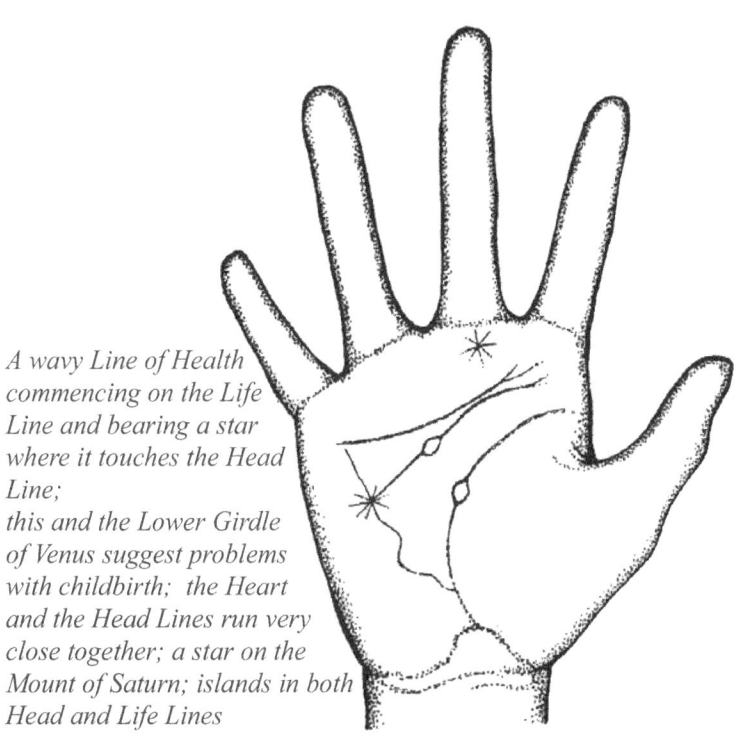

A wavy Line of Health commencing on the Life Line and bearing a star where it touches the Head Line; this and the Lower Girdle of Venus suggest problems with childbirth; the Heart and the Head Lines run very close together; a star on the Mount of Saturn; islands in both Head and Life Lines

and these or light blue marks may be explained as representing migraine or a recurrent nerve condition such as sciatica. Dark blue patches are also said to point to neurological disorders of a deeper origin and possibly to a tumour or other disturbance actually within the brain.

Along the Head Line too bluish patches are said to denote illness, in this case a serious organic condition which may be connected in some way with a timescale on one of the other lines. A dark yellowish patch along the Head Line or the Heart Line is said to indicate liver problems, while dark patches in general again indicate nervous disorders. Along the Heart Line bluish patches are said to denote serious infectious diseases.

Dark spots to be seen along the Head Line vary their implication according to the nearest mount. Beneath the Mount of Saturn, they denote problems with the teeth and gums. Beneath the Mount of the Sun they represent eye trouble, particularly if there is a star formation high on this mount near the base of the third finger.

When the Mount of Venus is particularly pronounced, these dark spots in general are said to indicate deafness.

The Life Line is the usual place where you would expect to find indications of ill-health, apart from the Line of Health itself. When the whole of the Life Line is noticeably pale, or unusually slender, this points to delicate health or general debility. Ongoing nervous disorders are suggested by a chained formation, while a clean break in the Life Line points to an isolated physical illness. An island, however, points to an illness of the depressive kind, with a mental or emotional rather than a physical origin.

Periods of emotional distress can also be indicated along the Life Line by an intersecting line running from the Mount of Venus, while a backwards fork from the Life Line, running a little way up the palm, indicates nervous illness. If this minor line runs through an area of dark skin, an acidic condition is suggested, which may give rise to gout.

Many of the signs which have been described earlier in the book may be given a different interpretation where health is concerned — one based on a purely physical level. Perhaps some palmists are more inclined than others to concentrate on physical ailments, but circumstances sometimes arise when such an interpretation is called for and plainly expected by the subject.

A Heart Line that has a considerable chained formation, for instance, interpreted on this physical level, indicates heart trouble, palpitations and anaemia. A break in this line below the Mount of Saturn also points to trouble with circulation and probably relates to a condition of low blood pressure. A star on the Mount of Saturn has been ascribed the meaning of a severe disabling condition or general paralysis. A star on the Mount of the Moon points to bladder and kidney troubles or dropsy.

A Head Line that is regularly broken along its length indicates recurrent headaches or possibly chronic forgetfulness. A single overlapping break, however, particularly if it occurs beneath the Mount of Saturn, indicates a physical injury, either to the head or to a leg. An island anywhere along the Head Line is indicative of nervous headaches. A star on this line usually suggests an actual brain injury, except that at the intersection of the Head Line and the Line of Health it will denote problems with childbirth. It may equally well indicate sterility, and this tendency is stressed if there is a blackish area of skin around the star formation. A distinctive small hollow anywhere along the course of the Head Line indicates the onset of neuralgia.

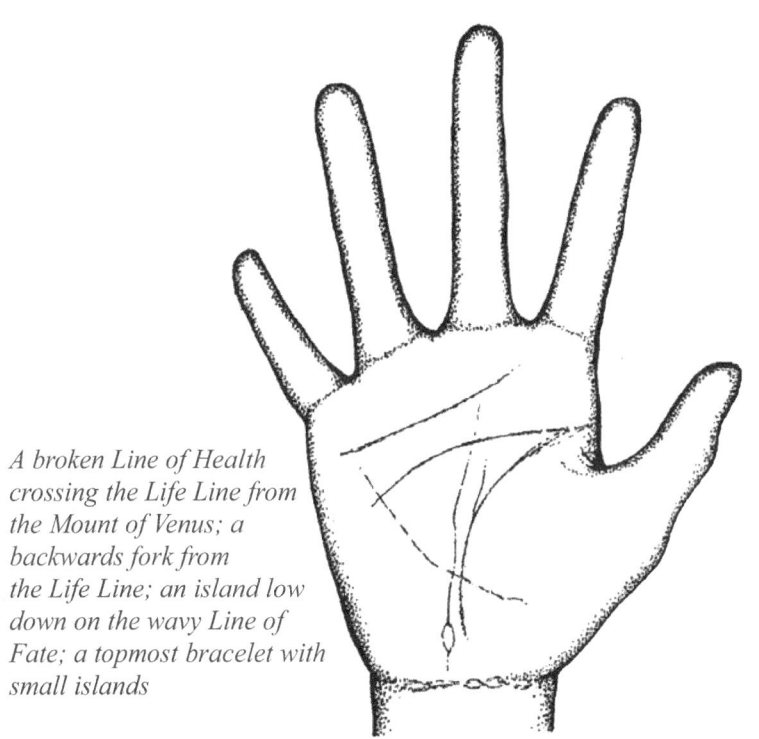

A broken Line of Health crossing the Life Line from the Mount of Venus; a backwards fork from the Life Line; an island low down on the wavy Line of Fate; a topmost bracelet with small islands

A Head Line which is particularly faintly traced is interpreted in the same way as one with a chained formation: it is said to indicate general debility and a tendency to feel faint. A Head Line intersected by several small lines indicates the probability of migraine. When the Head Line runs particularly close to the Heart Line, this is said to be a sign of breathing problems, particularly asthma. A large gap between Head and Life Lines at their rising, interpreted on this physical level, is said to be an indication of eye trouble early in life. The rising of the Heart Line and the Head Line with the Life Line, at the same point, has been taken by old-fashioned traditionalists to indicate the likelihood of stroke, while a break along the Life Line may correspond with the onset of heart problems according to the timescale.

It should be stressed that all these somewhat morbid interpretations need be dwelled upon only when the subject is plainly fascinated by the subject of his or her health and wants to hear such things. If not, it is best to leave them out!

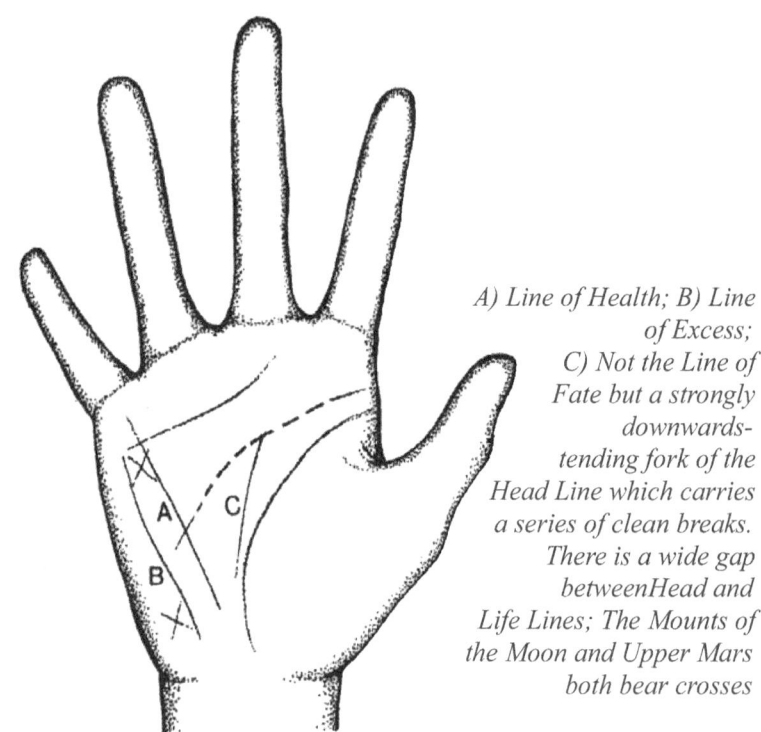

A) Line of Health; B) Line of Excess; C) Not the Line of Fate but a strongly downwards-tending fork of the Head Line which carries a series of clean breaks. There is a wide gap betweenHead and Life Lines; The Mounts of the Moon and Upper Mars both bear crosses

Like an inner version of the Line of Health, running between it and the edge of the palm, the Line of Excess follows a similar route, flowing between the Mount of Mercury and the Mount of the Moon, though it too may cross the Life Line and run into the Mount of Venus. In some ways it resembles a deeper-working, more intuitive version of the Line of Health. It hints at some form of apparently greedy or lascivious behaviour. Addictive personalities are liable to have the Line of Excess on their hand, and when addiction is a major problem, its course is likely to be wildly erratic, veering this way and that like the moods and feelings and sensations which it represents. When the Line of Excess runs straight and true, or is only gently curved, it implies a way of life that may be healthy enough, but only at other people's expense, for its wearer will have little regard for morality. When either of these lines occurs, it is useful to note if there is a link between them and one of the major lines. A link to the Head Line may give these matters the benefit of considered thought; a link to the Heart Line may mean that an emotional element will be

The Seal Of Solomon, composed of:
A) the Line of Excess, and B) the Line of Intuition

added to their excesses, their extravagances and over-concern with physical sensations.

When it occurs, the Line of Intuition, which will be discussed later in the book, shares the same area of the palm. Cases in which both the Line of Excess and the Line of Intuition are present on the same hand are rare, but when they occur, the lines may combine to form the double crescent of Solomon's Seal. This is a strange portent of a certain not very pleasant brand of inner magnetism, suggesting the dubious use of intuitive powers in order to gain some kind of advantage over others. It will operate chiefly in the sexual sphere, but quite often in the financial one as well. This sign can denote a dangerous Svengali-like charmer.

Some people are said to be accident-prone and this is indeed a problem, though not one of health. Accident-prone people may be basically very healthy – indeed, they may be exceptionally robust and vigorous – but they will certainly be inclined to be impetuous. Look for the tell-tale wide gap between the rising of the Head and Life

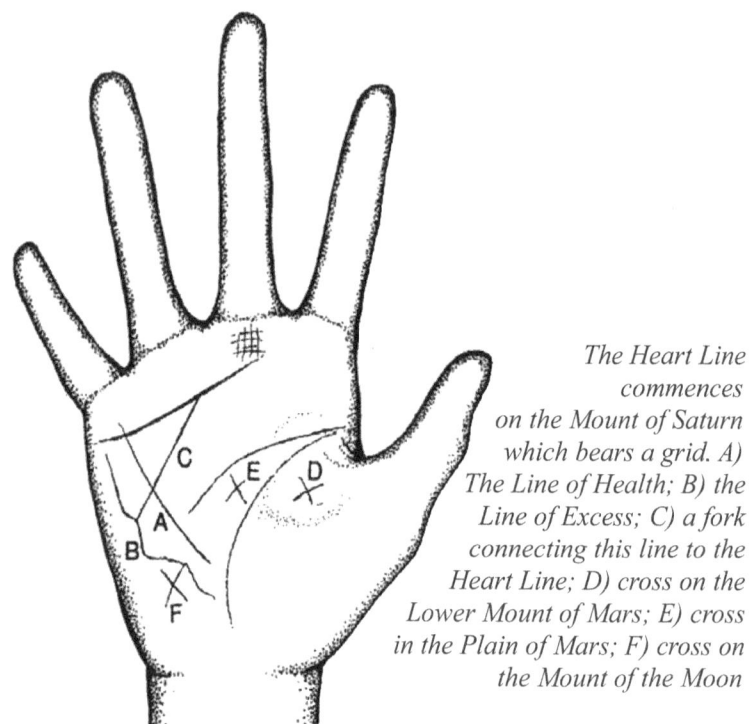

The Heart Line commences on the Mount of Saturn which bears a grid. A) The Line of Health; B) the Line of Excess; C) a fork connecting this line to the Heart Line; D) cross on the Lower Mount of Mars; E) cross in the Plain of Mars; F) cross on the Mount of the Moon

Lines, and the Head Line that slopes quite steeply towards the Mount of the Moon. The two Martian mounts may each bear a cross, as though warning of this propensity. The Mount of the Moon too is a likely place on which to find a cross or a star, symbolizing the ever-present danger of accident.

    A general prediction of gloom usually attends any grid formation of tiny, fine lines, particularly when this grid occurs on the Mount of Saturn – grim seat of depression – on the Lower Mount of Mars or on the Mount of the Moon. Grids often occur when people seem destined to lose money, whatever work they do, whatever they start out with, whatever good ideas they may have. In such a case, a cross too will probably be found on the Mount of Mercury, and another on the Mount of the Sun, as though to nullify financial luck. There may well be an island in either the Line of Fate or the Line of Fortune, or both, and an intersecting line from one of these to the Head Line may offer a clue as to the actual years of worst loss. When the Line of Fate actually ends in the Head Line, it speaks of a major failure of judgement that may well result in financial loss, or physical accident, or both.

General health and susceptibility to various less easily defined forms of illness can often be linked positively to hand-shape, and the fingerprints too need to be taken into account when assessing physical well-being. People with the 'pyknic' type of physique – stocky, heavily bodied stature with a short, thick neck and small, broad hands – are particularly prone to suffer from depression and depressive illnesses. The long, artistic hand, as we have already seen, suggests a certain intensity of emotional feeling, and intensity such as this will have a powerful physical effect on the function of the heart. Stressful symptoms such as high blood pressure and excessive adrenalin production are frequently to be associated with this cheirotype. Earlier in the book we noted that the whorled fingerprinter is more intensely focused than the other types. This again is related to habitual stress and is a sign of high-powered people constantly putting themselves under pressure at work and in society; this fact too is inevitably reflected in the physical action of the heart. In the case of a ten-finger whorled printer, or a mixed type whose whorls outnumber other patterns on their right hand (the hand of personally acquired attributes), it may be that high blood pressure is liable to be a problem, with its attendant risk of heart attack or stroke.

Fertility in men or women is quite readily predictable from the shape and size of their hands and fingers, as hinted at in a previous chapter. In a man, when one hand is larger than the other to a noticeable degree, the indication is a low sperm count. In both sexes, the comparative length of the Sun or ring finger and the Jupiter or index finger can be taken to predict fertility. When the two fingers are of very similar length (usually the ring finger is slightly longer) hormonal balance will be normal, but men with this feature will have a greater chance of suffering a heart attack while still below middle age. When a man's ring finger is noticeably longer, the indication is a higher than normal production of the fertility hormone testosterone, and a smaller chance of suffering a heart attack at a young age. In women the case is different: the longer the index finger in relation to the ring finger, the higher will be her body's production of oestrogen. Her fertility will be higher than most, but because of this extra boost of oestrogen her chances of contracting breast cancer while still fairly young will also be that much higher.

35 Creativity : Sideways Thinking

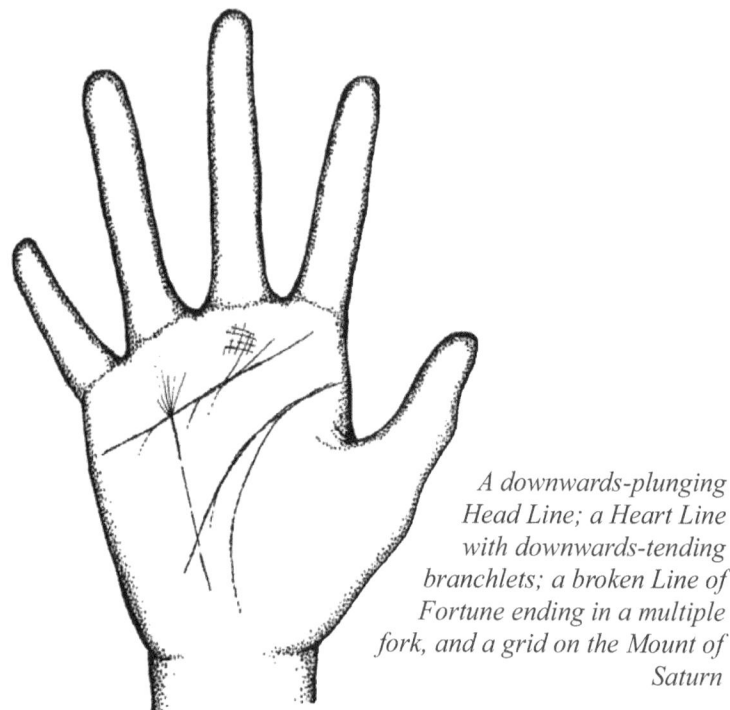

A downwards-plunging Head Line; a Heart Line with downwards-tending branchlets; a broken Line of Fortune ending in a multiple fork, and a grid on the Mount of Saturn

OUR DIVISION of hands and characters into cheirotypes has shown that a creatively artistic dreamer typically will have a finely shaped slender hand with narrow-tipped fingers. A long Head Line is always a sure sign of a keen brain. But you can be certain that the clarity of this good mind will be cloaked in strangely woolly ideas when the long Head Line slants down across the palm to reach well into the Mount of the Moon.

Of course, when its owner has chosen a career or way of life that calls for unusual imagination, this may not be a bad thing. The Mount of the Moon symbolizes the artistic or illogical side of life rather than the practical one. It is the territory of enigma, the home of 'sideways thinking', as well as the land of myth and fable.

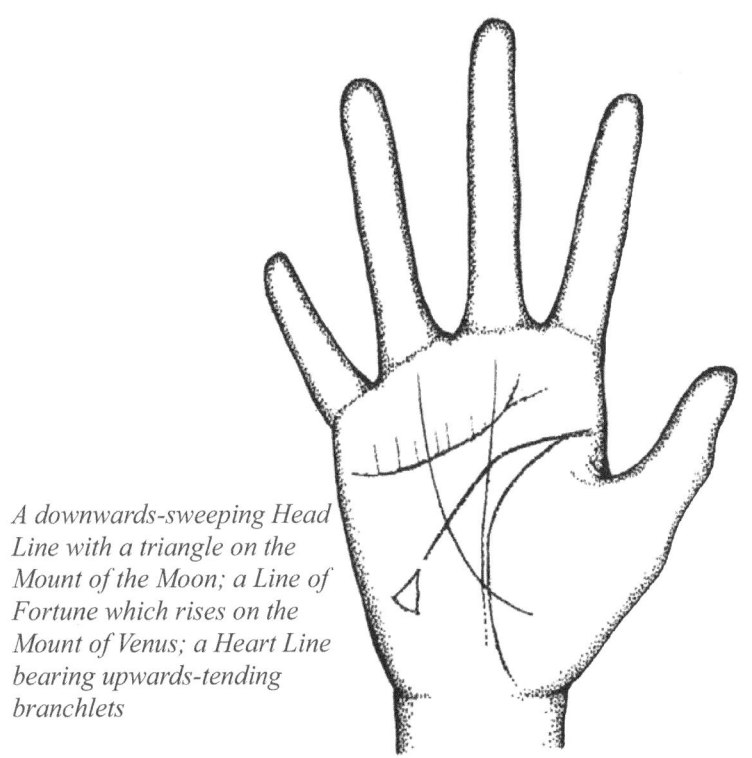

A downwards-sweeping Head Line with a triangle on the Mount of the Moon; a Line of Fortune which rises on the Mount of Venus; a Heart Line bearing upwards-tending branchlets

Compromise is the key to adaptability. In today's competitive world, for the imagination to be truly creative, it probably portends most favourably if the Head Line reaches just to the edge of the Mount of the Moon and stops there. Deeper penetration into this mysterious but unscientific area of the moon's subtly physical influence risks a profitless venture into the inactive world of dreams.

The dreamer whose thoughts and feelings float blissfully in the clouds instead of remaining purposefully on the earth will probably have a generously long, deeply curving Heart Line, the central portion dropping well down into the palm, most likely with several fine minor branchlets leading from it. Such a person will take nothing too seriously for very long. He or she may seem to concentrate furiously on some project, only to drop it absent-mindedly after a while and start on something else.

The dreams of such people are likely to be about what they will do 'when their dreams come true', rather like a dog chasing its own tail. This woolly lack of direction is all the more pronounced when the Heart Line has a double rising, one tributary on the Mount of Jupiter, the other on the Mount of Saturn. The interplay of abstract Jovian impulse and the braking effect of Saturnian materiality make for intermittent action and unfulfilled imagery.

The born dreamer may have a strong Line of Fortune, but it will carry all the signs of efforts and opportunities doomed to go astray, lost in idle fantasy. There will perhaps be frequent breaks throughout its length, but it is just as likely to be unbroken, only to end in a network of fine lines forking out and losing themselves on the Mount of the Sun, as though dividing and diluting the 'luck' until most of its value is lost. However, if a strong Line of Fortune, after rising across the palm on the Mount of Venus, sweeps up in a curve, crossing the Life Line in its course, the indications are that the imaginative mind can be put to good use in a very creative way. Many successful artists combine this feature on their hand with a long, sloping Head Line.

The forecast is greatly improved if there is a clear triangle of fine lines on the Mount of the Moon, near the end of the Head Line. Sited just there, this pyramid-like symbol of the intellect shows that even the fuzziest thoughts can be given a creative outlet and turned to profitable use.

The omen is not so good if there is also a criss-cross grid below the second finger, on the Mount of Saturn, as though cancelling out the wise use of material resources. It certainly implies a lack of concentration. But a good strong Line of fate is always a redeeming feature and suggests that even the most unusual, illogical ideas will be put to good use.

36 Sensitivity : Intuition, Concern, the Occult and the Spiritual

THE CONICAL HAND, Cheirotype BB, has a sensitive, otherworldly look about it. It is difficult to imagine owners of so fine a hand doing heavy manual work – unless perhaps they are those dissident political poets we read about, banished by some totalitarian regime to toil in a forgotten labour camp in the back of beyond.

We are already familiar with the 'sensitive' pattern formed mutually by the Heart Line and the Head Line – the former curving deeply, rising at its conclusion to cut across the communicative Mount of Mercury; the latter plunging steeply down the palm to reach the unpractical Mount of the Moon. There will probably be a branch line from the Head Line to the Heart Line too, as though to rob the mind of any last trace of non-emotional thought.

The Mount of Venus, though slender, will be fairly prominently fleshy. Its abstract equivalent on the opposite side of the palm, the Mount of the Moon, will show a distinct fleshiness towards the Rascette, as though heavy with the weight of mysterious, illogical contents. An extra line may well be present, linking this nether region of the hand with the Mount of Mercury, the seat of communication. This is the Line of Intuition, which curves upwards as though to outline the psychic zone of abstract values, embracing both creativity and the tenacity to put it to use, receptivity and the mind's reaction to it.

When most people think of intuition, they conjure up a vision of a head-in-the-clouds person; of very non-masculine 'feminine' intuition. But intuition is not a function limited exclusively to psychically sensitive people, nor is it by any means exclusively characteristic of the female sex. Great soldiers and statesman often possess this line too, faithfully reflecting their psychological 'type'. A good general certainly needs to use the faculty of intuition a great deal, if only to assess what his enemies are about to do.

On the Mount of Mercury, the Marks of Concern will often be found to share a palm with the Line of Intuition. This sign consists of several short, fine minor lines running closely together down the Mount of Mercury from the base of the little finger. When they are present, they suggest an ability to see into the minds of other

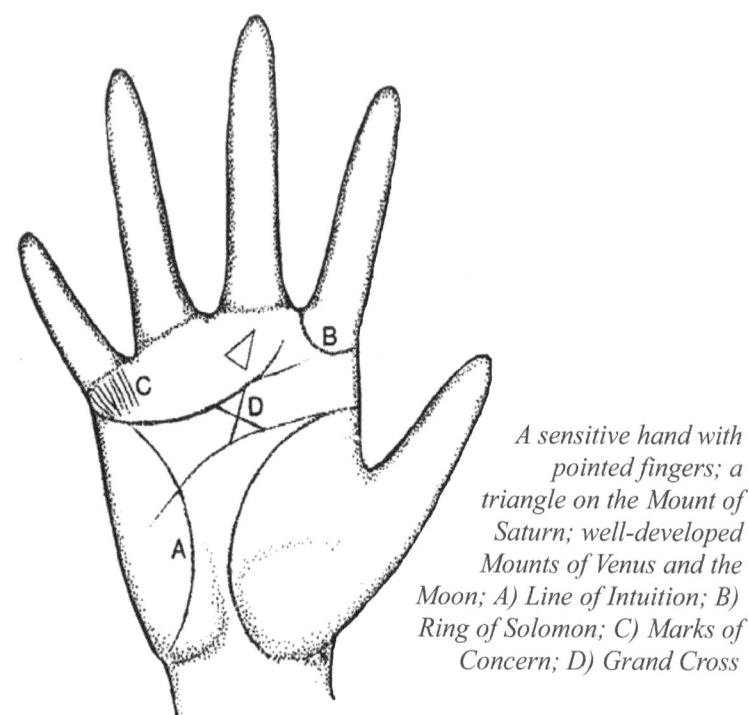

A sensitive hand with pointed fingers; a triangle on the Mount of Saturn; well-developed Mounts of Venus and the Moon; A) Line of Intuition; B) Ring of Solomon; C) Marks of Concern; D) Grand Cross

people, sometimes literally to 'read their minds' but more often denoting positive sympathy with their psychic contents, an aptitude which perhaps lies at the heart of intuition. These lines may also feature in the hands of 'caring' people, and as such are included in the next chapter.

The Line of Fate can carry with it signs of sensitivity in the occult sphere. The 'occult' is the subtle side of life, but not in its proper sense the spiritual side. If you see a ghost, for instance, this will certainly be an occult phenomenon, but not necessarily a spiritual one. Actually, 'occult' includes all that is abstract and immaterial within the world of materiality – the subtle side of materiality. 'Spiritual' includes those influences which reach the material world from beyond materiality, and is not at all the same as 'spiritualism'. The difference between the two is not always clear, but it is quite possible for someone to be 'spiritual' in every sense, without possessing any facility for the occult. Similarly, a person skilled in the occult may be very far removed from spirituality.

The Supernal Zone is a highly significant area of the hand when looking for signs of this nature. The Grand Cross is usually formed by a line crossing the Line of Fate between Head and Heart Lines, or, if the Line of Fate is absent, it may feature on its own. It will thus appear more or less beneath the Mount of Saturn. A cross symbolizes a cancelling-out or overcoming of a particular influence – in this case the powerful influence of materiality. By negating this power to some extent it indicates that its wearer is able to experience something of the world of spirit without succumbing to the misleading influence of the occult. Conversely, On the Mount of Saturn itself, a triangle is said traditionally to signal knowledge and skill in the occult sphere – the brain is to some extent 'given over' to abstract materiality, which is the essence of the occult. The Supernal Line has already been mentioned as the stamp of spiritual awareness. Like an unattached fork to either the Heart Line or the Head Line (depending on one's personal approach to these matters), it rises within this Great Quadrangle to symbolize a psychic function between thinking and feeling – an ability to suspend the workings of these two, opening a way for independent consciousness of the soul.

Finally, the Ring of Solomon is the sign that most palmists would give their eye-teeth to wear on their own hand (and, of course, some do possess it). It signifies an ultimate store of occult knowledge becoming available to its owner. Like so many other unusual signs, this is a splendid thing to have, but not at all something to covet. It symbolizes the knowledge and wisdom of King Solomon himself, and by tradition that biblical king is said to have reached the heights of attainment, while still within the sphere of materiality. But, of course, even the height of abstract materiality is still represented by the Mount of Saturn – in practice it is still governed by mortality and death.

On the hand, the Ring of Solomon has the effect of closing off the index finger, as though preventing the flow of influences through the soul. It is rather like a dam, holding back an enormous amount of energy that should by nature be cycling freely. The energy can be put to work for good or for ill, but its retention is not really contributing to the smooth running of the universe. It crystallizes or solidifies something that should be fluid, mobile and developing. In lighter vein, it is said to enable its wearer to converse with the animals. But, converse or not, the saintly individual can still be brought to destruction by the teeth of a crocodile. Similarly, the man or woman intoxicated by the occult can unsuspectingly forgo the possibility of true spiritual development, rebuffing the chance to actually transcend the earthly power symbolized by Saturn, the Grim Reaper.

If the Ring of Solomon can be said to represent a dam preventing the flow of influences, in a different sense the Upper Girdle of Venus can have this significance too. When the girdle is operative, or even when the Heart Line itself curves strongly upwards at its termination, it will pass above the Marriage Lines, thus cutting them off from the little finger – from the communicative power of Mercury. This often signifies an actual block, or a bar to the reality of marriage or normal sexual relations.

When this happens, it can have great significance regarding sensitivity. There is a little-known and rarely formulated fact concerning the damming-up of marriage, or male-female affairs, a fact that to some extent reflects the ancient tradition of celibacy as a religious custom. In any marriage, whether the contract is official and legally binding or not, or even in a seemingly casual sexual union, whether the participants realize it or not, an interflow of contents takes place – a karmic 'averaging out', resulting in either a lowering or a raising of the 'level of being' for one or other of the participants, a modification of their spiritual place in the universal order of things.

This can be expressed in a different way: in a sexual relationship, during the normal course of events, the female partner acts as an unwitting receptacle for inner contents of the karmic type. She becomes a mixing pot wherein all these subtle ingredients are blended and modified, and from which the modified results are redistributed. Her male partner acts as an involuntary channel for spiritual life forces, which we in palmistry have visualized as a flow of energy between wrist and forefinger, via the Supernal Zone and the Mount of Jupiter – an intercourse between soul and spirit, nourishing the mounts, replenishing the reservoir of the Supernal Zone, colouring feelings and relationships. Where marriage has been precluded for whatever reason, the likely result is a tremendous store of spiritual contents which, because they are normally unconscious, cannot be communicated through the 'normal' channels. This is particularly true in the case of people who set their store on religious values and have religious expectations.

37 Compassion : Caring, Sympathy, and the Mark of Mercy

THE SHAPE of people's hands and fingers can tell you a great deal about their readiness to care for others. Angels of mercy are practical people, and they often have large, practical hands. The owners of small, dainty, willowy hands may look angelic, and they will probably tell you how concerned they are about the plight of others less fortunate than themselves. But when it comes to the crunch, they will probably leave the actual nursing, cleaning, tending, fetching and carrying to somebody else — and the tedious but unselfish chore of fetching and carrying is usually the biggest part of caring!

Really caring people will probably have a squarish hand, with rather large, knobbly fingers. Their fingers may appear stiff, but the thumb in particular will be quite supple, curving backwards with ease. It will also be fairly narrow-waisted over its central phalange. When they lay their hands flat on the table, you may notice that both the second finger and the little finger are unusually long. The little finger may have a slight inward curve towards the third finger. The nails too will be long and pointed, whether they are kept well trimmed or not. And when these people open their fingers, they will spread them quite generously far apart, in particular the gap between thumb and index finger.

The 'caring Head Line' will probably be long and slightly sloping — not too far down into the unpractical Mount of the Moon, but far enough away from the other extreme of straightness, whose owners would probably see it as a waste of time to bother very much about others. The Head Line may well have a wide fork at the end, showing broad-minded sympathy for all sorts of people.

The 'caring Heart Line' will be long and firmly engraved, and will probably curve around the edge of the palm as it reaches the end. It will very likely rise from small tributaries on the Mount of Jupiter, or it may just as likely begin with two fairly lengthy tributaries, one from the Mount of Jupiter, the other rising midway between the first and second fingers, adjacent to but not on the Mount of Saturn.

The personal feelings of a deeply caring person are often overruled by the outside needs of the moment, and to illustrate this as a trait in their character there may be a strong branch line from the

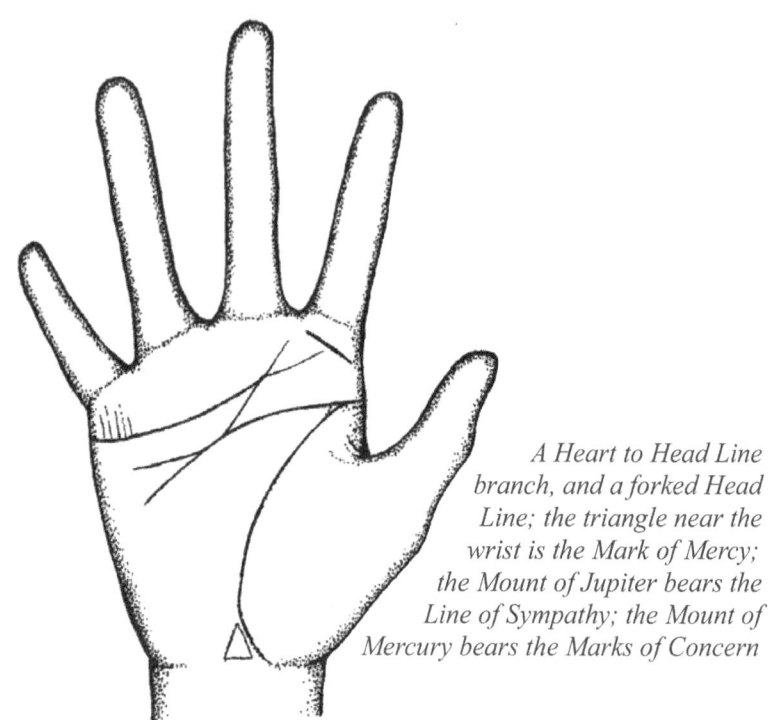

A Heart to Head Line branch, and a forked Head Line; the triangle near the wrist is the Mark of Mercy; the Mount of Jupiter bears the Line of Sympathy; the Mount of Mercury bears the Marks of Concern

Heart Line to the Head Line. These are the really practical carers, who use their common sense first and foremost.

But many sincerely caring people have the opposite connection — a Head Line that branches upwards into the Heart Line. In this case, their interest in others will tend to be less practical, more emotional. Their feelings are more easily hurt and they may find their own involvement in others' problems upsetting at times. They should guard against feeling hard done by or 'put upon'. They really need to keep away from the more distressing cases, for their own good, and they should be careful not to become too emotionally involved with troubled people outside their own immediate circle of family and friends.

The so-called Line of Sympathy is to be found below the index finger, slanting across the Mount of Jupiter as though to cut off the flow of psychic energy. It is something like a less decisive version of the Ring of Solomon, discussed in the previous chapter. As we saw, the Ring of Solomon proper symbolizes the

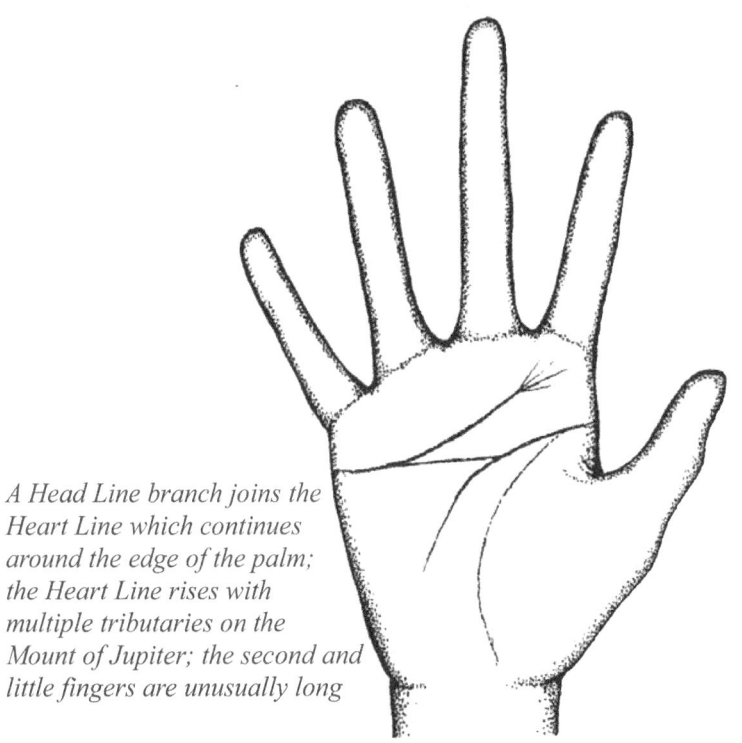

A Head Line branch joins the Heart Line which continues around the edge of the palm; the Heart Line rises with multiple tributaries on the Mount of Jupiter; the second and little fingers are unusually long

psychic 'collection' or keeping to oneself of all spiritual influences that enter the soul, and is therefore really a selfish sign. In a similar vein, this straight version, as the Line of Sympathy, has a somewhat selfish connotation too, despite the appearance of sympathy and the aura of caring which it symbolizes in its wearer. It expresses the reluctance some people have to share their *unpleasant* feelings, to tell others about their worries and weaknesses. They prefer to keep them to themselves.

In a way, it is a sign of pride. It is often said that 'a problem shared is a problem aired', or 'a sorrow shared is a sorrow halved'. Whichever of the many versions of this saying you know, the meaning is similar: the majority of people feel the need to 'talk to someone about it' as soon as they encounter problems or feel uncomfortable about something. Most of us like a shoulder to cry on, need a confidante. A few, however, would rather take their worries with them to the grave than share them with anyone. Good things, warm feelings, they are willing to share freely, but for them 'a worry shared is a worry doubled' and they will have none of it.

So in this sense, wearers of the Line of Sympathy are indeed sympathetic, compassionate even. Perhaps they are basically very private people, but the result for them is unfortunate: they cannot readily throw or project faults and problems from their soul, but keep them hidden from view, much as they detest having them. To all around them, of course (apart, perhaps, from the excessively curious, to whom they are a source of great frustration), they spread only light and hope. They never bother anyone else with their troubles and they are usually good listeners. Because of this peculiar trait, however, they carry about with them a quiet air of sadness, and in practical terms they are apt to preserve a skeleton or two in their cupboards.

We have already seen how a sensitive person may carry the Marks of Concern on the Mount of Mercury. They are often to be found on the hands of dedicated nurses, doctors and others drawn to the caring professions. They are rather close, in every sense, to the Child Lines which we discussed earlier: minor branchlets which are attached to the Marriage Line. And, indeed, to the wearer of such marks the helpless and sufferers in general may take the place of their own children, and their heart goes out freely to anyone in need. This sign in the hand of a childless person suggests a subliminal diversion, perhaps, of the basic parental instinct.

The clinching sign that identifies a real angel of mercy is the Mark of Mercy — a clearly defined triangle near the wrist, near the end of the Life Line. When seen on the hand that lacks this general picture of a caring personality, the Mark of Mercy *could* indicate a morbid preoccupation with thoughts of death — a sign, as the poet William Dunbar put it, of *'Timor mortis conturbat me'*. In this case it would be better known as the 'Mark of Morbidity'. But on any otherwise compassionate hand, it shows a genuine practical concern about old age, suffering and death in others. Certainly, it is not the sign of a pushy person, or of a retiring one. Familiarity with death can carry several connotations. Rumours from India have it that the late Mother Teresa of Calcutta had this triangular Mark of Mercy on each hand. The most modest of people, who put her own welfare last, her gift lay in caring for those in need, in the most practical way possible.

38 The Grand Cycle : The Basis of Ancient Psychology

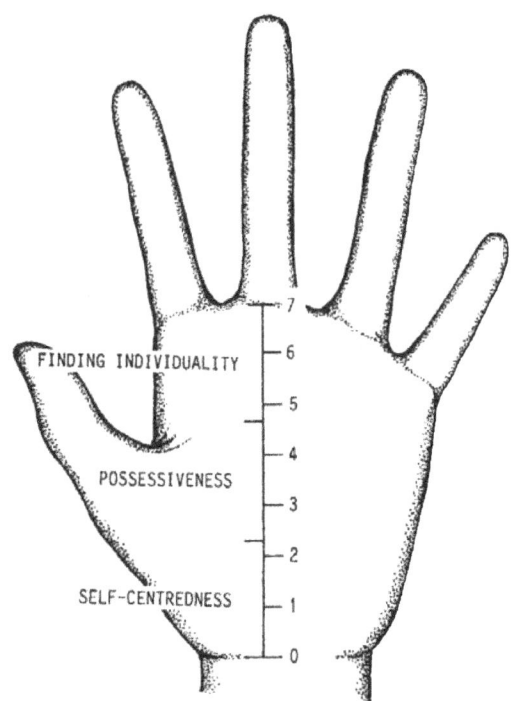

Ancestral Cycle following the Line of Fate on the left hand

OF INCREDIBLY ANCIENT ORIGIN, the Grand Cycle is connected with the cycle of the sun — the twenty-eight year cycle at the end of which the days of the month fall once again on the same days of the week. During this twenty-eight year period, the world in relationship to the sun is said to have traversed or sampled all the possibilities open to it, and all the world's people too will have lived through all their potentialities, limited only by their current psychological and spiritual levels of development.

Three of these twenty-eight year cycles following in succession constitute this so-called Grand Cycle, a triad of past, present and future; of raw material, developing skill and creativity; of body, soul and spirit. The whole adds up to the Age of the

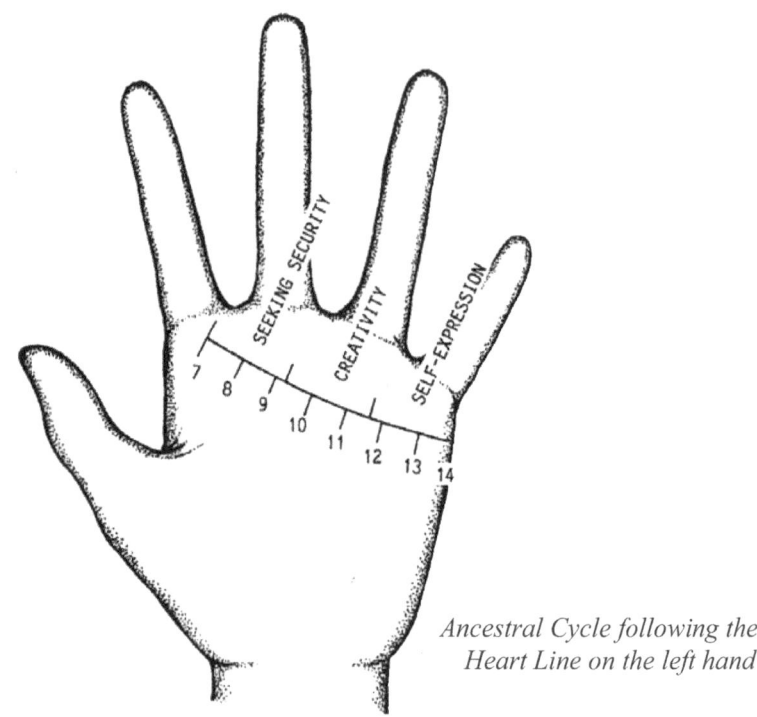

Ancestral Cycle following the Heart Line on the left hand

Patriarch, or, as it equally well may be, the Age of the Matriarch, the full life span of the completed person — eighty-four years.

It is not a very practical method of divination, but if you need to assess a person's psychological content and, in particular, his or her spiritual progress, it is really essential to complete the whole picture in this way. The cycle proceeds in definitive seven-year steps, like the degrees of a chronometer or the hours of a clock. Within each seven-year step are three compartments of concern, corresponding with the Mundane Houses of astrology.

The first twenty-eight year cycle, when completed, is known as the Ancestral or Bodily Cycle — that is, the cycle of the past. During this period of a person's life, from birth to young adulthood, he or she is governed chiefly by family background, by inheritance, by cultural, racial, religious and parental rules. This cycle is recorded on the left hand. True independence begins with the second twenty-eight

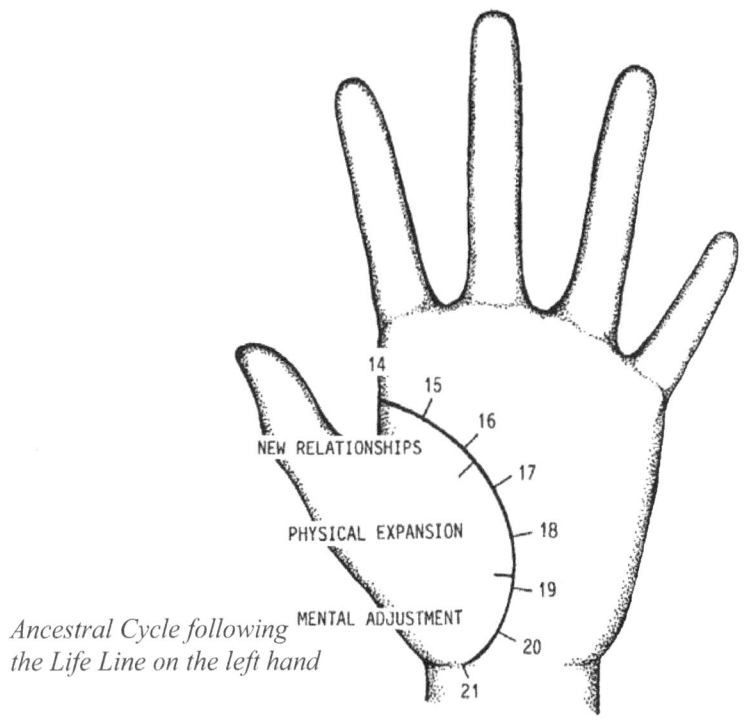

Ancestral Cycle following the Life Line on the left hand

year cycle. This is known as the Individual or Soul Cycle — that is, the cycle of the present. Having started at the age of twenty-eight, it lasts until the age of fifty-six. During this period, the person of destiny will have cast off the shackles of parental guidance — though everything of value will have been retained in the memory, as the basis of his or her character. During this second cycle, the whole independent individual — or his or her own soul — will be the guide. This implies guidance that will include all contents and experiences, both good and bad, rather than merely the inherited and cultural parts. This period will be recorded on the right hand.

The third cycle is called the Communal or Creative Cycle, or the Cycle of Spirit — that is, the cycle of the future. This final period of a person's life is the time when all his or her contents can be put to creative use and devoted towards building for the future. Both hands taken together are supposed to record this period, from the age of fifty-six onwards; but in practice, if the previous two cycles have really worked and gelled, palmistry should no longer apply. The

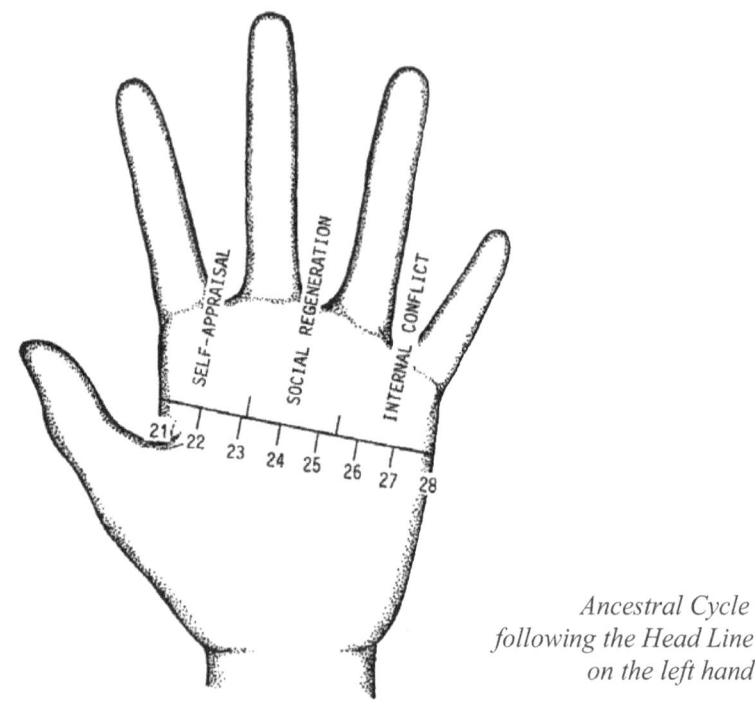

*Ancestral Cycle
following the Head Line
on the left hand*

subject should now be free from the type of personal karma that is recorded in the hand, and free to that extent from preordained fate. So as palmists, we can use this method only to the age of fifty-six. Thereafter, it is little more than a parlour game for so exalted a subject.

The method, as distinct from conventional palmistry, will present a clear picture of a person's *centre of gravity* – their main concern – during any particular period of their life. This factor can be read off, and its progress interpreted according to the conventional signs and symbols to be seen along the *representative line*, with any associated tie lines to the mounts, or branches linking with the other lines, and their particular psychological functions. In doing this we use the set of meanings which we have already learned.

The representative line is decided by the subject's age. Each of these twenty-eight year minor cycles passes through four phases, during which one psychological function is more in evidence than the

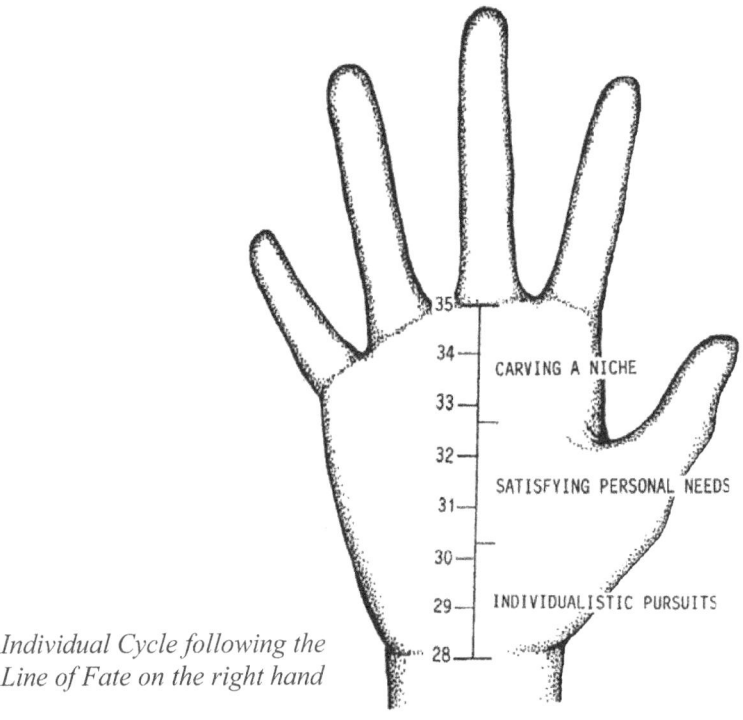

Individual Cycle following the Line of Fate on the right hand

others. The truth of this is readily recognizable in your own life. The first seven years of childhood are governed mainly by purely instinctive intuition which, in this system, is recorded by the Line of Fate. During the second seven-year period, to the age of fourteen, you are governed chiefly by the emotions, and this passage of time is recorded by the Heart Line. The third seven-year phase, lasting until the age of twenty-one, is governed chiefly by the physical sensations, and is recorded here by the Life Line. The fourth seven-year period of the first cycle, until the age of twenty-eight, is governed chiefly by the intellectual function, and in this system progress between these ages is recorded by the Head Line.

    Once you have passed the age of twenty-eight, and assuming the first cycle has been successfully completed and the psychological change-over accomplished without a hitch, the process starts over again. From twenty-eight to thirty-five, the chief function is instinct or intuition, to be recorded once again by the Line of Fate. From thirty-six to forty-two, the main function is emotional, to be recorded again

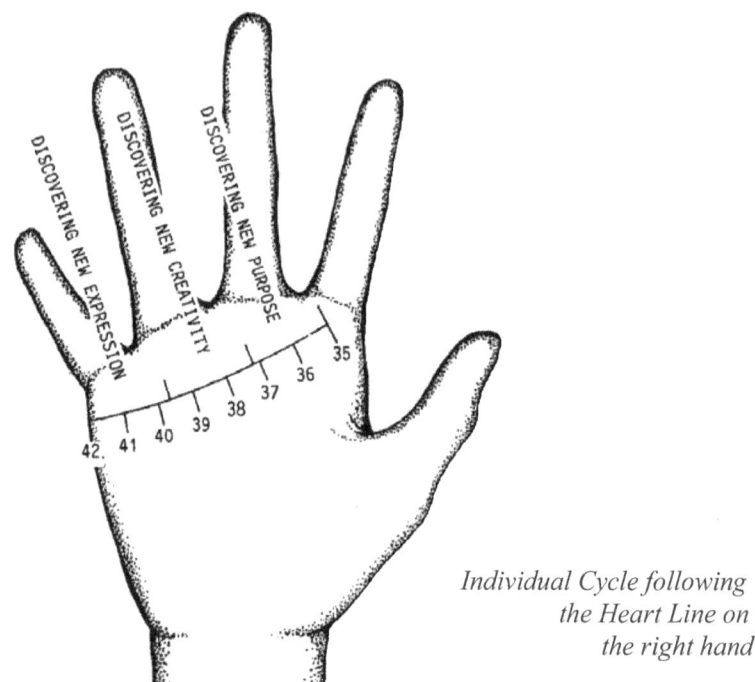

Individual Cycle following the Heart Line on the right hand

by the Heart Line. From then to forty-nine, the chief function being physical sensation, recording once more is done by the Life Line; and from the age of fifty to the completion of the second cycle at fifty-six, intellect is the main guiding principle, and this seven-year phase will be recorded once again by the Head Line.

When setting out to analyse the hand on the basis of the Grand Cycle, it is necessary to take each 'compartment of concern' in turn, beginning at the rising of the Line of Fate, which is equivalent to birth on the first cycle and to rebirth on a new and subsequent cycle. Psychologically, rebirth at the age of twenty-eight or fifty-six entails sudden freedom from the symbolic womb of becoming; freedom, often, from all-too-real stifling depression, a sense even of desolation. It may be experienced as a brilliant release into daylight from a dark period when everything has seemed pointless, purposeless and totally frustrating.

It is not merely an obscure, theoretical state of mind. The new cycle can commence with dramatic suddenness. Often enough it arrives as a sudden flash of new intuition, shedding old inhibitions and

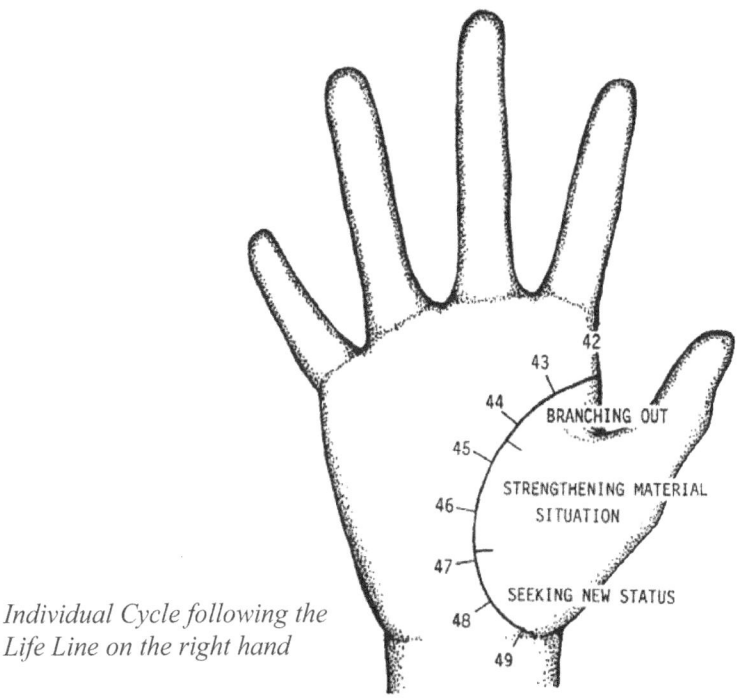

Individual Cycle following the Life Line on the right hand

setting the subject on a completely new path – a selfish path, it is true, in the sense that a new-born baby is selfish. But it is a path which makes full use of all the soul's contents, all individual experiences, and by that fact alone it implies the commencement of a process that works towards an eventual state of wholeness.

It sometimes happens that the Line of Fate rises within the encircling Life Line, on the Mount of Venus. In such a case on the second cycle, the Line of Fate carries extra significance when you are following this ancient method of understanding the human psyche. It means that the subject's sex impulses will be allowed to function freely, as never before, having escaped the 'womb of the past' – the hampering confines of parental rulings and even of conventional morality.

In simplistic terms, a man or woman 'of destiny' is liable to 'go off the rails' to some extent, soon after having passed the age of twenty-eight. But this type of behaviour, from the individual viewpoint, and in the long run, will be all to the good. If the Line of Fate merges with the Life Line and the two lines run together for a

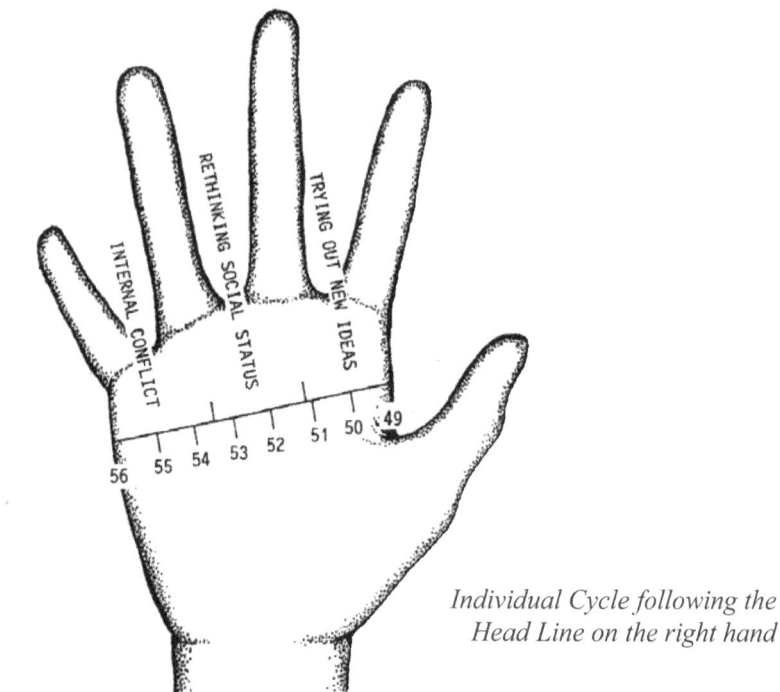

Individual Cycle following the Head Line on the right hand

short distance this will represent a period of recrimination, the accelerated karma of the past two years catching up with the subject, carrying the consequences of his or her uninhibited behaviour. As the Line of Fate separates itself from the Life Line and traces its upward course on the palm, the individual too will seek new horizons with mounting confidence. While still wholly freed from the old inhibitive restrictions, he or she should now have learned how to live with this new-found freedom and how to put it to good use in the world.

The person will feel an increasing sense of responsibility regarding ownership and family security, and will feel the need to put down new roots. Lines of Influence from the Mount of Venus will be significant at this time, representing his or her surviving ties with the parental home and memories of the past, no longer a hindrance. Ties from the Mount of the Moon will symbolize his or her new and growing relationships with the outside world in general, and in particular with individuals of the opposite sex. This is the time when the Line of Dominance, if the subject has one, will make its real-life meaning known.

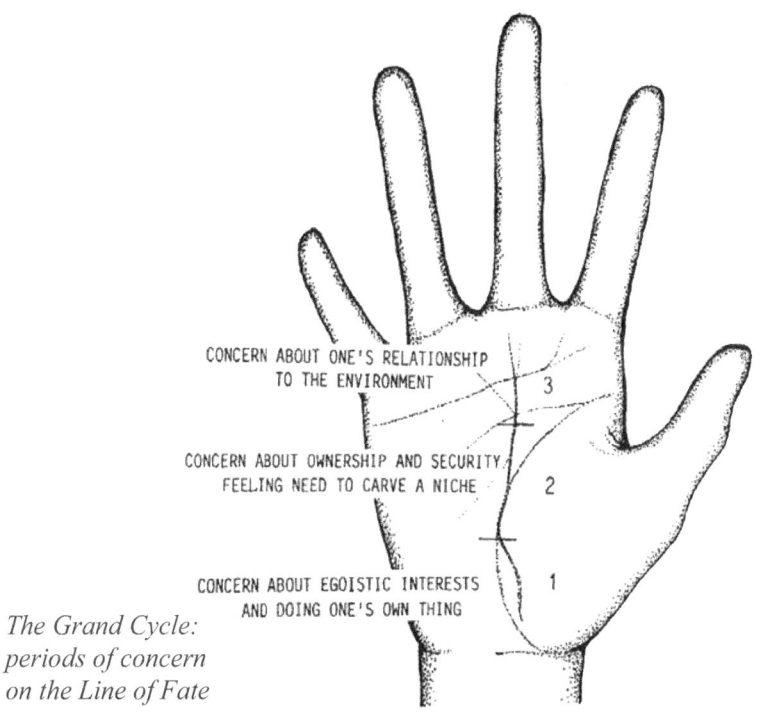

The Grand Cycle: periods of concern on the Line of Fate

Quite suddenly, the person's outlook will become less selfish, far less self-satisfied, and he or she will look beyond themselves and their physical needs to broader horizons. Now more than ever before he or she will feel concern about the environment in its broadest sense and will seek to start a new relationship with that wider, impersonal horizon.

As the cycle switches to the Heart Line, our subject's centre of gravity will have become more emotional, less intuitive. New affections will arise, new loving relationships that were never previously suspected. The actual rising point of the Heart Line will have particular significance at this time, with the division that it represents between Jupiter and Saturn. If there are tributary rising points there will be a corresponding sharing of the inner and outer needs of the world, dividing the responsibilities of life between soul and materiality, for both need their share of attention if a person is to become well balanced in the long-term.

Travelling now towards the cultural Mount of the Sun, the subject's concern will be the inner 'new person' fast developing within.

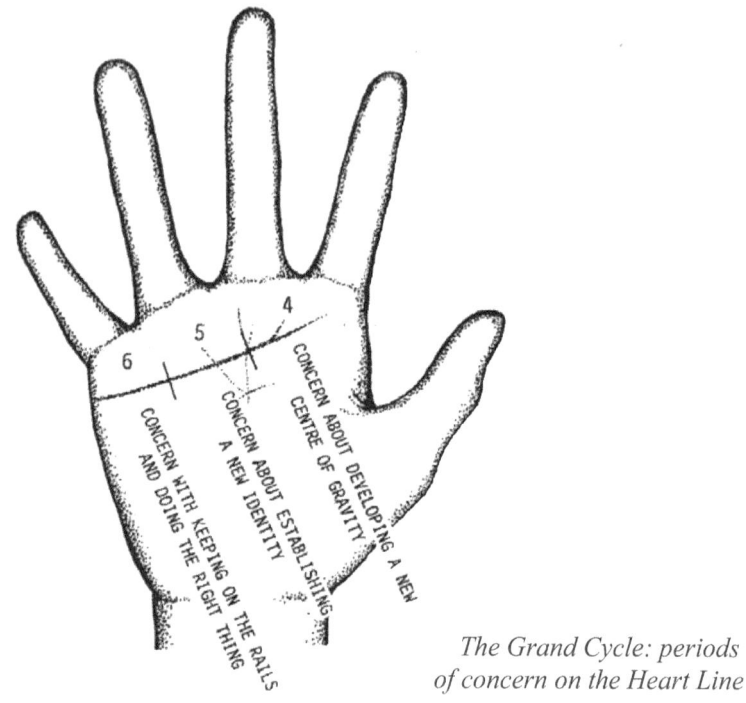

The Grand Cycle: periods of concern on the Heart Line

This is psychological change at depth; he or she will begin to sense a completely new cultural centre taking practical shape deep inside what can now be seen as the true self. As the Heart Line runs out at the edge of the palm, so will the current pattern of emotionally inspired life come to an end. The need for a complete change of milieu will become increasingly apparent, quite literally, as old securities lose their power of protection and take on instead a restrictive nature. At this point on the first cycle, the subject arrived at puberty. On this second, adult life cycle of individuality, the similarity is clear. The subject will look eagerly beyond their environment for new relationships, on a wider scale than before.

The person's course now is downwards along the Life Line, and the existence and extent of that line's tie at its rising with the Head Line is of deep significance. The subject has to break away from control by the minds of other people, and quite often will realize that, for the past few years, he or she has been used by these others, perhaps unwittingly, for their own purposes. The subject's new

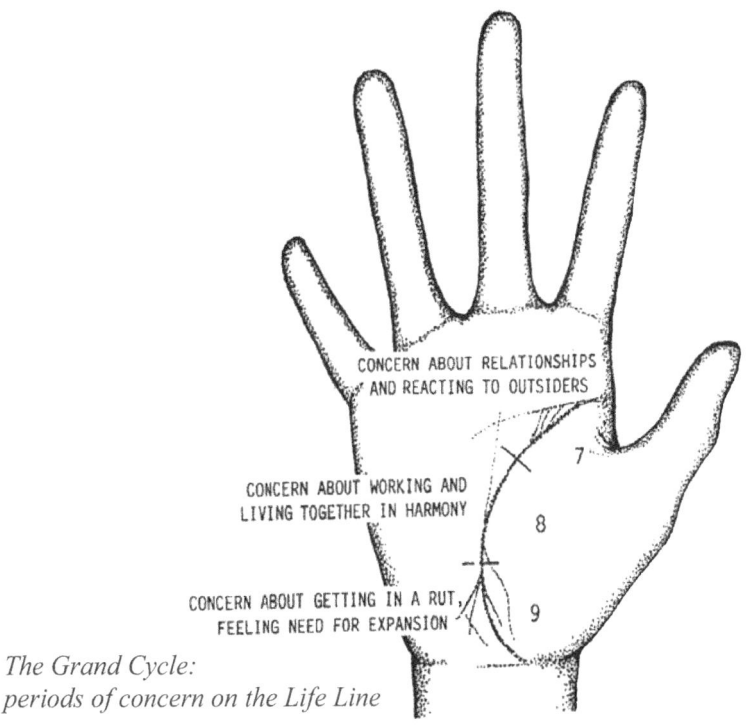

*The Grand Cycle:
periods of concern on the Life Line*

physically orientated independence will not now have a selfish nature; it will involve living and working with others in confident equality, in a completely new scale of harmony.

But seven years on, towards the end of the physically inspired career marked by the Life Line, the old familiar feeling of restriction will return. The subject's life will have been running smoothly for some time, but to what end? It seems to be getting nowhere. The Life Line itself is often fragmented at this low point, and this fragmentation symbolizes his or her feelings well, reaching this way and that for a new line, a new kind of future. The past seven years have been spent in vigorous style, stamina has seemed endless. But now he or she will feel the need for a more intellectual approach to life.

The subject's course now in the Grand Cycle has reached the rising point of the Head Line, and again, the possible initial tie between this and the Life Line will symbolize his or her struggles in breaking free from the physically orientated mode of living. The subject's concern now will the need to do something more important, more significant, more satisfying than their work in the

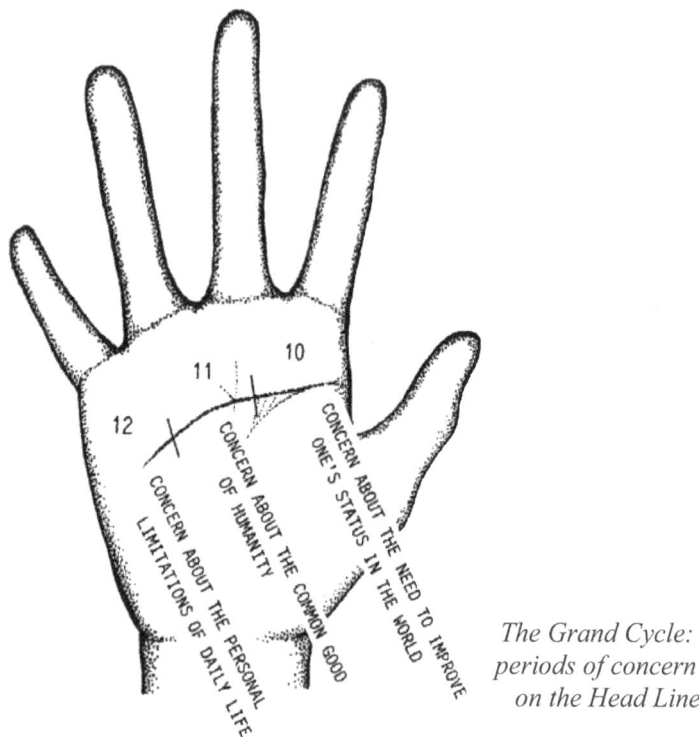

The Grand Cycle: periods of concern on the Head Line

past. On top of this is a growing awareness of far wider horizons, and the feeling of being drawn by fate towards the impersonal destiny of humanity as a whole – though he or she is unlikely to express it in such terms. The whole process will be taking place on the inner plane. It is not a particularly outgoing phase of the subject's life, but the inner attainments can be very real, able to have significant impact on the world.

      At last approaching the final phase, the final compartment of concern which will complete the current cycle, our subject is again fated to lose confidence in his or her ability to achieve, to become, to attain. The subject will sense the drawing to a close of the cycle and approaching symbolic death. The subject's mind at this stage may well be in a continual whirl, and he or she may find themselves unable to complete whatever intellectual projects they may have begun. Only now can we see the full significance of the Supernal Line, if the subject possesses one, or at least if he or she has the inner strength which that line represents. Having risen a few years earlier in the

Supernal Zone of the inner self, in the centre of his or her concern for the common good, it can now carry on towards a safe rebirth in the next cycle. As the Head Line itself fades out, as the mind declines, this Supernal Line symbolizes the inner momentum that will carry the soul across the final great divide.

ANCESTRAL, INDIVIDUAL AND COMMUNAL CYCLES

LINE OF FATE	HEART LINE	LIFE LINE	HEAD LINE
Intuition or instinct	*Feelings or emotions*	*Sensations or energy*	*Intellect or thoughts*
age 0-7 Birth Freedom from the womb Developing selfhood	age 7-14 Selfish expression Growth of ego	age 14-21 Practical expression Adjusting to the world	age 21-28 Mental expression Beset with limitations
age 28-35 First rebirth Freedom from moral restrictions Building for the present	age 35-42 New emotional guidance Concept of a new identity	age 42-49 New practical energetic guidance Turning point in career	age 49-56 New intellectual guidance Increasing power of reason
age 56-63 Second rebirth Freedom from mental limitations Building for the future	age 63-70 Heightened emotional awareness Orientated towards immortality or death	age 70-77 New physical outlook Disruption bringing new rhythms and broader horizons	age 77-84 New intellectual strength Change of understanding Growth of serenity

39 Giving a Reading : Basic Principles; Permanent Impressions

IF YOU ARE A NEWCOMER to the art of palmistry and have read thus far, now is a good time to recap the basic principles involved. Once you have learned to associate the mounts with their traditional meanings, and the major character lines with the functions they represent, you will automatically be able to relate a person's history with all the various human activities, instincts and impulses, and see in which direction the fates seem to be leading – where the strengths lie and where the weaknesses.

You will have learned to associate a fork, a break or a sudden change of direction in one of the lines with a dividing of the ways or an interruption to the flow of that function. The time of change, you will have seen, can often be pinned down – at least within a year or two. Although it is not the usual practice to count a person's years with a time-scale plotted along the Head Line or the Heart Line (unless you are studying the Grand Cycle), wherever a distinctive warning mark occurs along one of these lines some indication of its owner's age at the time of impact can usually be gained by noting the point at which it is crossed by the Line of Fate.

This is not a very exact method of timing, because the mounts beneath which the lines pass will 'exert their influence' at any or all ages in the subject's lifetime, and they are, of course, distributed above the full length of both these lines. But if you are looking for 'destiny' rather than mere 'fate', any break or fork that occurs to the right of this crossing point will refer to the first half of a person's life. To the left of the Line of Fate, these lines trace the second half of a person's life. The Line of Fate is considered to touch the Head Line at its owner's thirty-fifth year. If the Head Line should fork at exactly this point, for instance, it means that the age of thirty-five – a highly significant age in anybody's life – will bring with it a new way of thinking, a new sort of career, a new inner orientation. Another method is to note any tie lines that reach the Head or Heart Lines from the Life Line or the Lines of Fate or Fortune, and apply the timescales from these lines.

When there is a strong fork in the Head Line, you can take it that half the subject's mind will be pursuing a no-nonsense business-like course, straight across the palm to the zones of tenacity and

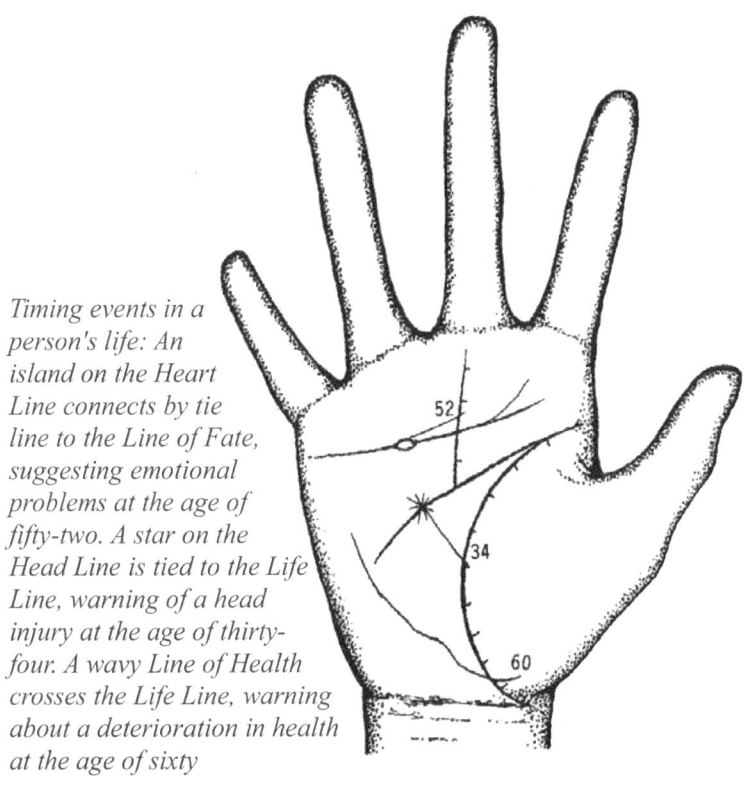

Timing events in a person's life: An island on the Heart Line connects by tie line to the Line of Fate, suggesting emotional problems at the age of fifty-two. A star on the Head Line is tied to the Life Line, warning of a head injury at the age of thirty-four. A wavy Line of Health crosses the Life Line, warning about a deterioration in health at the age of sixty

communication. The other half, however, will probably be relaxing in an easy-going, imaginative curve, down towards the Mount of the Moon. Or one of the prongs may lead to the Upper Mount of Mars, the seat of tenacity, while the other rises slightly to approach the Heart Line. This will suggest a tendency towards extreme views and a stubborn outlook on life.

If one prong is much stronger than the other, and particularly if one grows in strength while the other gradually fades out, the stronger tendency will seem to take over that person's life. Any line that grows in strength and deepness means that the function it represents will strengthen itself as the person grows older. Similarly, a line that fades towards its end means that this particular area of activity tends to weaken with age.

Small forks at the end of a line do suggest a certain dissipation or dilution of that line's function. But large forks are not necessarily divisive; they don't necessarily weaken the function. A long Heart Line that curves upwards and a long Head Line that curves downwards are in some ways similar. They both show less-than-logical tendencies that could well appear sentimental and unbusinesslike. A fork in a Head Line or Heart Line of this type, carrying either the intellectual or the emotional function straight across the palm, can represent a powerful influence towards prudence and common sense, serving to keep that person's feet firmly on the ground.

It is only in cases where a downwards-curving and an upwards-curving prong are equally strong that people will seem to be torn between two opposing tendencies. They may be indecisive characters, with a touch of 'anxiety neurosis'. Or they may make good decisions, only to lack the determination to carry their ideas through. Their will to succeed in any undertaking will tend to be distracted, so that their best plans all end in daydreams.

Never forget to check both hands. The left hand of inheritance often gives important clues to the meaning of forks, breaks and changes of direction. You can get the picture of a natural break away from parental influence and the gradual growth of independence. And it is always useful to be able to blame your ancestors for your own shortcomings!

Once you have this background picture, fortified with what you have gleaned from the size and shape of the hands, fingers and thumbs, you can start giving meaning to all the signs and portents regarding luck, love, money, travel, partnerships, special interests and so on. When giving a reading, make sure you are in a relaxed frame of mind and feeling pleasantly disposed towards your client. If you are both relaxed and at peace, with no negative vibrations in the air, you will start to 'feel' all sorts of information about the other person. When anxieties have gone, inner contents can flow freely, intuition will really work, and you as a palmist will gain an amazing insight into your client's general personality, past experiences, health, hopes and fears, and give a really rewarding reading. But let your subject chat freely if he or she wants to; listen to everything being said and take an interest. It will help the session along.

As people get older, the skin of their hands often becomes rather dry and wrinkled, sometimes concealing the true lines and marks of the palm. Hold your client's hand and gently smooth the palm out, this way and that, with your thumb. Your other hand will be holding a large magnifying glass. Even if your eyesight is young and keen and you don't need it, it will help to give the impression that you know what you are looking for!

As has been mentioned from time to time, lines and marks can appear or disappear at some definite stage during the subject's life; they are not all present at birth, or at death. For instance, a Line of Health may well make its appearance during the subject's sixties and early seventies – sometimes earlier, if there happens to be an alteration and particularly a deterioration in health. Minor marks and link lines often fade out and disappear. Take special note of particularly deeply marked features, especially lines which deepen and strengthen as they follow their own course. These represent the function that will sustain a person into old age.

Make an estimate of the subject's age (unless, of course, they want to tell you their actual age) and remember that, as a rule, the lines which carry a timescale 'run out' at the age of seventy. If your subject is elderly, it will be mainly a matter of concentrating on what 'you did' rather than what 'you are going to do'. Occasionally the Life Line carries on beyond its normal finishing point at the Rascette and continues around the wrist, or curves towards the thumb, climbing back up the Mount of Venus. This is an excellent point of discussion, indicating a long and meaningful life ahead; but, as I have already stressed, never feel tempted to foretell an age of death. Better to say 'It goes on for ages yet.'

So, if the subject is obviously 'past seventy', there is really very little point in ascertaining his or her exact age with regard to predictions for the future; but a point of reference is still needed in order to establish the past timescales of the Life Line and the Line of Fate. It often happens that elderly subjects are eager to tell the palmist (and anyone else who is interested) their age and past history, and this, of course, makes the reading a great deal easier for the palmist. The alternative is to identify and isolate some outstanding event in the person's life and tie it to their age at the time.

If you can do this, and obtain the subject's agreement about their age and the year concerned, it is sometimes safest for the sake of good relations to refer to the year only: so, for example, you can say, 'And then, in about 1987 ...' Because people so often *are* touchy about having their age known and spoken aloud, this is a time when you need to tread carefully. But as the year seldom causes offence, no one can object to you mentioning it (provided it is not too early in the subject's life). It is all a matter of pride, of course. Almost invariably there comes a time in such a person's life when a certain line is crossed, a barrier breached, and from then on it is a point of pride for them to proclaim their impressive age: 'Of course, I'm ninety-two, you know!' It pays to discover tactfully which category your client currently belongs to and play along.

Many palmists ascribe meaning to the sometimes numerous minor lines which are often to be seen running up the fingers. They have been described as lines of 'electric energy' or, more frequently, as 'tired lines', indicating that the subject has been overdoing things and should be advised to rest or take a holiday. As often as not, however, these lines are simply creases caused by a dry skin and they cannot be given any better interpretation than that. Some people have dry skin to such an extent that the lines of their hands actually crack – a painful condition. Characteristics such as these are really beyond the province of palmistry, unless you want to recommend an appropriate hand-cream!

In certain circumstances it can be a good idea to take an impression of your subject's hand, to be studied at leisure. This is where the photocopier can prove a real boon. Hold the subject's hand firmly on to the glass, pressing gently so that the centre of the palm touches evenly, otherwise this most important area will 'blank out'. You may need several goes before you get it right. Lacking a photocopier, you can follow the police fingerprinting procedure, modified to suit our needs: using a washable endorsing ink applied evenly to the palm, fingers and wrist (removing surplus ink with a tissue) press the hand firmly on to a sheet of paper. A pad of sponge rubber or something similar beneath the paper is helpful. Again, apply pressure to the back and sides of the hand and the base of the fingers, so as to include any hollow spots. The imprint may turn out a little 'squashy' at the edges and this needs to be taken into account when assessing the cheirotype.

Of course, if you are technically orientated, you may be able to reject these 'Stone Age' methods and use the technique of digital photography instead. You can then store perfect colour images on your computer, which you can study at leisure. A print-out of the client's hands with a full written report will be greatly valued and have lasting interest as a keepsake.

Finally, practise reading hands upside-down, as you would see them when sitting opposite somebody at a small table. This arrangement helps the session go smoothly and ensures a more professional job. If you rely on sitting very close, side by side, to see the hands as you are used to seeing your own, you are in danger of

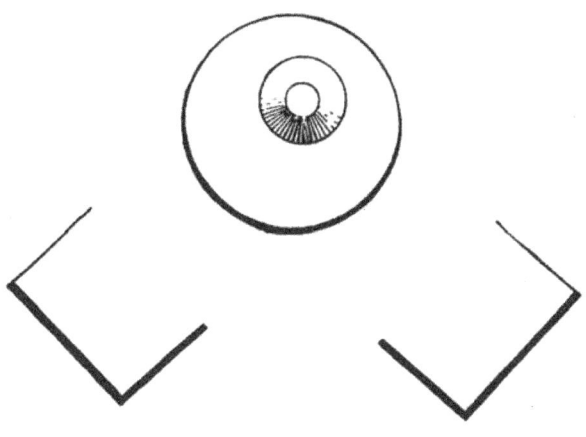

A harmonious seating arrangement

invading your prospective client's 'privacy zone'. If he or she is at all a private person, you can wave goodbye to any intuitional rapport you may have hoped to establish. The subject will be unable to relax and negative feelings will predominate. Even sitting directly opposite to someone can seem confrontational and vaguely threatening. Try to strike the happy medium: take your seat and allow your client to move the other chair to the position in which he or she feels most at ease.

When learning palmistry, you need to be able to relate the various features to your own hand, and for this reason all the diagrams in this book show the hand as you are used to seeing it. But when studying these diagrams, turn the book round and get used to seeing the features of the hand from another viewpoint.

40 Practical Analysis : Outward and Inward Events

THE FIRST SUBJECT, Joan, is an elderly lady who, though frail with age, is plainly healthy and happy, with a keen brain. She has retained a great interest in everything that goes on and there is obviously none of that sad withdrawal into private memories that does so often characterize old age. This type of assessment, and the degree of confidence, an aura of inner serenity and general sharpness of mind (not to be confused with clarity of hearing, for deafness can often give the impression of loss of interest in the world around), all this can be defined instantly through general observation. But it also goes to form a very important part of the 'reading'.

Elderly subjects, though not necessarily easier to analyse, make better samples for analysis than young ones. In the case of a young person having his or her hand read, of course, there is no way that predictions can be verified; it is a case of 'wait and see'. In the case of an older person, all these occurrences which can only be surmised from a study of the hands can actually be confirmed (or denied) by the subject's memory.

RAY: You obviously have a beautifully calm temperament. Even as a child, you seldom lost your temper and never got the sulks. I can see a lot of love in your early childhood. Your life started off on a sound basis; you had a very happy and secure family background. You never had to go without, either affection or material things. But you did suffer a great loss which affected you very deeply, when you were about twelve. The death of a parent?
JOAN: Yes, my father died when I was twelve.
RAY: It certainly did affect your emotional life, quite apart from the obvious sadness of it. I think you disliked people feeling sorry for you, and for a few years after your loss you did have this feeling that people were feeling sorry for you, and this made you feel isolated and not very happy. But you soon got over that phase in your teens, when you became more independent. As a young woman you used to enjoy going out and having a good time, but you never overdid it. Not like some of your friends! You enjoyed yourself with moderation. But then, of course, you met a young man and settled into a steady relationship. No... I think there were

two young men, weren't there? Your first love was very attractive and attentive, but he wasn't really responsible enough for a long-term commitment. You married the *second* young man in your life. Your marriage was very successful in material terms, and almost always happy. You were well matched. But you still remember your first love with affection ...?

(Joan smiled and nodded as the memories came flooding back)

Of course, your marriage has had its ups and downs. What marriage doesn't? But you have never regretted your choice.

JOAN: Yes, Keith was a good friend, but I never regretted marrying Peter. We were very happy together.

RAY: And, of course, it was a great blow for you when you lost him – quite recently, about five years ago?

JOAN: Just six years ago now.

RAY: Yes. You didn't keep in touch with Keith, of course?

JOAN: Oh no, I made a clean break when I married Pete.

RAY: Well, it's just a feeling, but Keith could be unattached himself now, and I'm sure his memories of you will be just as fond as yours are of him. He will be more responsible now that he's older! I can see a lot of happiness and romance for you in the years ahead. You have plenty of time to run yet, so you might think of contacting him.

JOAN: I could try ...

RAY: I'm looking for Child Lines now and I shall need the magnifier.

JOAN: There should be some!

RAY: Ah yes, one ... two ... three ... four ... five, I think. Four quite close together and the last one some distance away – a latecomer, perhaps?

JOAN: Yes; Frank came as a complete surprise. *(She lowered her voice and glanced at the door.)* I thought we had finished with all that ten years before he arrived!

RAY: Is that Frank waiting for you outside – the young man who was with you when you arrived?

JOAN: Now, how did you know that?

RAY: Sheer guesswork!

JOAN: Well, you are quite right. Of course, he's forty-eight now – a lot younger than the others.

Joan then started talking about her children and their own familes, and their various occupations and talents and characters, all of which told me a great deal more about Joan herself – information which, of course, helped me to give a satisfyingly full reading.

The second subject is male and in his sixties, his cheirotype on the practical side of the normal range. Looped fingerprints and flexible thumbs indicate versatility and a tolerant, adaptable nature. His Mercury finger tends to separate itself more widely than the others, suggesting that here is an independent sort of person with a dislike for convention. The palms display an intricate network of fine lines in addition to the three major ones. The Lines of Fate and Fortune are present but not very clearly marked, and that fact in itself is very significant. A well-developed Mount of Venus shows a great capacity for sensuality, and the lower part of the Mount of the Moon has a certain prominent fleshiness which suggests a proclivity for things mystical or spiritual. In this respect, one of the first things to strike me was the Grand Cross on the right hand.

I noticed too that the lines of the right hand are clearer and more deeply marked than those of the left. To me this indicates an individual who has left his inheritance behind – who has long since moulded his innate characteristics to fit an independent lifestyle. The Grand Cycle, in other words, is very much in operation. It is difficult to analyse hands such as these in the ordinary, practical, material way. Everything seems to be pointing towards the mystical explanation. Besides the Grand Cross, I noted the Line of Sympathy and the Supernal Line, all these in the right hand of the Soul Cycle. Everything so far points to a highly complex and, judging by the plethora of fine lines, probably a somewhat temperamental character.

Complicated hands like these are a challenge to palmistry skills. As they contain many of the minor lines and signs described in previous chapters, they offer useful diagnostic practice. This subject is obviously one of those soul-orientated people whose life seems to be governed by the spiritual and who is, as is usual with such people, somewhat isolated and highly enigmatic. It is probably normal for him to experience inner upheavals from time to time, particularly at seven-year intervals. What follows is my practical analysis recorded during a session with the subject, whom we shall refer to here as Martin.

RAY: First of all, I am struck by the process of development to be read across your two hands, from left to right. Your left hand shows a strong fork from the Head Line, carrying it across the palm to meet the Heart Line beneath the Mount of Mercury. The Heart Line then carries on to the percussion – to the edge of the palm – and even partly curves round it. It's obvious that you have inherited a compassionate nature, and as a basic function your emotions are more powerful than your thoughts – though, needless to say, your brains are pretty efficient too! Now, on your right hand, the situation is completely changed. You have left your inheritance behind...

MARTIN: I remember that my father had this fork from the Head Line to the Heart Line, but in his *right* hand.

RAY: That is exactly what I would expect. On *your* right hand the fork has become independent and separated from the Heart Line. But first, I have to say something about the Heart Line. On your left hand again, you have the Upper Girdle of Venus – both the open and the closed versions. The closed Girdle, which passes between the Sun and the Mercury fingers, encloses what is known as the area of 'conscious occurrence'. This implies that all those deep karmic influences that are vibrating through the hand, flowing from the undercurrent of life at the wrist – all these will have been felt by you fairly strongly since your childhood days, even though you may not have realized it. Now, your open version of the Girdle, curving around the edge of the palm beneath the Mercury finger, surrounds the area which relates to communication and compassion. In itself it almost amounts to a fork in the Heart Line. In your right hand, the closed version of the Girdle is still faintly visible. But the course of the open Girdle has been adopted by the Heart Line itself, taking over its function. Your right-handed Heart Line now curves *above* your Marriage Lines, as though to seal them in. This is a special area of communication and you have an emotional barrier over it. I'll bet you're not married, are you?

MARTIN: No.

RAY: Karmic causes can be very complex, and your hand is very complex indeed. But this unusual formation of the Heart Line is certainly the outward sign of rather chaotic personal emotions. It means that you brood. It is as though the past never really weakens its hold. You do tend to dwell on the past, don't you?

MARTIN: I suppose I do.

RAY: And, talking about chaotic emotions, there is an overlapping break in your left-handed Heart Line beneath the Mount of the Sun. This represents quite a lengthy period of emotional disturbance of some kind, an inner wrestling match with yourself – uncertainty, depression. There is a tie line to this break running from the Line of Fate. It was during your twenties – twenty-five, twenty-six, twenty-seven?

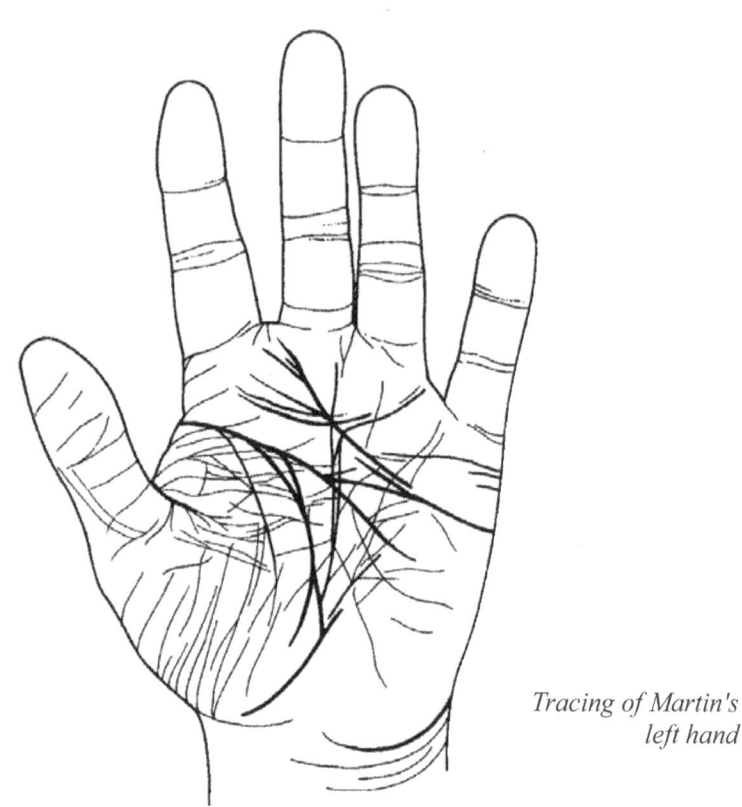

Tracing of Martin's left hand

MARTIN: Absolutely right. Those were the worst years of my life, psychologically speaking. Idyllic conditions outside; chaos inside!

RAY: I just have to give a spiritual bias to this analysis. To come back to the right hand, not many people can separate the ordinary emotional feelings from the deeper feelings that are inspired by the soul – the inner feelings. Nobody can make the distinction unless the emotions themselves cease to flow. But in your case, the added fact that this Girdle of Venus-track Heart Line rises only partially on the Mount of Jupiter (which is the motte and bailey of the soul), and partly between the mounts, makes me fairly certain that it's not the pursuit of worldly ambitions that flows along your Heart Line. It's a flood of *inner* feelings. And so, in your right hand, it comes as no surprise to find that the Marriage Lines have been over-ruled or superseded by the Heart Line. Let's have a look at these Marriage Lines

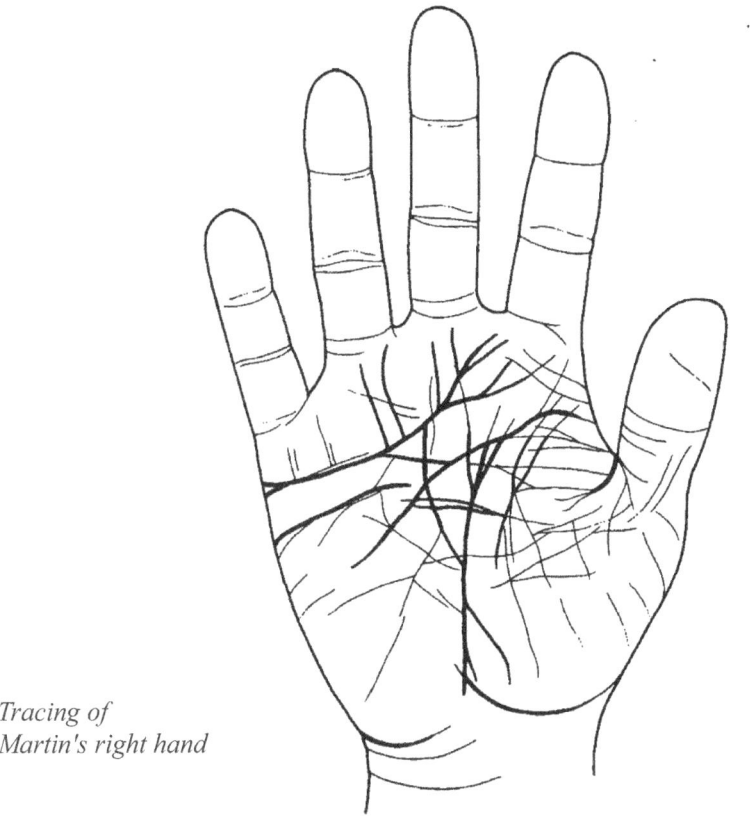

*Tracing of
Martin's right hand*

more closely. These three small lines on the edge of the palm are clearly defined and show three distinct periods of 'attachment'. The first can be placed in the late teens, the second around the age of thirty, the third a little later, but still in the fairly early thirties. The final line is clearly the strongest – the longest-lasting in effect. Does this make sense?

MARTIN: Yes, absolutely.

RAY: Well, now, in the left hand they are still in their proper place, above the Heart Line. But in the right hand, the last two at least of these lines make their appearance parallel with those on the left hand, but this time *below* the Heart Line. The first teenage attachment does not appear on the right, and to me this implies that the switch-over from the left-handed to the right-handed course must have taken place after your teens, and most likely during the

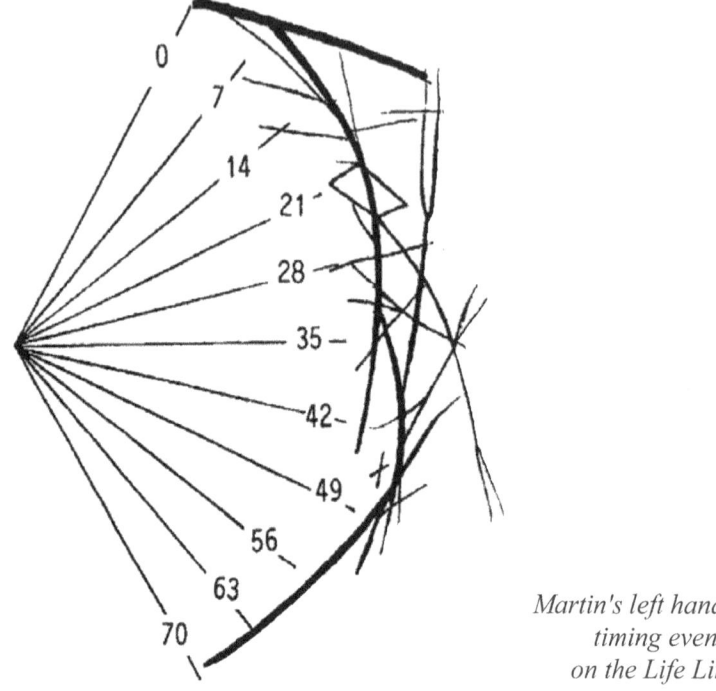

Martin's left hand: timing events on the Life Line

late twenties. It was probably a deeply emotional period of your life: a shedding of the old and a welcoming in of the new. Does that ring a bell?

MARTIN: It certainly does. I remember it very well. In fact I think I remember the exact moment.

RAY: And, of course, they do refer to attachments, despite their popular name of Marriage Lines. There is another traditional meaning given to a Heart Line that curves up strongly beneath the little finger – it implies an interest in the 'inner life', a familiarity with occult realms, or even the truly spiritual dimension. Now to return to the right-handed Head Line, the major fork to the Heart Line as seen in the left hand has become detached – separated from the Heart Line. In fact, it is no longer really a fork at all, though at first glance it looks like one. It has formed a new line of its own, which we call the Supernal Line. Its rising is entirely separate from the Head Line itself, if you look closely, and this point of origin is

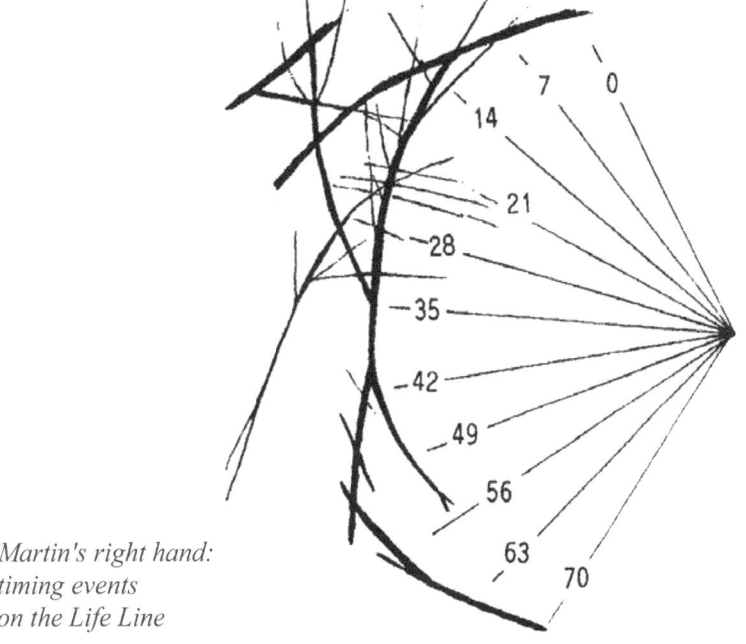

Martin's right hand: timing events on the Life Line

associated with a very distinct Grand Cross. This strengthens what I have said about familiarity with the dimension of spirituality – of mysticism. I shall come back to this in a minute. First, let's find the material base for your life. I can see that you were well used to heavy manual work earlier in your life. You have an Inner Life Line which extends to about your fiftieth year. Up to then I guess you had pretty well boundless energy?

MARTIN: I certainly did. When I was about forty-nine I finished with the heavy work and concentrated on more intellectual stuff. I have been pretty well sedentary since then.

RAY: And this was not just physical energy. There is a tremendous sense of nervous energy in your hands, not least because there are so many minor lines all over the place – it makes your hands very difficult to read!

MARTIN: I'm sorry about that!

RAY: Now, on your left hand again, I'll have a look at your Lines of Travel. You seem to have had a substantial journey just before your twenty-first year – about eighteen or nineteen?

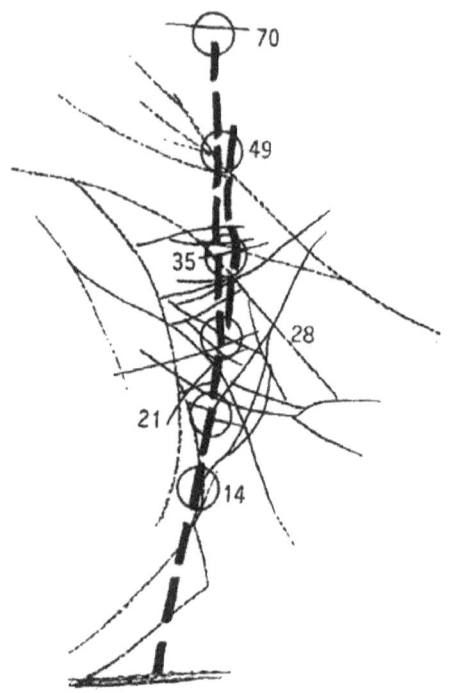

Martin's left hand: timing events on the Line of Fate

MARTIN: Yes. I went abroad in the army.

RAY: And around twenty-three there was another and much more significant journey?

MARTIN: Yes. That's when I went to live abroad.

RAY: Good, then the timescale is probably about right. Now, at twenty-eight, there is a back-link with that Travel Line. Is that when you came back to this country?

MARTIN: Yes, I did, but only for a few months. Then I went abroad again.

RAY: And there is another return a couple of years later, when you were about thirty.

MARTIN: Yes, I came back then for good.

RAY: Your left-handed Life Line changes course soon after that point, so it all seems to have been inevitable and preordained. A major change of lifestyle at about thirty-four – a new job, perhaps?

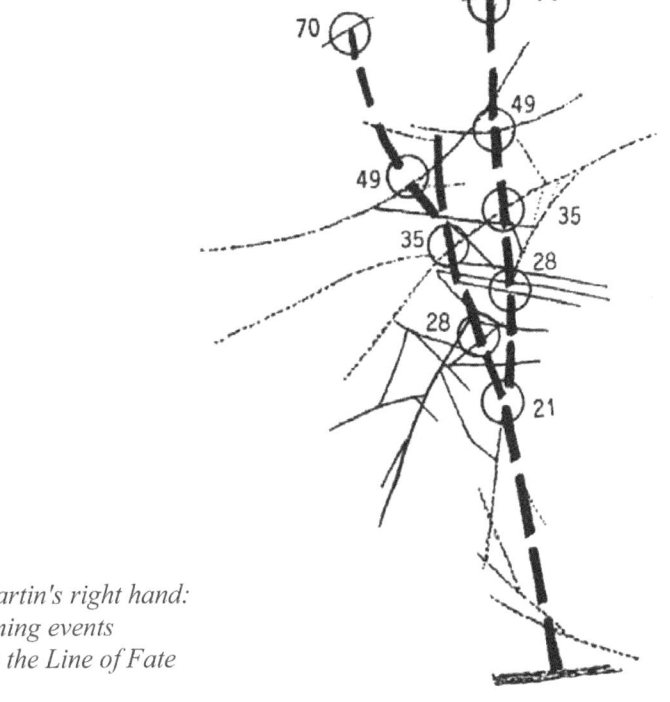

Martin's right hand: timing events on the Line of Fate

MARTIN: A new occupation altogether. A completely different lifestyle

RAY: And possibly another change of course – or change of lifestyle – seven or eight years later. This fork of the Life Line has its origin in the Mount of the Moon, so it would involve other people rather than family?

MARTIN: Yes. I moved to a different part of the country and became self-employed, and started employing others for the first time.

RAY: Looking at your left hand again, corresponding with about the age of twenty-eight on your Line of Fate, I see there is a cross, followed by a double section of the line which goes on and on. I don't want to pry, but to me this implies some sort of threat to your reputation, followed by a sort of double life – some part of your life, perhaps, that you would want to keep from your family, if not from the rest of the world. Is that a fair assessment?

MARTIN: Absolutely true, I'm afraid.
RAY: And you wouldn't care to fill in the details?
MARTIN: Absolutely right again!
RAY: OK, we'll drop the subject. But don't forget that your left hand shows the inherited side of your nature, so all this was really cut-and-dried before it happened. Now, let's move on to your right hand. That should show events from a more spiritual angle – the deeper meanings. The Life Line changes course at around the age of forty-two – that fits in with your new-found independence, self-employment. And another major change of course at around fifty-two or fifty-three.
MARTIN: Yes, that fits. I had a major reorientation within the spiritual brotherhood I belong to.
RAY: Now, your Line of Fate. Actually, there are two courses here – you can take either to represent the Line of Fate, and I think they are both applicable, or you can say that one is the true Line of Fate, the other a variation of the Line of Fortune. I shall work out a timescale for both and read them together. There is a major Line of Influence with a couple of prongs, each approaching the Line of Fate – at the ages of thirty and thirty-four, or thereabouts. That corresponds pretty well with your Marriage Lines – or perhaps now I should call them Lines of Affection. The first is the deepest – someone you remember with fondness? But the second is the most enduring, I would say. But no marriage, of course.
MARTIN: Exactly as you say. G– had a big effect on me when I was thirty; but I met D– when I was about thirty-four, and we are still the best of friends.
RAY: In fact, there is another minor prong between the other two which does not actually touch the Line of Fate itself. This minor prong is itself forked more than once, so it represents several people. I don't suppose they were very important to you. Above that, you have three cross-links which rise between the Mount of Venus and Lower Mars, running as far as the Head Line. They cross your 'new' Line of Fate at about the twenty-eight year mark and your 'old' Line of Fate a few years later, in your thirties. This looks to me like a new form of energy coming into your life – a sort of aggression or self-confidence. Did you go through a particularly outgoing phase of your life around that time?
MARTIN: Yes, I certainly did. Those were the most self-confident, uninhibited years of my life, from twenty-eight to thirty-five.
RAY: And I notice that the Lower Mount of Mars on both your hands

bears a cross. This points to some kind of physical risk through obstinacy or indiscretion. I would guess those were your indiscreet years too? But don't say anything about that now, because all this was leading you to the most remarkable features in your right hand – the Grand Cross and the Supernal Line. They both rise as you become thirty-five and cancel out a host of indiscretions. I imagine you know exactly what they imply.

MARTIN: This is related to the spiritual brotherhood I mentioned just now. I joined at thirty-five. This was the start of reality for me – the most incredible experiences.

RAY: You have a large and very pronounced cross on the Mount of the Moon – on both hands – and a good selection of stars there as well. Traditionally, this would be taken to mean indiscreet travel involving a risk of death by drowning. I don't mind telling you this because it is not to be taken literally. The water in this case is the emotional flood or tide of sexual feelings, and this is where the element of danger for you personally has always arisen. Does that ring a bell?

MARTIN: Well, I see that's how it is. Some while back I had a vivid dream: I was standing near the beach when an enormous tidal wave came sweeping in – a wall of water hundreds of feet high – demolishing everything in its path. There was nothing I could do about it. Then the wave broke over me and passed on, leaving me unscathed and not even wet. I woke feeling very relieved!

RAY: Well, there you are. That is the nature of your Moon Cross and the stars. Your hands are more symbolic than most. You have to experience these things but, as I see it, you will win through in the end. Your Line of fate ceased to be divided from the age of forty-nine or so. From then on your fate has been running more and more clearly for you. You are single-minded now and achieving solid things for the future.

MARTIN: So I am, and thank you for your analysis.

41 Quick Character Sketches:
Distinctive Types

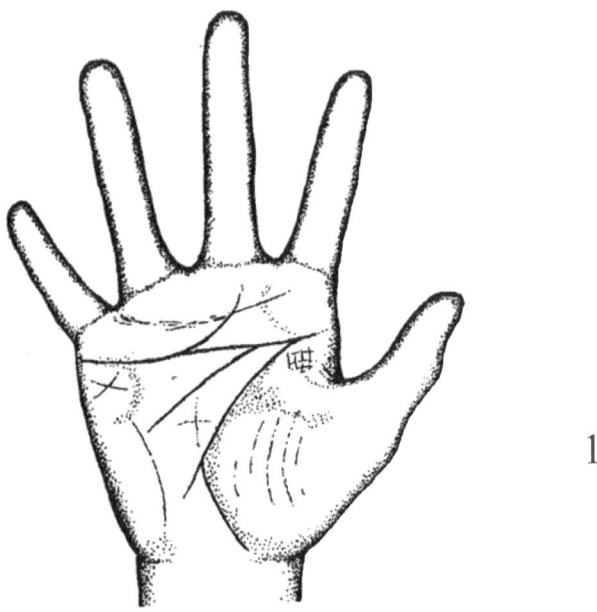

1

This is a somewhat strange and rather moody character who can be extremely emotional when others are being logical. There is tremendous depth of emotion and a keen capacity for affection, but it is not shown freely to just anyone. The emotions do not entirely overrule the intellect, however, and this person's mind is very perceptive and penetrating. His value judgement is sound. It would be easy to receive the impression that here is an irreligious and somewhat coarse person. In a sense this is true, but the 'irreligion' stems from an understanding of what lies at the root of religious impulses and the 'coarseness' comes from awareness of the continual undercurrent of sexual desires that are common to everyone but not always acknowledged. Not a particularly outgoing personality, but one who is always happy to meet new people and begin new relationships. This person can be very impatient at times and sometimes bad-tempered, but only for a short while. Enjoys travel with constant changes of scene.

2

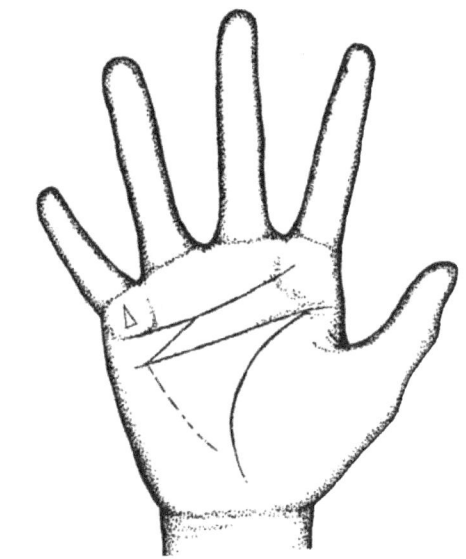

First impressions on seeing this hand are: here is a quiet, gentle person who is always striving to attain perfection. Highly intelligent, this person is probably well at home with the most complex of problems. The intellect, 'thinking', is far and away the most important psychological function, and it invariably overrules the emotional feelings. We get the impression of a sense of superiority over others less intellectually inclined; palmists are well used to being patronized by intellectuals who probably classify their art as 'mumbo-jumbo'! But there is an undercurrent of kindness here too, and this is plainly a person who likes to be friendly. This combination of characteristics add up to rather lonely person. If we see emotion in others as a sign of weakness, and neglect our own function of feeling, we tend to become isolated. Like all isolated people, this subject would agree that a degree of suffering is inescapable when experiencing the ups and downs of life: he is rather prone to illness, probably associated in particular with the liver. Suffering here is borne stoically; the bodily functions and physical symptoms tend to be pushed into the background of awareness. This is a person who depends for success on his own abilities rather than seeking the support of society in general. The hand shows great qualities of leadership and analytical skills, but they are unlikely to come fully to fruition because potentially influential people may feel that they are not required to help.

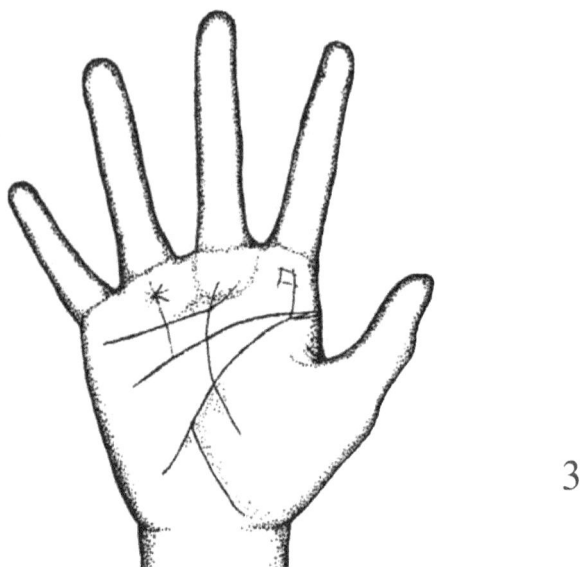

3

Examining this hand, we could say that here is a particularly stable personality who is unlikely to go off the rails. Eminently sociable and outgoing, but not necessarily friendly with all and sundry, we can see quite clearly a wise ability to discriminate and select only what is useful, whether these be opportunities, things, friends or partners. There is a tremendous appetite for living, and a powerful instinct for fair play. This person may seem in some people's eyes to be selfish or self-centred, but he is unlikely to take any unfair advantage of anyone. This is a person destined to succeed, a person who sees life as a series of steps to be climbed to reach the top, and every effort will be made to climb as high as possible. Many people would see this characteristic as a materialistic and somewhat selfish one, but he is unlikely to tolerate any injustices, and will go out of his way to lend a helping hand if he considers it is really needed and deserved. This wholehearted leap into life will be tempered by common sense; he is unlikely to give way to irrational impulses and will remain true to the ideals acquired during his upbringing. Petty, transitory pleasures will tend to be rejected, and everything profitless will soon be discarded. Periodically, this subject will stop and take stock of his life so far: everything will be open to inspection. He will not go along with the mob, nor will he let his standards drop. He seems destined to go far, carving a niche in the fields of business and society.

4

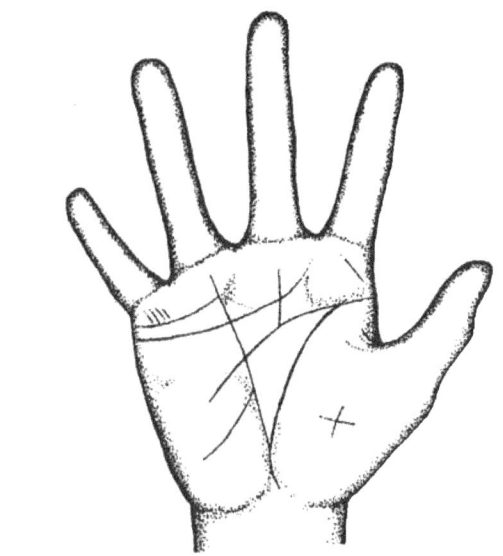

Here is the hand of one of whom we could say, 'still waters run deep' – a quiet person with powerful emotions. But being orientated towards the principle of privacy, this trait is not usually noticed by others. A complicated person, therefore, who dislikes displaying those emotions in public. One of the 'purest' of people, we would say, as near as one is likely to get to the truly 'pure in heart'. This person can act impulsively at times, but the brain is very active as well as the emotions, and decisions are usually made with great care. Kind and gentle, one who genuinely feels that selfless giving is more important in the long-term than material advantage. Those with whom this person comes into contact are likely to sense that here is a 'good' person, one who will prove a valuable friend in times of trouble. We get the impression that during this person's youth there was a dedicated interest in material and social considerations, perhaps political conviction. But in later life something like spirituality grew out of these emotions as awareness of the abstract nature of life grew with maturity. Marriage will be considered as much a spiritual obligation as a practical, domestic arrangement, though these ideas are unlikely to be expressed openly. The sexual experience too is likely to be taken as a spiritual rather than merely a physical one. Tedious routine for this person is to be avoided, and finding the right occupation will be all-important. One of the caring professions will seem the best choice.

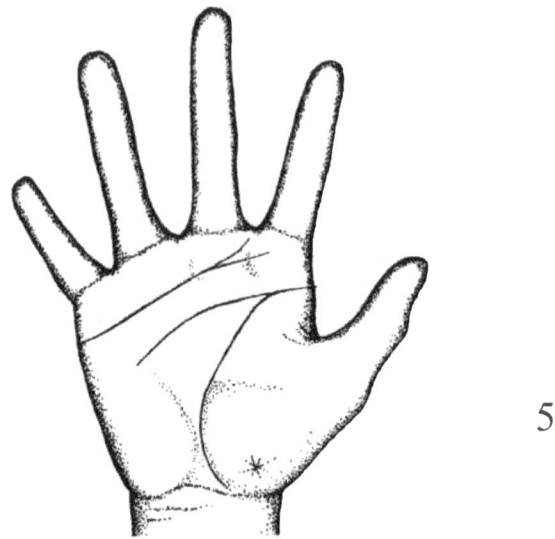

5

This is a somewhat contradictory character. After a quick glance at this palm we would say how calm and peaceful this person was – someone who could be relied upon, always ready to face up to their responsibilities; a great home-lover, quite contented with the intimate family circle. But this type of phlegmatic nature is somewhat overly self-concerned. He or she is unlikely to have a wide circle of friends, despite the apparent openness and tranquillity portrayed by the palm. A friendly person, certainly, but as soon as an acquaintance is out of sight, they tend to be out of mind too. The appearance of introspection is a somewhat false one, because people of this type do not look very deeply into themselves, their own motives. A naturally cautious person, who seldom rushes into decisions and who considers new ideas very carefully before either accepting or rejecting them. When made to feel at all guilty about some aspect of relationships, this person is likely to try to overcome these feelings by plunging into activity. A good manager of money and other assets, we would say, but he or she would far rather be managing a household than some kind of business consortium. An independent person; the sense of ambition displayed in this hand is strong, and self employment would be advisable. Despite the easy-going appearance of dependability and reliability, being an underling would not suit this character at all. There would be constant disagreements.

6

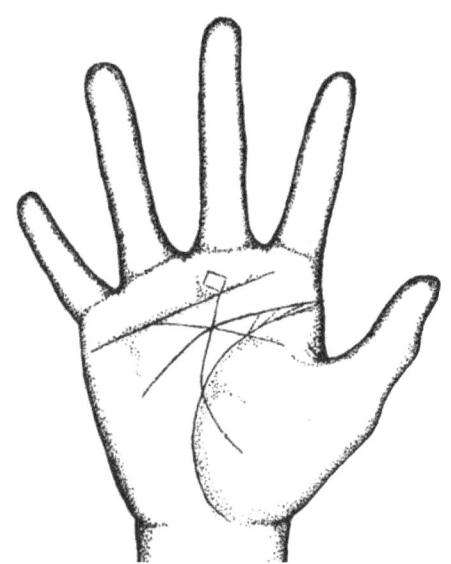

We can say immediately that here is a remarkably powerful personality, and a strongly emotional one. Well able to intel-lectualize any problems and arrive at logical conclusions, certainly, but nevertheless the chief psychological function is emotional feeling. Sincerity stands out on this palm (and sincerity is not the same thing as honesty), a trait which makes us think of politics as a profession. Here, perhaps, is a potential politician who will fight for a cause with ardent zeal – not merely because it is the party line, but because it is what he or she believes in, for the time being. The trouble is, emotions are notorious for swelling and diminishing, ebbing and flowing, and such a person will seem changeable for that reason. We suspect that this person has a knack for remaining isolated psychologically from colleagues and opponents alike. This characteristic makes him or her look vulnerable and in need of a caring companion; but in fact the powers of self-sustainment shown here are considerable, and even when times prove hard, there will be no letting up of confidence. This person obviously likes exploring new ideas and new places, but always needs a reliable home-base to return to. The family will be all-important here and loyalty will be unquestionable. Artistic, strong on material planning, completely self-confident in company, this person is unlikely to be attracted to any spiritual ideas – introspection would seem an unprofitable and somewhat morbid pursuit.

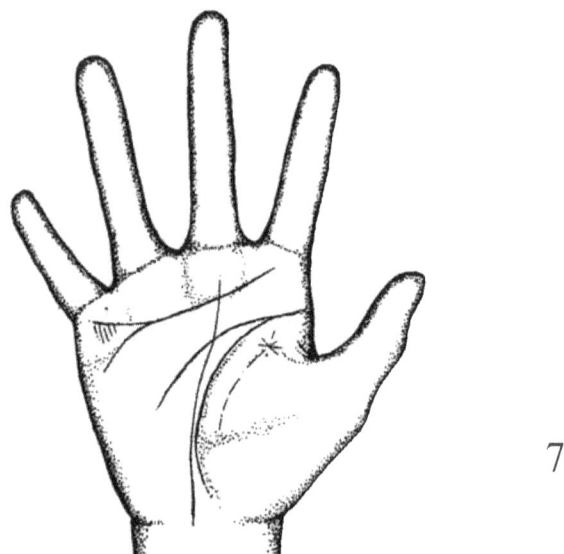

7

The owner of this hand could possess only a most unusual personality, because there is a powerful split at work in the psyche, and this always makes a palmist's job more interesting. There is a dual nature which probably leads to occasional wild flights of fancy, but these flights are very quickly overruled as the subject snaps back to mundane reality. This propensity could be put to valuable use in a creative situation, but it could be disastrous within the confines of a business environment where cold, clear, sober decisions are called for. While this person would prefer to be able to exercise his or her romantic imagination, there is no aversion to occasional spells or even long periods of hard work: the physical 'sensations' are powerful, drawing strength from the emotions. We could see this person projecting or creating poetry or music, which are both physical expressions of emotion. Frivolity is sometimes allowed to get in the way of serious personal relationships, and misunderstandings are liable to arise because of this. When others see this subject as an impulsive, changeable person, an amiable eccentric, they find it difficult to take him or her seriously. But there is a serious side to this nature and at root there is a sense of responsibility; this person's family is unlikely to find themselves short of the basic necessities of life, or even a few luxuries. An evident predilection for robust, even exuberant, physical pursuits suggests a fit and energetic state of health.

8

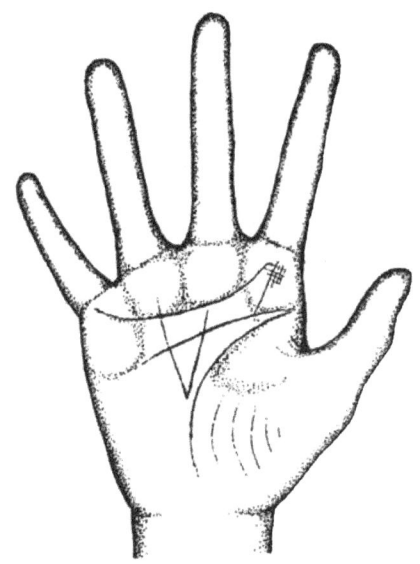

We can see all the signs of ambition in this hand, exceeding the mere desire to do well in a trade or profession. Here is a person determined to leave his or her mark on the world, and if others are not willing to yield, one who is quite prepared to take the top place by force. We can imagine this character going about the daily rounds whistling 'I did it my way...', for this is the prevailing mood to be read in the palm. This person does not care about what others think, or what the neighbours may say. The aggression and tenacity to be seen here are capable of carrying that drive through to the bitter end. Unscrupulous, prepared to exploit others perhaps, but this is not for material gain in particular; it is simply in order to consolidate that personal advancement, that climb towards a personal goal. We suspect that this subject's luck is being stretched too far, and is liable to give out before many years have passed; he or she is liable to reach a broken rung on the ladder of success. Emotional feelings will tend to be ignored as a sign of weakness. The physical senses are powerful too, giving almost unbounded energy, provided it is aimed always towards that basic drive to the top. Outwards-looking in the extreme, introspection here is something to be despised. Sexual desires feature quite strongly in the palm. If the subject is married, establishing equality in all things will be important, but for that reason, perhaps, the act of taking responsibility for a partner's welfare will not be a strong point.

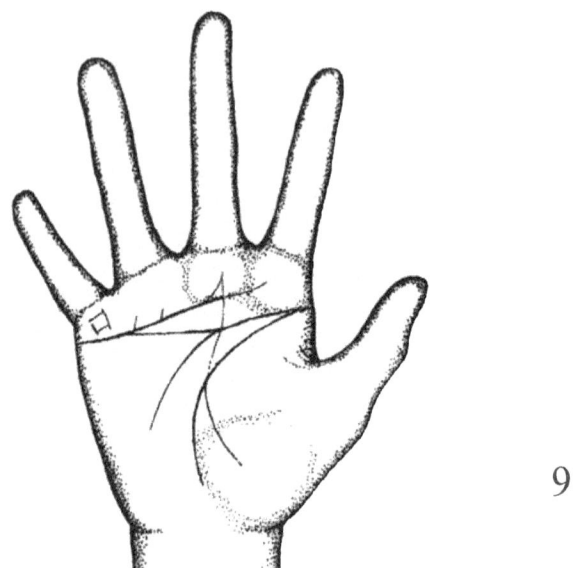

9

We can recognize an extremely emotional character here, one who values warm feelings far more highly than cold carefully considered judgements. But there is a practical, down-to-earth side there too. If asked, he or she would probably insist that intellect is to be valued over emotion, but this is a 'false front': not a case of dishonesty, but simply that this person's heart is a private if not a secret place, and the powerful emotions it feels are kept strictly private also. What the public are allowed to see is a practical, somewhat hard-nosed image. This means that the subject is able to live 'in a world of his own', a world where the feelings can float above the stark realities experienced by everyone else. Other peoples' emotions are to be shunned, or scorned, or pitied. While some might weep over a sad movie while actually enjoying it, this subject will probably refuse even to watch it: It would be a secret torment. One result of this feeling of emotional privacy is that while others may complain and suffer, he or she will always seem peaceful and content. It is an inner world that does not bear close comparison with the world being experienced by everyone else. The practical side of this contradictory nature comes to the forefront when emergencies arise. The apparently dreamy state of languor can change instantly into a whirl of useful activity. Secretly, this person probably likes to associate with people who seem in need of help, and over whom he or she can feel superior.

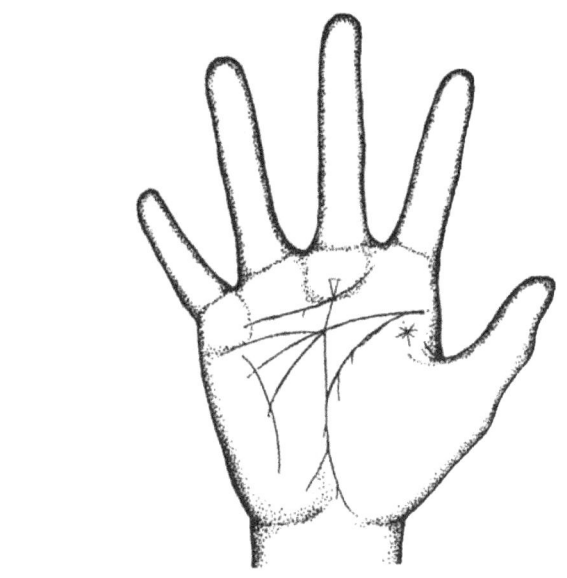

10

This is plainly a person with great strength of mind: an intellectual whose logical thoughts are given pride of place and emotionally-held opinions are dismissed out of hand as sentimental nonsense. 'We have to be realistic about this' could well be this person's favourite phrase, and 'getting emotional' about some issue is not being realistic. The next most often used psychological function for this person is intuition – which is very different from emotional feeling. This is abstract thought, and sentiment plays no part in it. This person, we would say, has the ability to grasp complicated issues instantly and make speedy and accurate decisions. He or she will be a good judge of character, provided the character being judged is not primarily an emotional one, and will quickly see in which direction someone else's talents lie. Almost inevitably, there will be a sense of superiority and an accompanying element of sarcasm which may well alienate sensitive people. These characteristics may lead to neglect not only of emotional values (such as friendship and honesty) but of physical considerations as well. We get the impression that this person was beset with physical problems as a child, and this factor helped to forge the character of adulthood. It probably taught him or her how to influence others by strength of mind, and while such an approach may seem to be aggressive, physical aggression will never be used. This is a person who likes new ideas, and has never stopped learning.

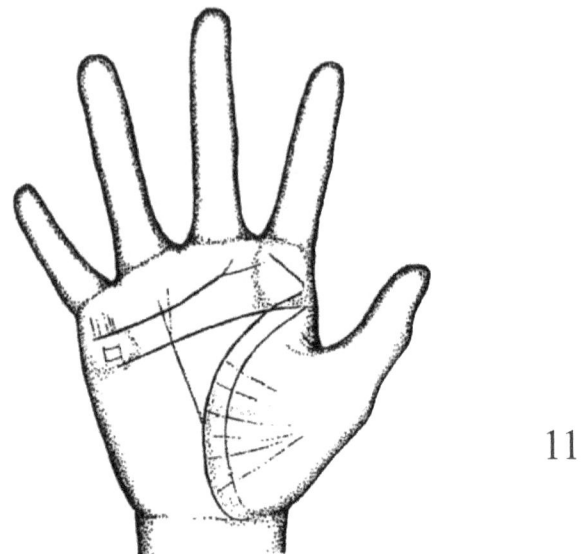

11

The quality that seems to leap out of this hand is independence. This is a physically-orientated person with an enviable balance of mind and heart, thoughts and feelings, to make the background for a markedly physical, energetic lifestyle. A self-sufficient person with the ability to make good use of all available materials – a good person, perhaps, with whom to be shipwrecked on a desert island. Any lessons learnt by this person will seldom be forgotten, and past mistakes will be put to good use. The practical ingenuity seems to shine out of the palm, so that solutions to emergencies and problems will seem to arise as if by magic. What others may discard as useless – whether material objects or ideas – will be seized upon and put to work. There is an element of aggression to be seen here, and strangers may well gather the impression that this is a bad-tempered person; but what they see as bad temper is not enmity but strictly controlled aggression. There is nothing personal in this: it is simply a civilized way of putting the caveman's fighting instincts to good use. There is a deal of promiscuity to be seen in this hand, and the sexual impulse is also used in an entirely practical manner: it is not a means of conquest or power, or even lust, but mainly a means of getting to know and understand people whom the subject finds at all attractive. Those in need will likely find this person to be caring and generous, but they may be put off in equal measure by what might seem to them to be arrogance.

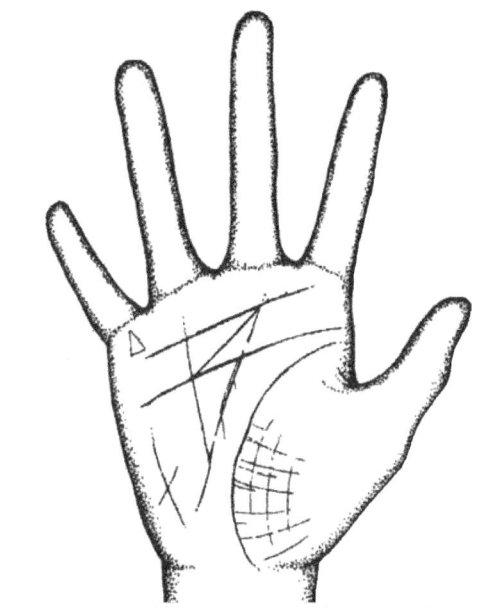

12

Here is a person who plainly believes in the power of mind – if not mind over matter, then certainly mind over emotional feelings. He or she will be well aware of the subtle difference between thinking and feeling, and would certainly maintain that the brain must take precedence and remain supreme. In fact, we would have to disagree with this, because we know there is a far superior function of understanding than that which we call the intellect. This subject tends to carry the thoughts-feelings argument to excess, to the extent of caring little about the feelings of others considered to be less intelligent. There is an element of ruthless arrogance here; he or she will probably strive to cultivate relationships thought likely to be profitable. Ordinary friendship is likely to be neglected. Knowledge, to this person, will be considered more important even than the basic material needs of society. Opinions and ideas will be dispensed liberally, but they will not necessarily be wise ones. We guess that here is someone liable to rush into new ventures or high-flown schemes with something approaching careless abandon – schemes that may prove to be less than practical. Such people are quite capable of leading others astray with their rashness coupled with that strong sense of conviction. Ideas which fly ahead of value-judgement are best expressed in abstract symbols such as we might find in mathematics. He or she would probably make a good teacher.

Summary A : Signs on the Mounts and Lines

STAR  *Principle:* Increase, additional impact, accumulation, excess

On mounts

JUPITER	High on mount – increase in fortune; Low on mount – influential friends
SATURN	Tragedy (an excess of materiality)
SUN	Social attainment; prestigious friends
MERCURY	Success in ventures and mental challenges
MOON	Indiscreet sex; danger of accidents
LOWER MARS	Excessive aggression
UPPER MARS	Quarrelsome stubbornness
VENUS	High on mount – romantic success; Low on mount – home attachment at the expense of romance

On lines

HEART	Happiness in love; serenity
HEAD	Injury to head; at end of line – tragedy
LIFE	Accident; shock
FATE	Danger to material security; risk of accidents
FORTUNE	Good luck; at top of line – Star of Success
HEALTH	Sterility; complications in childbirth
INTUITION	Living in serene dream world
MARRIAGE	Serenity in marriage
RASCETTE	Money coming in; happiness in old age

On plain

Adjacent to the Line of Fate – good fortune

CROSS

Principle: Strengthens the relevant function; antagonism by others; barrier caused by outside interference

On mounts

JUPITER	Secure marriage; advancement through romantic attachments
SATURN	Violent death or ignominy (reaction to excess of materiality)
SUN	High on mount – loss of reputation; Low on mount – temporary loss of prestige
MERCURY	Liability to be cheated
MOON	Danger of travel accidents
LOWER MARS	Risk of violent death caused by aggression
UPPER MARS	Risk of physical injury through obstinacy
VENUS	Single lover; faithful in marriage

On lines

HEART	Traumatic experience
HEAD	Self-deception
LIFE	Period of hardship
FATE	Threat to reputation, security or wealth
FORTUNE	Threat to social status and self esteem
HEALTH	Serious illness
INTUITION	Danger of serious misunderstandings
MARRIAGE	Dangerous opposition to marriage
RASCETTE	Hardship or bereavement in youth

On plain

Beneath Mount of Saturn – mysticism, Grand Cross
Beneath Mount of Jupiter – money skills, Gambler's Cross
Beneath Mount of Mercury – fascination with the occult
Central Plain of Mars – bad temper
Adjacent to the Line of Fate – good luck

SQUARE

Principle: Security; safety; protective reassurance

On mounts

JUPITER	Protection of ambitions and integrity
SATURN	Protection in money matters
SUN	Protection of prestige
MERCURY	Protection against mental strain
MOON	Protection when travelling
LOWER MARS	Protection in dangerous occupations
UPPER MARS	Protection against loss of temper and bodily harm
VENUS	Protection against broken romances

On lines

HEART	Overcoming risk of emotional stress
HEAD	Overcoming risk of mental stress
LIFE	Overcoming threats to life
FATE	Overcoming threats to wealth and well-being
FORTUNE	Overcoming threats to prestige
HEALTH	Overcoming threats to health
MARRIAGE	Overcoming threats to relationships

On plain

Adjacent to any line – protection to the smooth flow of that basic function

Note: A square surrounding any threatening sign protects against its worst effects. The predicted event may take place, but the end result will not be life-threatening. A square surrounding a line-break predicts the smooth healing-over of the interrupted flow of that particular life force.

TRIANGLE

Principle: Intellectual ability; concentration of brain power

On mounts

JUPITER	Ability to organize diplomatically
SATURN	Ability to research, analyse
SUN	Ability to handle wealth and fame wisely
MERCURY	Ability to communicate, do business, and influence others
MOON	Ability to succeed in artistic or literary work
LOWER MARS	Ability to take courage and keep a cool head
UPPER MARS	Ability to organize resistance against oppression
VENUS	Ability to manipulate marriage partners; jealousy

On lines

HEART	Ability to apply intellectual solutions to emotional problems
HEAD	Strengthens mentality according to the nearest mount
LIFE	Intelligent behaviour; diplomacy
FATE	Ability to solve problems of finance
FORTUNE	Ability to solve problems of prestige
HEALTH	Ability to solve problems of health
INTUITION	Ability to solve intuitively sensed problems
MARRIAGE	Ability to solve problems of partnership

On plain

Above topmost bracelet adjacent to Life Line – concern with suffering and death, Mark of Mercy, Mark of Morbidity

GRID

Principle: Negative impulses

On mounts

JUPITER	Domineering nature; selfishness
SATURN	Morbid introspection; lack of concentration
SUN	Unscrupulous publicity-seeking
MERCURY	Cunning; dishonesty
MOON	Nervous tension
LOWER MARS	Habitual trouble-seeking
UPPER MARS	Bad temper
VENUS	Antagonism to the course of true love

ISLAND

Principle: Uncertainty; interruption of smooth flow

On lines

HEART	Emotional stress according to the nearest mount; guilty romance
HEAD	Stress; mental disturbance; indecision according to the nearest mount; headaches
LIFE	Severe illness; depression
FATE	Money problems. Elongated island – leading a double life
FORTUNE	Scandal; financial loss
HEALTH	Internal illness
INTUITION	Tendency to paranoia
MARRIAGE	Extramarital affairs
RASCETTE	A considerable handicap to be overcome

CHAIN

Principle: Troublesome periods

On lines

HEART	Emotional instability; stress; heart trouble
HEAD	Mental instability; stress; depression according to position relative to mounts
LIFE	Illness; strain; stress; nervous disability
FATE	Difficult times; uncertainty; insecurity
FORTUNE	Obsession with undesirable pursuits
HEALTH	Problems of respiration
INTUITION	Insanity
MARRIAGE	Troubled relationships
RASCETTE	Relatively minor problems to be resolved

CROSS BARS

Principle: Obstacles to the smooth flow of relevant function

On lines

HEART	Emotional upsets
HEAD	Migraines; loss of memory
LIFE	Periods of depression
FATE	Personal attacks on wealth and well-being
FORTUNE	Personal attacks on reputation
HEALTH	Recurrent illness
INTUITION	Unfounded suspicions
MARRIAGE	Opposition to marriage

BREAKS

Principle: Interruptions to smooth progress

On lines

HEART	Quarrels with close friends; circulation problems
HEAD	Stress; injury to head; headaches
LIFE	Isolated illness
FATE	Upheavals in lifestyle
FORTUNE	Failure of enterprise
HEALTH	General debility; liver condition
INTUITION	Forgetfulness
MARRIAGE	Separation

Note: Overlapping breaks are less decisive than clean breaks and imply temporary disruption followed by a restoration of the flow

Summary B : Detailed Features

RASCETTE

Star: Happiness in old age. Traditional sign of an inheritance or unexpected wealth.

Cross: On or just above the topmost ring denotes hardship or bereavement experienced during childhood.

Chained formation: Relatively minor problems to be overcome.

Island: A considerable problem to affect the wearer's life.

Breaks: Awareness of signals from the unconscious mind.

MOUNT OF JUPITER

Pronounced development: Ambitious; determined.

Star: High on mount denotes good fortune or effortless success. Central to mount denotes pre-eminence in one's chosen field. Low on mount denotes plentiful influential friends.

Cross: Secure marriage. Social and professional advancement is likely by way of romantic attachments.
Beneath the mount – the Gambler's Cross; success with financial arrangements.

Square: Ambitious aims successfully carried through. Threats to professional integrity easily overcome.

Triangle: Diplomacy. Great ability to organize affairs.

Grid: Selfish; domineering nature.

MOUNT OF SATURN

Pronounced development: Resourceful; materialistic.

Star: Warning of tragic consequences following reckless materialism or ruthless actions.

Cross: Wholly on the mount – the 'Sign of the Scaffold', warning against pursuing material gain to the detriment of other people. Beneath the mount – the Mystic Cross, denoting an awareness of the spiritual dimension.

Square: Effortless good fortune in financial matters.

Triangle: Ability to carry out research and analysis.

Grid: Morbid introspection and lack of concentration.

MOUNT OF THE SUN

Pronounced development: Cultural interests.

Star: Effortless social attainment. Influential friends.

Cross: High on mount – danger of losing prestige.
Low on mount – temporary loss of reputation likely.

Square: Held in high esteem despite occasional setbacks.

Triangle: Ability to handle wealth and fame wisely.

Grid: Tends to attract fame of the wrong sort. Prone to unscrupulous publicity-seeking.

MOUNT OF MERCURY

Pronounced development: Compassionate. Communicative.

Star: Welcomes mental challenges. Probable success in business ventures.

Cross: Somewhat gullible and liable to be cheated.
Beneath the mount – a certain fascination with the occult.

Square: Ability to withstand stress and mental strain.

Triangle: Ability to communicate effectively and influence others in business matters.

Grid: A cunning streak. Dishonesty.

MOUNT OF VENUS

Pronounced development: A sensuous, voluptuous nature.

Star: High on mount – the 'Rising Star of Venus', denoting romantic happiness.
Low on mount – the 'Setting Star of Venus', denoting close ties with home and family which tend to preclude romantic attachments.

Cross: Faithfulness in marriage, with a single lover.

Square: Well protected against the possibility of broken romances.

Triangle: Jealousy. Tendency to manipulate family and marriage partners.

Grid: Romantic success seems unlikely. Obstacles always seem to appear, hindering the course of true love.

LOWER MOUNT OF MARS

Pronounced development: An aggressive nature.

Star: An aggressive nature; warning against the use of violence.

Cross: A stern warning. An over-aggressive attitude could result in an unfortunate outcome.
Adjacent to the mount on the Plain of Mars – a bad temper.

Square: Attracted by high-risk occupations. A seemingly charmed life in dangerous circumstances.

Triangle: Courageous. Ability to keep a cool head in difficult circumstances.

Grid: A habitual trouble-seeker.

UPPER MOUNT OF MARS

Pronounced development: Tenacity; stamina.

Star: Quarrelsome. Stubborn.

Cross: A warning against the risk of physical injury brought about through stubbornness.

Square: Denoting tremendous energy and stamina: the ability to keep going without coming to harm. Forthright but good-tempered.

Triangle: Ability to organize effective resistance against oppression or exploitation. A tireless care-worker.

Grid: Bad temper.

MOUNT OF THE MOON

Pronounced development: Creativity; mysticism.

Star: Indiscretion, especially with regard to sexual exploits. Prone to take unnecessary risks. A warning to take special care when travelling away from home.

Cross: Prone to exaggeration. Fond of grandiose schemes. Indiscrete tendency to venture 'where wise men fear to tread'.

Square: Ability to endure apparent hardships, especially when travelling.

Triangle: Ability to succeed in artistic or literary work.

Grid: Nervous tension.

HEAD LINE

Star: Injury by accident, usually to the head itself. A star at the end of the line is traditionally associated with danger involving water.

Cross: Suspicious thoughts; mental confusion.

Square: Resilience. Resistance to the long-term effects of stress.

Triangle: Great strength of mind (refer to nearest mount).

Island: Stress; migraine. Indecision (refer to nearest mount).

Parallel doubling: Inconsistency. Unusual behaviour.

Chained formation: Mental breakdown. Stressful periods. Nervous disability (refer to nearest mount).

Breaks: Trauma. Injury to head or limbs. Headaches.

Overlapping breaks: Forgetfulness; inconsistencies.

Crossbars: Loss of memory. Migraine

HEART LINE

Star: Happiness; romance; good fortune.

Cross: Traumatic experience; misfortune.

Square: Capacity to absorb and overcome emotional hurts.

Triangle: Capacity to think one's way out of emotional dilemmas.

Island: Guilt; emotional stress (refer to nearest mount).

Parallel doubling: A secret side to one's emotional life (refer to nearest mount).

Chained formation: Emotional instability (refer to nearest mount).

Breaks: Quarrelsome nature; emotional upsets.

Overlapping breaks: Tendency to quarrel with partners only to make up later.

Crossbars: Emotional disturbances; interrupted romances.

Note   When the Heart Line and the Head Line are combined into one single line, this suggests a genetic malfunction. It is frequently symptomatic of Down's syndrome.

LIFE LINE

Inner Life Line: Extra energy; a reliable reserve of stamina. Also known as the Line of Mars.
(May be limited in length – refer to the timescale).

Star: Trauma. Accident (refer to the timescale).

Cross: Period of hardship (refer to the timescale).

Square: Any difficulties will be safely overcome, particularly when surrounding a break or other warning sign.

Triangle: Diplomatic lifestyle. A general indication of intelligence. Not usually subject to timing.

Island: Usually denotes a severe illness or period of deep depression (refer to the timescale).

Parallel doubling: (Not to be confused with an Inner Life Line which is distinctly separate). A period of confusion, quandary or insecurity (refer to the timescale).

Chained formation: Period of severe stress or nervous disability. May denote a recurrent illness (refer to the timescale).

Breaks: Isolated illness (refer to the timescale).

Overlapping breaks: Illness with the promise of complete recovery (refer to the timescale).

Crossbars: Periods of depression (refer to the timescale).

Tie lines: Connecting the timescale to other features on the palm.

LINE OF FATE

Star: Risk of accident. Threats to material security. Close to line – success arising from an apparent setback.

Cross: Below the Head Line – an ongoing threat to career and material wealth. Low down on or close to the line – tragedy within the family. Elsewhere close to the line – material gain arising from a change of circumstances (refer to timescale). On the Mount of Saturn itself – the 'Sign of the Scaffold' warning against reckless or violent behaviour. Below the Mount of Saturn formed by a single line crossing the Line of Fate – the Mystic Cross denoting spirituality.

Square: Good arising out of hardship. Protection against the effects of threats to material well-being.

Triangle: Overcoming financial difficulties. Large triangle at the base of the line – the Mark of Mercy or Mark of Morbidity, implying an unusual concern with death and suffering.

Parallel doubling: Leading a double life; a side of the personality being kept secret (refer to timescale).

Island: Financial difficulties (refer to timescale).

Chained formation: Unforeseen difficulties; period of insecurity (refer to timescale).

Breaks: Interruptions to routine; disruptions to normal lifestyle (refer to timescale).

Overlapping breaks: Temporary upheavals in routine (refer to timescale).

Crossbars: Drain on financial resources. Some kind of personal attack on material well-being (refer to timescale).

Changes of direction: Changes of occupation or lifestyle (refer to timescale).

Wavering Line of Fate: Negativity; wasted energy.

LINE OF FORTUNE

Star: A sign of good fortune, particularly actually on the Mount of the Sun, where it is known as the Star of Success.

Cross: Threat to reputation; antagonism from envious people (refer to timescale).

Square: Ability to overcome any threats to prestige.

Triangle: Intellectual ability to achieve success.

Parallel doubling: Implies that a potentially scandalous situation is being kept secret (refer to timescale).

Island: Sudden loss of prestige with a drain on resources (refer to timescale).

Chained formation: Pursuing a scandalous course, apparently seeking notoriety (refer to timescale).

Breaks: Failure of enterprise (refer to timescale).

Overlapping breaks: Severe but temporary setbacks successfully overcome (refer to timescale).

Crossbars: Personal attacks threatening prestige.

Changes of direction: Changes in career (refer to timescale).

MARRIAGE LINE

Star: Serenity in marriage.

Cross: Finding opposition to marriage.

Square: Relationships are stable enough to overcome threats from outside the marriage.

Triangle: Denotes an intellect capable of surmounting any marital problems.

Island: A guilty secret; an extramarital affair.

Parallel doubling: Split loyalties. Or enduring memories of a previous relationship.

Chained formation: Troubled relationships. Seething emotions.

Breaks: Predict separation.

Overlapping breaks: Separation followed by reunion, or an improved arrangement.

Crossbars: Outside interference; threats to marital stability.

Tributaries: An initial period of separation; or dual loyalties.

Fork: Freedom from excessive ties; or split loyalties.

Downwards curve: Separation; or widowhood.

Upwards curve: Happy marriage.

LINE OF INTUITION

Star: An extremely intuitive personality; a contented but impractical dreamer.

Cross: Warns against antagonism from others brought about through misunderstandings.

Square: A profitable combination of intellectual and intuitional resources.

Island: Unprofitable imaginings; paranoia.

Chained formation: Brooding. Psychic imbalance.

Crossbars: Displays a tendency to distrust people and suspect their motives.

Breaks: Absent-mindedness.

LINE OF HEALTH

Star: Sterility; or problems with childbirth.

Cross: An isolated serious illness.

Square: Serious health problems successfully overcome.

Triangle: Given to pondering over health matters.

Island: Serious internal illness.

Chained formation: Serious lung condition.

Breaks: General debility.

Overlapping breaks: Emotional rather than physical problems.

Crossbars: Recurrent illness.

Summary C: The Principle Lines

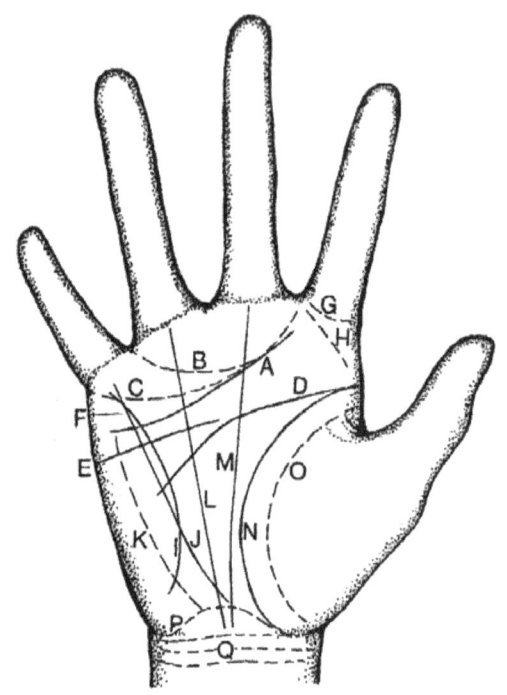

A	Heart Line
B	Upper Girdle of Venus, closed version; (Inner Heart Line)
C	Upper Girdle of Venus, open version; (Inner Heart Line)
D	Head Line
E	Supernal Line
F	Marriage Line
G	Ring of Solomon
H	Line of Sympathy
I	Line of Intuition
J	Line of Health

K	Line of Excess; (Inner Line of Health)
L	Line of Fortune
M	Line of Fate
N	Life Line
O	Line of Mars; (Inner Life Line)
P	Lower Girdle of Venus (Extended upper bracelet of the Rascette)
Q	Rascette

Other minor lines commonly to be seen include Child Lines above the Marriage Line, and Marks of Concern on the Mount of Mercury. Lines of Influence which rise on the Mount of Venus indicate family influences and romantic encounters. Those which rise on the Mount of the Moon indicate non-family, outside influences. They may include (on the left hand) Lines of Travel, and (on the right hand) Lines of Dominance.

Index

Page references in *italics* refer to diagrams

accident, risk of 125, 190, 246, 247
accident-prone 189
'actual barrier' 110
addictive personality 188
affection 79-83, 154, 231
aggression 25, 95, 114, 165, 171, 179, 181, 241, 244, 246, 247
  area relating to 42, 43, 114
ambition 61, 111, 114, 130, 164, 166, 241
  seat of 42, 43, 114
anatomy of the hand 16, 17
Ancestral Cycle 203-206, 215
anxiety neurosis 218
artistic type 21, 192
assertive personality 180
athletic types 171, 172
atonement 126-128

bipolar disorder 65
bisexuality 81
Bodily Cycle 203, 204
branchlets *123,* 124, *134,* 136, 168, *192, 193, 242, 243, 244*
branch lines 117, *see also* Head Line *and* Heart Line

chain formation 251, *see also individual lines*
characteristics, inherited 16-19
Child Lines 82, *83,* 202
childbirth, difficult 68, 185, 187
children and parents, compared 51-52, 225
cheirotypes 20
collective unconscious 37, 44, 48
Communal Cycle 204, 205
communication, area relating to 43
compartments of concern 204, *211-214*
compassion 102, 106, 199, 202

compassion, area relating to 43
compatibility 59, 150
concentration, difficulty in 112, 193, 250
Concern, Marks of 82, 195, 196
'confusedly discursive' type 74
conscious occurrence, area relating to 47, 67, *68,* 225
Creative Cycle 204, 205, *215*
creativity, 94, 192, 193, 239
  area relating to 42, 43
  opposing conformity 89
crime and fingerprints 28, 29
cross 247 *see also individual lines and mounts*
crossbars 250 *see also individual lines*
cycles, psychological 140, 141, 178, 179, 203-215

depression 41, 42, 95, 111, 191, 226
dominance *see* Line of Dominance
doubling of lines *133,* 175
  see also individual lines
dreaming personality 90, 192
dual-natured personality 89, 178, 218

Earth, symbolism of 38
elderly subjects 218-220
'electric energy', lines of 210
emotional feelings, strength of 60, 72, 104, 106, 191
  instability 72, 73, 110, 186, 251
  traits, incoming and out-going 18
emotions and intellect 12, 14
  lack of 104
energy, physical 113, 114, 123
entrepreneurial signs 94, 104, 251

faithful personality 150, 237
faith interacting with will 46
'faith-greed' type 66
fate 17, 18
Fate Line see Line of Fate
'fate people' 127
fertility 191
fickleness 72, 157, 158
finance 105, 149
finger joints 20, 66
fingernails 184, 199
fingerprints 25-29, 191
  and crime 28, 29
fingers, curved 32-34, *162*, 163, 167
  length of 29-32, *165*, 167, 179, 181, 191, 199
  set of 34-35
  spatulate *168*
  spread of 35-36, 199
  suppleness of 166, 199
fingertips 21, *22*
fluctuating moods 63, 178
forks see *individual lines*
Fortune Line see Line of Fortune
fund-raiser 66

Gambler's Cross 163, 165, *168*
Girdle of Venus, Lower 68, *69*
  Upper 67, *68*, 70
Grand Cross *196*, 197, 224, 228, 229, 232
Great Quadrangle 107, 197
grid 190, 250 see also *individual mounts*

hand, shape of 20, *21*, 171, 191, 192, 195, 196, 199
  size of 179, 199
Head Line 12, *13*, 84-97, 110-112 257
  branch to Heart Line 98-103, *99, 100, 101 104, 106*, 195, 201, *234, 242*
  breaks in 110, *111*, 173, 174, *184*, 187, *188*, 252, 257

Head Line, chained 110, *111, 175*, 252, 257
  close to Heart Line 187
  colour of 185
  combined with Heart Line 14, 258
  crosses on 247, 257
  curving *88, 94*
  'domineering' 181
  finishing point 165, 178, 179, 190, 192
  forked *89, 90, 176*, 177, 178, 199, 218, *243*
  in Grand Cycle *206, 210, 214*
  islands on 110, 111, *112, 185*, 187, 251, 257
  linked to Mount of Jupiter *241*
  plunging *192*
  rising point *95*, 97, 181
  square on 248, 257
  star on *184, 185, 217*, 246, 257
  straight 84, *85*
  tied to Life Line *88, 91, 92*
  timing on *217*
  triangle on *249*, 257
  upwards curving *93, 162*, 163, 164
  widely separated from Life Line *85, 86, 87, 88, 94*, 164, *165, 172, 176, 177, 178, 180*, 187
health 119, 120, 183-191, *see also* Line of Health
Heart Line 12, *13*, 56-66, 72-78, 258
  branch to Head Line 104, 105, *158, 172, 200, 235, 245*
  breaks in *75, 76, 77, 150, 158, 184*, 187, 226
  chained *72, 73, 158, 174, 184*, 187, 251
  close to Head Line 187
  colour of 185
  combined with Head Line 14, 258
  cross on *145*, 245, 258
  curving 58
  'domineering' 181

Heart Line, forked *190*
  in Grand Cycle 204, 206, *208*, 210, *212*
  Inner 67 *see also* Upper Girdle of Venus
  islands on 74, *75, 145,* 150, *158, 175, 217,* 250, 258
  length of *56, 57, 58,* 178, 199
  rising point *60, 61, 62, 63, 64, 65,* 66, 153, 157
  short *57, 96*
  star on 258
  straight *56,* 153, *155*
  timing on *217*
  tributaries *see* rising point
hollow palm *145,* 146
homosexuality 68
hypochondria 183

illness 119, 120, 183-191
  see also Line of Health
imagination opposing logic 89, 192
immoral traits 77
impressions of the hand 220
indecision 90, 218
independent personality 92, 238, 243
indiscretion 58, 232
Individual Cycle 203, *207, 215*
infidelity 157
influence *see* Line of Influence
inheritance of characteristics 16-19
  of money 117, *118*
inhibitions 13, 67, 91
  lack of 87, 232
injury to head 110, 173, 187, 217, 246, 252
inner feelings 227
Inner Heart Line *see* Upper Girdle of Venus
Inner Life Line 171, *172, 240, 244*
inner turmoil 77, 98, 125, 225
integrity, area relating to 39, 43
intellect and emotion 12, 14
'intelligence-hate' type 85
introspection, excessive 111, 250

introversion 67, 90
intuition, area relating to *17,* 39, 43, 195 *see also* Line of Intuition
irritability, inbuilt 95
islands 250 *see also individual lines*

Jupiter, symbolism of 38, 40, 41, 43 *see also* Mount of Jupiter
Jupiter-heart person 60, 61, 62

karma 10, 11, 198
knuckles 166, 179

length of fingers 201
Life Line *13, 113, 114, 259*
  breaks in *124, 125, 175, 184,* 186, 187
  chained *175,* 184
  colour of 175
  forked 120, 121, *122, 124,* 125
  fragmented 121
  in Grand Cycle 204, *205, 209,* 212, *213*
  Inner *114,* 115
  islands on *174*
  rising point *115,* 116
  separation from Head Line 164, *165, 172, 176, 177, 180,* 187
  slender 186
  tied to the Mount of Jupiter *116*
  timescale on *113*
Line of Dominance *133,* 134, *159,* 160
  in Grand Cycle 210
Line of Excess *188, 189, 190*
Line of Fate *126*-136, *147,* 148, 260
  branchlets on *168,* 169
  breaks in *135,* 136, *169, 246*
  cross on 135
  crossbar on 135
  curtailed *130, 145,* 191
  doubling *133,* 136, *158, 175, 230,* 231
  forked *132, 134,* 136

Line of Fate in Grand Cycle
203-204, *211*
  islands on 134, *135, 155,* 156, *186*
  merged with the Life Line 129, *243*
  rising point 129, *131,* 155, *165, 236, 239, 242, 245*
  square on *169*
  star on 135
  timescale on *129,* 140-141
  wavering 132, *158, 177, 180,* 182, *186*
Line of Fortune 138, 161, 261
  breaks in 142, *192*
  chained *141,* 192
  cross on *141,* 143
  crossbar on *141,* 142
  forked 192
  island on *141,* 142, 143
  rising point *138, 139, 140,* 141, *168, 193,* 194, *237, 244, 245*
  star on *141,* 143, *168,* 169
  timescale on *137,* 140-141
Line of Health 183, *188, 190,* 219, 263
  broken 183, *188, 190,* 219
  chained *184*
  coloured 184-185
  inner *188, 189, 190*
  island on *184*
  star on *185*
  timing on *217*
  wavy 183, *185*
Line of Influence *134,* 161, *162, 167, 239*
  in Grand Cycle 210
Line of Inheritance 108, 109, *110,* 153
Line of Intuition *189,* 195, *196, 234,* 243, 263
Line of Marriage *see* Marriage Lines
Line of Mars *114,* 115
Line of Sympathy *200,* 201, 202, 224, *237, 244*

Lines of Travel 120, *121, 122, 231*
lines appearing and disappearing 38, 210
  fading and strengthening 217
  of 'electric energy' 212
link lines *117*
Lower Girdle of Venus *185, 238*
Lower Mount of Mars *38,* 43, 256
  signs on *165, 169, 190, 234, 240, 243*
'lucky in love' *147*

manic-depressive syndrome 65
Mark of Mercy *200, 202*
Mark of Morbidity 202
Marks of Concern 82, 195, *196, 200, 202, 236, 240, 244*
Marriage Lines *79, 147, 150, 151, 262*
  breaks in *159*
  cut off 198
  down-curving *81,* 148
  family interference 151-152
  forked *80,* 81, 148, *149*
  island in *82, 148,* 151
  long 81
  overruled 226-228
  straight 148
  timescale *79*-80
  upwards-curving 148, *150, 158, 237*
Mars, Plain of *107, 190, 234*
  symbolism of *38,* 40, 42, 43
  see also Lower and Upper Mounts of Mars
Mercury, symbolism of *38,* 42, 43
  see also Mount of Mercury
Moon Cross 232, 257
  symbolism of *38,* 43
  see also Mount of the Moon
Mount of Jupiter *38,* 40, 43, 164 253
  cross on *145, 147,* 150, 162
  grid on 154, *155,* 180, 181, *240*
  square on *169,* 235
  star on *165,* 168

Mount of Mars, Lower *38*, 43, 256
  Upper *38*, 43, 256
Mount of Mercury *38*, 43, 46, 255
  cross on 190
  square on *242*
  star on *169*
  triangle on *162*, 163, *168*, *234*, *244*, *249*
Mount of the Moon *38*, 43, 162, 164, 258
  fleshy 195
  cross on *188*, *190*, 232
  star on *184*, *244*
  triangle on *193*, 194
Mount of Saturn 38, 41 43, 254
  cross on 145, 188
  grid on 154, *155*, *192*, 194
  square on *168*, *169*, *239*
  star on *185*, 187
  triangle on *196*, *197*, 243
Mount of the Sun *38*, *43*, 45, 254
  cross on 190
  star on *147*, *165*, *168*, *185*, *236*
  triangle on 169
Mount of Venus *38*, 43, 255
  cross on *148*, 152, *237*
  curving lines on *151*, 153, *240*, *245*
  fleshy 157, 186
  grid on *148*, 152
  radiating lines on *150*, 152, 157, *158*, *244*, *245*
  square on *148*, 152
  triangle on *148*, 152, 154, *155*
mounts, symbolism of 37-43, *38*, *41*, *42*

nervous tension 183, 250
Neptune, symbolism of 37, 38

obsession 111
'occult' and 'spiritual' 196
organizers, effective 93

phalanges 31
'planetary rulership' 30, 38-43

Pluto, symbolism of 37, 38
practical types 20. 21
privacy zone 221
pyknic physique 191

Rascette 37, 44, 47, 68, 172, 253
  chained 172, 174, 181
  fading 49
  island on 172, 180, 181
  star on 162
right and left hands 50-55
  transfer between 225
Ring of Solomon *196*, 197, 201
Rising Star of Venus *147*

Saturn, symbolism of 38, 40, 41, 43
  see also Mount of Saturn
Saturn-heart person 62, 63
Seal of Solomon *189*
Setting Star of Venus *147*, 148-149, *238*
seven-year cycles 178-179
sexual relations 198
shyness 176
Sign of the Scaffold *133*, 135
Solomon's Ring *196*, 197
Solomon's Seal *189*
Soul Cycle 203-204
  nature of 39-43
Spirit Cycle 204-205
'spiritual' and 'occult' 196
Squares of Protection *134*, 136, 170
Star of Success 169
stars 165-166, 246 *see also individual lines*
Sun Line *see* Line of Fortune
  symbolism of 38 *see also* Mount of the Sun
Supernal Line *108*, 109, 197,214, 224, 227, 228, 232
  Zone *107*, 109, 197
Sympathy, Line of 200, 201

thinking and feeling, difference
  between 12-14
thumb, clubbed 180
  flexible 25
  length of 24
  pugilist's 25
  supple 199
tie lines *117*
timescales 216 *see also
  individual lines and
  Grand Cycle*
timidity 179
'tired lines' 120
Travel, Lines of *120, 121, 122*
triangle 249
'trigger points' 120
tributaries *63, 64, 65, 80, 117*

twins 19
Upper Girdle of Venus 197, 225, *234*
Upper Mount of Mars *38,* 43, 256
  signs on *169, 180, 188, 234, 244, 256*
Uranus, symbolism of 37, 38

Venus, symbolism of 38, 40, 42, 43
  see also Upper *and* Lower Girdles of Venus *and* Mount of Venus
versatility 144

width of the hand 21, 191
wrinkled palms 218-219

Notes

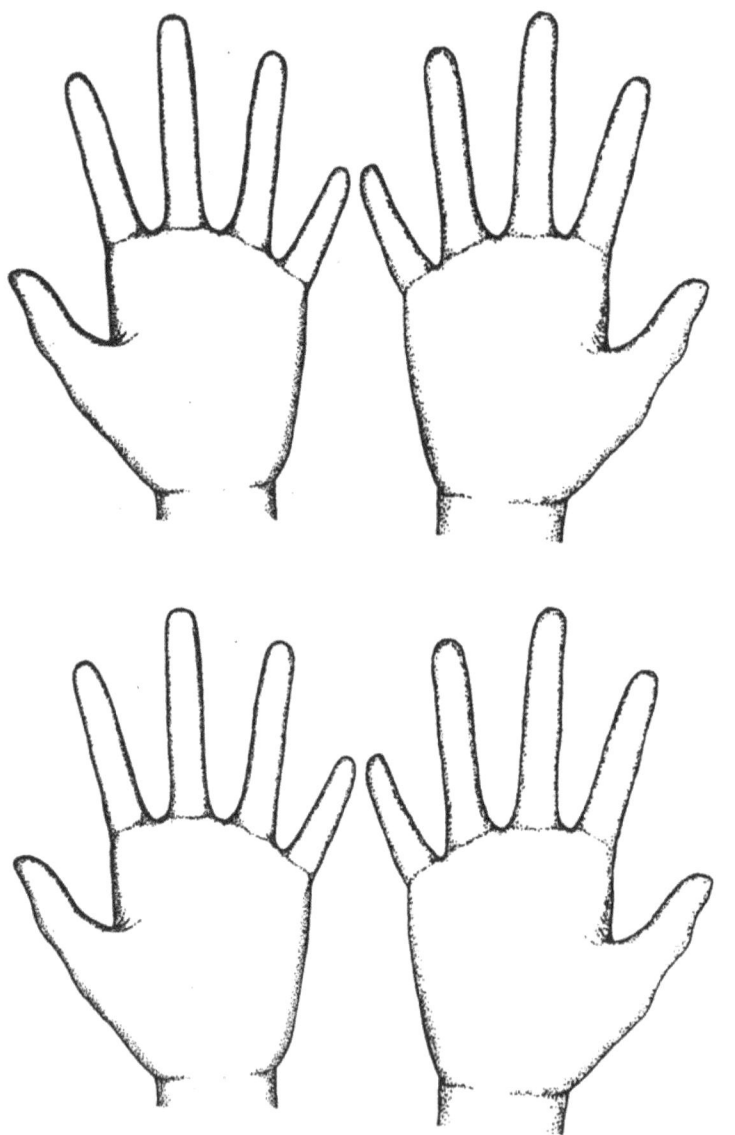

www.ingramcontent.com/pod-product-compliance
Lightning Source LLC
Chambersburg PA
CBHW031947080426
42735CB00007B/295